A CITIZEN'S
RIGHT
TO KNOW

Risk Communication and Public Policy

A CITIZEN'S
RIGHT
TO KNOW

Risk Communication and Public Policy

Susan G. Hadden

WESTVIEW PRESS
Boulder • San Francisco • London

Published in 1989 in the United States of America by Westview Press, Inc., 5500 Central Avenue, Boulder, Colorado 80301, and in the United Kingdom by Westview Press, Inc., 13 Brunswick Centre, London WC1N 1AF, England

Library of Congress Cataloging-in-Publication Data
Hadden, Susan G.
    A citizen's right to know.
    Includes index.
    1. Freedom of information--United States.
2. Hazardous substances--Government policy--United
States.   3. Hazardous substances--Law and legislation--
United States.   I. Title.
JC599.U5H23 1989   323.44'5   89-5801
ISBN 0-8133-0913-1

Printed and bound in the United States of America

The paper used in this publication meets the requirements of the American National Standard for Permanence of Paper for Printed Library Materials Z39.48-1984.

10   9   8   7   6   5   4   3   2   1

Contents

Part 1
What Is Right to Know?

Part 2
Aspects of Right to Know

Tables and Figures

Tables

Figures

ix

Preface

On December 3, 1984, a cloud of toxic gas was released over Bhopal in central India, ultimately killing thousands and causing injuries to many more. Efforts to try to prevent similar accidents in the United States culminated in October 1986 when Congress passed the Emergency Response and Community Right-to-Know Act, which gave citizens the right to learn about the hazardous materials present in their communities through reports submitted by industry.

Does the fact that citizens know, or can know, about the presence of chemicals in their communities reduce the chances of another Bhopal disaster occurring? On the surface, this seems unlikely. In order to prevent a release of toxic gas--or of a toxic liquid--managers of plants where the materials are used must ensure that procedures for storage and manufacturing are appropriate to the characteristics of the chemical and that the correct procedures are followed. How can citizens affect decisions by plant managers? Should they be able to? After all, plant managers are responsible to owners and stockholders, and they possess a lot of technical expertise that citizens who live in the area could duplicate only with years of study, or never.

For what else can citizens use right-to-know information? If they experience health complaints, they might tell their doctors about substances to which they had been exposed. They could also tell their lawyers, perhaps preparing to file suit for damages. Some citizens in states with right-to-know programs have used information about hazardous substances in their neighborhoods to justify requests to public officials for regulatory actions ranging from testing air or water to inspecting facilities. The fact is, however, that very few citizens have exercised the right to know as it applies to hazardous chemicals, and fewer still have taken action based on that information.

There are many reasons that this is so. The data have been unavailable except in a few states and in some cities with right-to-know laws that predate the federal law. Even when the data have been collected, ensuring that they are accessible is still difficult, and even when accessible, understanding their purport is not always easy. Some data are suppressed as trade secrets, and sometimes the data are divided up among two or more government agencies, forcing users to put information together for themselves. Knowing which agency to approach for action once the information is obtained and analyzed is another potential barrier to exercising the right to know.

Despite these problems, there is--there should be--a right to know. People have the right to have information that will enable them to make decisions that affect their own lives and health. But a law that merely ensures the availability of the raw information about amounts and locations of hazardous materials may turn out not to be adequate to ensure the right to know; citizens may need additional information and may need help in interpreting the data or in finding ways of affecting decisions.

This book, then, is first a study of the right to know as embodied in a particular piece of legislation. Part 1 provides a brief history of right to know, followed by a study of two state programs. This discussion tries to infer the goals of the legislators and evaluate the programs on their own terms.

As I have tried to indicate, however, right to know is not a straightforward concept. A brief consideration of its premises suggests that there are several different forms of right to know, some or all of which are embodied in the legislation. The ambiguity of the statute is a result not only of the usual push and pull of interest groups in the political arena but also of a more basic question, unanswered after two hundred years: To what extent should government merely provide information as opposed to ensuring actual participation of citizens in decisionmaking? In the case discussed here, the decisions concern the acceptability of risks posed by hazardous materials stored and used by private companies in their communities. Thus, a second purpose of the book is to examine the underlying premises of all information policies. In Part 2, I consider five issues that must be considered in trying to make information available and useful to citizens in a responsible way.

In Part 3, the two themes are pulled together; I provide both suggestions for improving right to know as we presently have it and an analysis of the ways in which right to know is typical of other information policies that raise similar questions about the proper roles of government and citizens.

The result, I hope, is a study that goes beyond the examination of a particular law to pose fundamental questions about our society. The trend toward providing information to citizens is growing; California's Proposition 65, although treated only occasionally in the text, was an important motivation for my study. Another motivation was my concern that the implications for social change of the right-to-know statute would be lost in its widespread designation as a "risk communication" law. In the final chapter, I suggest that one conception of this law and other information programs is that they fulfill the Jeffersonian dream of empowering citizens through knowledge. Whether the reader endorses this conception is much less important than the fact that he or she has consciously thought about what the law should achieve. Data take on meaning only in the context of questions; I hope to have raised the right questions about right to know.

A note on nomenclature: Although the phrase is most often written as "right-to-know," using hyphens, I find this usage intrusive and inconsistent. Other rights are not hyphenated with the words describing them; why should this one be different? Therefore, throughout this book, right to know is used as a three-word phrase, or else, more often, in its abbreviated form, RTK. It is hyphenated only when used as an adjective.

Susan G. Hadden

Acknowledgments

A study such as this, of a policy that is both new and potentially revolutionary, depends for its success on the candor of scores of people. In return for their kindness, I must refrain from thanking them by name, albeit at the cost of documentation for readers. It is to these people, in both the public and private sectors, that any success I have had in accurately portraying right-to-know activities must be attributed. Officials at the federal, state, and local levels, members of a wide variety of interest groups, and a host of industry representatives from CEOs to line engineers all contributed points of view not as divergent as I had originally expected. Among the most helpful, of course, have been the right-to-know staffs of the states of Massachusetts and New Jersey, who assisted with the survey as well as consented to long interviews and repeated phone calls. Without in any way implicating them in my conclusions or analysis, I must also especially thank two Texas officials, Mike Scott of the Division of Emergency Management and Bill Elliott of the Texas Department of Health, who willingly provided documents and tried to overcome the inherent barriers of bureaucracy to bring right to know to the people of Texas.

Colleagues also contributed by reading the manuscript; Brandon Johnson and Jerry Zeitz added much to the merit of the analysis as well as forestalled many errors. Others whose comments and conversations were helpful include Jurgen Schmandt, John Slavick, Frances Lynn, and Dan Fiorino. Although much of the merit of the present study is due to their help, the remaining errors are, of course, mine alone. Several students of June Fessenden-Raden and Sheila Jasanoff in the Science, Technology, and Society Program at Cornell University provided many helpful comments as well: Rebecca Efroymson, Garrett Keating, and Jim Wilmer. Leigh Boske codirected the project in which the field survey of Texas counties was conducted. Fellow members of the Steering Committee of the Texas Risk Communication Project provided a wide range of insights. Chandler Stolp, as always, provided cheerful, timely, and appropriate technical and methodological advice.

Financial support is always essential to a wide-ranging project. The University Research Institute of the University of Texas at Austin provided a leave during which writing was begun. The Chemical

Manufacturers Association funded the workshop that provided the basis for the information formats in Chapter 9, and the Administrative Conference of the United States (ACUS) funded the research presented in part in Chapters 5 and 8; it is reported in a different form in one of ACUS's reports. The Texas Department of Highways and Public Transportation funded the project of which the Texas field survey constituted a small portion; none of the interpretations presented here should be attributed to the department. The LBJ School and the Stephen H. Spurr Centennial Fellowship supported some of the travel and research.

The project could not have been completed in such a timely fashion without help from research assistants Letitia Flores, Jennifer Mason, Andy Gilmour, Mike Vanchiere, and Jay Schmidt, as well as from Barbara Jann. To the anonymous geniuses who made it easy for me to switch the text from one computer to another and to Caren Troutman and Carl Ratliff in the LBJ School computer office go another set of thanks. Andy Gilmour's computer virtuosity accounts in large part for the book's format, and his persistence in some measure for its timeliness. The book was typed and formatted on a variety of Apple Macintosh computers using Microsoft Word.

My deepest debt is to my family, who, as usual, cheerfully discussed hazardous chemicals and emergency response rather than more felicitous topics. James Hadden helped with some of the more tedious typing tasks, and Jim Hadden assisted with the computer and the editing as well as in many different ways. His contributions are beyond words.

S.G.H.

PART 1
What Is Right to Know?

I conclude, That a clear knowledge of all these particulars, and many more . . . is necessary in order to good, certain, and easie Government. . . . But whether the knowledge thereof be necessary to many, or fit for others, then the Sovereign, and his chief Ministers, I leave to consideration.

--John Graunt, *Natural and Political Observations
Mentioned in a Following Index and Made Upon
the Bills of Mortality, 1662*

1 / The Need for Right to Know

On the afternoon of October 17, 1988, a resident of a small but heavily industrialized city in Texas looked out her window and saw a large dark cloud hanging in the east, in the direction of one of the larger petrochemical plants. As she watched, the cloud grew in size; soon she began to smell a foul odor and her eyes started to run. She turned on her radio to see if there were emergency information for residents, but there was no mention of the cloud at all. Concerned, she called the city health department, but they had no information. After a few hours, her symptoms disappeared and the cloud dispersed. The morning newspaper contained a small article about a fire at one of the local plants but failed to state what substance had been released. When she called the health department, the citizen was referred to the emergency planning department, which, in turn, stated that it had no information on the substance released. In desperation, she called the facility itself; she was told that the information was not public.

Should the citizen have been able to find out what substance was burning? If so, in such cases should the information be made public through the media, or should it only be available if a citizen takes the trouble to ask? Who should make it available--government or the management of the facility? Should just the name of the substance be given out, or should additional information about its health effects, uses, and physical chemistry be available? Again, whose responsibility might it be to make such information public?

It seems logical that people should be able to know about the chemicals stored and used in their communities, but the right to know that kind of information was not won until 1986. Indeed, the date on which the spill mentioned in the first paragraph occurred entails some irony, as it was two years earlier on that very day that Congress had passed the Emergency Planning and Community Right-to-Know Act, which provided that citizens should have access to information that local facilities would submit about the hazardous chemicals they were storing, using, or emitting. But the right to know, as this occurrence in Texas suggests, is not absolute; although the law requires that information about the quantities and potential health effects of accidental releases of chemicals be reported to local officials, this provision applies only to about 400 "extremely hazardous substances." Perhaps this incident involved another substance, one of the nearly 60,000 chemicals in commercial use in the United States to which the law requiring the reporting of releases does not apply. Perhaps local officials or the plant manager were not fulfilling their duties under the law. Perhaps the citizen called the wrong people.

But even if she had obtained information about the chemical, what would she have done? Knowing its name enables her to find out more about the chemical itself, but it tells her nothing about the level at which she was exposed, and little about what the effects of such an exposure might be. Supposing these facts were also available, what then? The citizen might want to work with her doctor to mitigate the health effects, or she might want to mobilize her neighbors to complain to the facility manager or to the government to try to reduce the risks of future accidents. Many obstacles intervene between the desire to take action and the achievement of an actual reduction in risk. Would the costs to the political system and the manufacturer be worth the benefits in reduced risk?

The right to know is a complex concept, belying its simple name. The term has been used throughout U.S. history, from the first Constitutional Convention, when James Wilson of Virginia argued that "the people have a right to know what their agents . . . have done," through World War II, when a representative of the press worried about censorship argued that "there cannot be political freedom . . . without respect for the right to know."[1] Its application to hazardous materials is only the most recent manifestation of a long-standing ideal. But even applied to hazardous chemicals it seems to raise more questions than it answers--questions about the nature of government in the information age, about the duties of citizens, about the rights of corporations. These are the questions that I intend to explore in this book.

By definition, right to know is an information policy. Although we have realized for more than a decade that we have entered the "information age," our society has still not defined the proper role of government in creating information, making it available, or ensuring its accuracy. We have failed even to clarify who owns or may use information embodied in the not-so-new technologies of videotape, television, and computer. Our preoccupation with educational reform may stem in part from our inchoate understanding that our children and our society will not survive unless they can master the deluge of information that inundates us--acquire it, store it, understand it, assess its quality, and use it.

Precisely because it is only one small part of the information puzzle that confronts us, right to know about hazardous materials, which is usually called "community right to know" to distinguish it from its predecessor "worker right to know," gives us insights into many information policies, even those of considerably larger scope. At the same time that technological advances and, at least in the case of right to know, government policy continue to lower the cost of information, the same forces appear to be increasing the cost of the infrastructure needed to acquire and use the information: computers, modems, ability to find and manipulate complex databases. Thus, a policy such as right to know that should empower people by giving them information may instead empower only the few who can actually acquire and use the data; even more perversely, the policy may actually tip the balance of power further toward the regulated industries about which citizens wish to know by allowing these industries to overwhelm nonspecialists with vast quantities of technical data.

In this chapter, I lay the groundwork for consideration of these issues. First, I provide a brief introduction to chemicals in the environment, the problem to which community right to know was the response. I then suggest the kinds of questions that citizens may have about these chemicals--the things they want to know. The questions in turn imply that there are different kinds of right to know, each of which entails a different role for government, the private sector, and citizens. These different approaches serve as a framework for the discussion of RTK throughout the remainder of the book.

Chemicals in the Environment

Chemicals are central to the modern way of life. From telecommunications satellites to the laundry room, synthetic organic chemicals provide us with immeasurable benefits. Our diets, our health, our ability to travel have all become better and cheaper through advances in chemistry. As the rise of the automobile in the early part of this century forced scientists to learn more about petroleum, important new products were developed, including explosives and plastics. Shortages and new demands during World War II again provided the stimulus for chemical inventions, which modern industrial practices quickly turned into commercial products: DDT was first used to control typhus among troops in Italy in 1943;

nylon stockings first became common during the war; new detergents were developed as a result of a lack of animal fat from abroad.

Thus dawned the "chemical age."[2] From 1950 to 1974, chemical production expanded at a rate more than double that of the gross national product as chemical companies found more and more ways to substitute synthetic for natural or other traditional products in clothing, adhesives, drugs, pesticides, rubber, paper, building materials, and packaging. In 1974, the peak year, the synthetic organic chemicals manufactured in the United States had a commercial value of about $43 billion.[3]

As we now know, the manufacture, disposal, and use of some of these chemicals had unwanted and unintended side effects. Some chemicals turned out to cause diseases many years later or to affect unborn children when their parents were exposed; some were found to harm wildlife exposed to them in water or air. These are the "hazardous chemicals" to which community RTK applies.

The level of danger presented by such a chemical depends both on exposure--length, route, and amount--and on its toxic or hazardous characteristics. Hazardous effects are often divided into short-term, or acute, and long-term, or delayed. Among short-term hazards are explosivity and flammability. Two acute hazards to human health are toxicity and sensitization, or the ability to cause allergic reactions after exposure. A chemical can be toxic--that is, cause systemic damage as a result of a one-time exposure--by ingestion, inhalation, or touch. Long-term or delayed hazards, which are often more difficult to identify because they only become manifest long after an exposure, include carcinogenicity (tendency to cause cancer), teratogenicity (causing damage to fetuses), and mutagenicity (causing alterations in the genes of an individual).

Hazardous chemicals get into the environment in many ways. For many years, before the nature of the hazards that such chemicals posed were understood, people disposed of chemicals by dumping them into the water, burying them, or burning them in such a way that residues got into the air. Unintended emissions also occurred when a valve in a manufacturing plant developed a slow leak or an accident caused a chemical to spill. Many chemicals reached the water or soil through intentional and seemingly proper use--for many years it was not known, for example, that some pesticides and herbicides were leaching through the soil into the groundwater or running off into surface waters.

In 1962, publication of Rachel Carson's book *Silent Spring* focused public attention on the role of chemicals in the environment. But without knowing which chemicals were being used, it was difficult to decide which were causing the unwanted effects. Manufacturers and sellers of products did not want to lose their markets and argued that they could not be blamed for such effects; they said that people were using the products improperly, that producers had no way of knowing about the delayed effects, or that no one could prove that it was their product rather than someone else's that was causing the harm.

It took eight years for the United States to phase out use of DDT. And twenty-five years after the publication of *Silent Spring*, evidence of the presence and delayed effects of hazardous, man-made chemicals in the environment continue to be found in fish kills, in mysterious skin rashes that disappear when the person goes away from the neighborhood of chemical plants, or in clusters of a rare cancer.

So long as manufacturers and users of chemicals did not have to reveal what substances they were using and emitting, it was impossible to obtain an overview of the extent to which hazardous chemicals are present in our air, water, or soil and constitute a risk to human health or the environment. In a few places--where research was conducted, where an old waste site was detected, or where people tried to explain an apparent cluster of some disease--"snapshots" of situations were obtained. But with tens of thousands of different chemicals in use, the number that can be found is so great and the cost of testing for them so high that no study can look for more than a few preselected substances. Table 1-1, for example, shows the amounts of some hazardous chemicals found in water at a few sites, and Table 1-2 shows the results of a study of air pollutants in another set of locations.

In addition to the few direct measurements, there are indirect indications of the amount of hazardous chemicals in the environment, although interpreting these is also difficult. Table 1-3, for example, shows the residues of certain toxic materials in human fat--a measure not of the exposures to chemicals but of their results. By themselves, however, information on these residues does not tell whether they are too high or constitute a threat to human health. Many people argue that they do not constitute a threat, because the cancer rate in the United States has been declining. Table 1-4 illustrates that argument; it shows cancer deaths generally declining between 1950 and 1980. Others, however, believe that the data shown in Table 1-4 are misleading; they cite the data in Table 1-5, which show an increase between 1981 and 1988 in the number of new cases of cancer, especially those associated with chemical exposures such as leukemias and bladder cancer.

Why have we relied on indirect measures of exposure and scattered small studies to find out what hazardous chemicals are

TABLE 1-1 Concentrations of Selected Synthetic Organic Compounds in Raw and Finished[a] Groundwater

Compound	Number of Cities Sampled		Percent with Chemical Present	
	Raw	Finished	Raw	Finished
Trichloroethylene	13	25	38.5	36.0
Carbon tetrachloride	27	39	7.4	28.2
Tetrachloroethylene	27	36	18.5	22.0
1,1,1-Trichloroethane	13	23	23.1	21.7
1,1-Dichloroethane	13	13	23.1	23.1
1,2-Dichloroethane	13	25	7.7	4.0
Trans-dichloroethylene	13	13	15.4	15.4
Cis-dichloroethylene	13	13	38.5	30.8
1,1-dichloroethylene	13	13	15.4	7.7
Methylene chloride	27	38	3.7	2.6
Vinyl chloride	13	25	15.4	4.0

[a] "Raw" means untreated water and "finished" means treated water.

Source: Council on Environmental Quality, *Contamination of Ground Water by Toxic Organic Chemicals* (Washington, D.C.: CEQ, January 1981), p. 26.

TABLE 1-2 Summary of Annual Levels of Seven Air Contaminants at Six Sites (in micrograms per cubic meter)

Contaminant	Site						Screening Value[a]
	1	2	3	4	5	6	
Benzene	6.000	6.000	11.000	18.000	11.000	7.000	1.500
Formaldehyde	--	6.000	6.000	7.000	--	4.000	1.500
Lead	--	0.200	--	0.200	--	0.200	0.005
Benzo(a)pyrene	--	0.007	0.005	0.010	0.007	0.005	0.005
Benzo(ghi)pyrene	--	0.007	--	0.007	0.006	--	0.005
Pyrene	--	0.018	0.018	0.014	0.013	0.017	0.005
Chrysene	0.006	0.009	0.007	0.009	0.010	0.010	0.005

[a] A value without the force of a standard that is used for determining whether ambient air concentrations are too high.

Source: Texas Air Control Board, *Final Report: Gulf Coast Community Exposure Study* (Austin: TACB, March 1988), n.p.

TABLE 1-3 Residues of Toxic Materials in Human Fat, 1970-1983 (parts per million, geometric mean, lipid basis)

Chemical	1970	1975	1981	1983
DDT	7.95	4.34	2.38	1.63
Dieldrin	0.16	0.12	0.05	0.06
Oxychlordane	--	0.11	0.09	0.10
Heptachlor Epoxide	0.09	0.08	0.11	0.09
Hexachlorobenzene	--	0.04	0.04	0.03

Source: Council on Environmental Quality, *Environmental Quality: Fifteenth Annual Report*, (Washington, D.C.: CEQ, 1984), p. 604.

TABLE 1-4 Death Rates in the United States, 1950-1980 (deaths per 100,000 population)

Disease	Rate in Age Category			
	45-54		55-64	
	1950	1980	1950	1980
Heart disease	309	182	808	510
Cancer	175	179	393	443
Suicide	21	17	27	17
Motor vehicle accidents	22	21	29	18
Cerebrovascual disease	70	26	195	69

Source: U.S. Department of Health and Human Services, Public Health Service, National Center for Health Statistics, *Health United States: 1982* (Washington, D.C.: HHS, 1982), pp. 61, 63, 67, 69, and 73.

present in the environment? The answer in large part is that it never occurred to anyone that people needed to know. Government was regulating specific products that might present health hazards and had established emissions standards to protect the environment. Manufacturers of chemicals and of chemical-based products had no incentive to reveal the substances they were storing or using, as that might help competitors to learn their secret formulas. They certainly had no incentive to tell anyone what they were emitting into the water or air beyond the requirements of government regulations, as such

TABLE 1-5 Estimated New Cancer Cases and Deaths, 1981 and 1988 (in 1,000s)

	1981		1988	
	New Cases	Deaths	New Cases	Deaths
All sites	815	420	985	494
Oral	26	9	30	9
Digestive	194	110	228	122
Respiratory	135	110	168	144
Breast	110	37	136	42
Urinary Organs	55	19	69	20
Genital Organs	152	46	177	52
Leukemias	23	16	27	18
Other Blood/Lymph	40	22	51	26

Sources: Kathryn H. Salisbury and Eleanor L. Johnson, *The Indispensable Cancer Handbook* (New York: Seaview Books, 1981), pp. 316-317. *Cancer Facts and Figures* (Washington, D.C.: American Cancer Society, 1988), p. 8.

information might elicit additional regulation or encourage neighbors to file lawsuits against them. Finally, collecting information and making it available is itself a costly activity. In short, there were many incentives not to make such information public and virtually no incentives for the opposite course of action.

The absence of information about specific chemicals did not, however, prevent people from getting more general information. With great regularity, the media reported both new evidence about delayed harmful effects of chemicals and new evidence that people were unwittingly exposed to those chemicals. Surveys document the high level of concern that people feel about hazardous materials, and especially hazardous waste, in their communities. In a poll taken in 1980, 64 percent of the respondents felt "a great deal" of concern about disposal of hazardous industrial chemical wastes, and 46 percent felt a great deal of concern about the presence of toxic chemicals in the environment; in 1988, "active hazardous waste sites" were the highest environmental concern, called serious or very serious by 91 percent of the respondents to a Roper Poll.[4] A telephone survey of more than 600 Texans taken in February 1988 asked respondents to answer the question "How concerned are you about commercial activities involving hazardous materials in your community?" on a scale of 1 to 7. More than two-thirds of the people polled responded in categories 6 and 7, the highest levels of concern, for all three commercial activities-- transportation, production, and manufacturing; nearly 90 percent expressing this high level of concern about manufacturing of hazardous materials. In the same poll, however, 13 percent responded "don't know" and 47 percent responded "no" to the question "Are there hazardous materials in your community?"[5] Other studies report similar results for other areas of the nation.

The combination of ignorance and concern is politically explosive. People were bombarded with stories about hazardous materials, but they did not know which substances they were exposed to or even if they were exposed. Without that information, they could not take action to reduce their risks--either individual action such as drinking bottled water or collective action such as seeking stricter emissions standards for hazardous chemicals. Thus, they demanded the right to know.

Information, Regulation, and Individual Choice

It is probably not coincidence that the twentieth century, which has witnessed a vast increase in the use of chemicals, has also been a period of increasing governmental intervention to protect human health and the environment. Still, a general distrust of government in the United States has placed clear limits on its role as a regulator. Governments may deploy many different tools to reduce unwanted side effects of industrial activity. Arrayed on a continuum from least to most interventionist, these include: providing people with information about risks; limiting the uses of a product; imposing standards (such as the amount of a pollutant that may be emitted or requiring lawnmowers to be designed to turn off when the operator's hands are lifted); and banning products.

From the beginning of this century, when the first federal regulatory statutes were passed, U.S. policy has leaned heavily toward information provision as the preferred form of regulation. The Food and Drug Act of 1906 and the Insecticide Act of 1910, for example, required manufacturers of packaged food, drug, and pesticide products who provided a list of ingredients to be accurate and not to mislead potential purchasers deliberately. In the 1930s and 1940s, when public distrust of private industry was greater, stronger disclosure standards were enacted that forced manufacturers to list ingredients and required regulatory agencies to assess products before marketing to ensure that they were both safe and effective.

As a government regulatory strategy, information provision has many advantages over standard setting or banning. It is more consistent with the notion that government should "perfect" rather than alter the economic market: By ensuring that consumers had information, the government maintained their freedom to choose, whereas imposing standards narrowed the range of choice. Moreover, information provision is often cheaper than setting or complying with standards, so it is advantageous to both regulators and the regulated community.

Gradually, however, it became clear that certain kinds of risks were not appropriately regulated through information provision. For example, children could neither be expected to read warnings on flammable nightwear nor to act reasonably in response to such warnings. Therefore, it was appropriate for government to enact standards. Similarly, air, water, and wild animals needed direct protection, being unable to act in their own interests. The environmental laws of the 1960s and 1970s required government agencies to set standards limiting emissions of various chemicals into the air or water. These standards were to be set so as to achieve "swimmable waters" or to limit "significant risk." Reasonable people could differ over precisely what standards would achieve these goals, and many times industry challenged the standards in court.

Although there was some evidence that the standards were effective--fish returned to rivers they had abandoned because the water had been too polluted, people found breathing easier even in manufacturing towns[6]--people realized that the standards did not affect many of the substances that present long-term hazards to human health and the environment. When they experienced burning eyes or saw wild animals giving birth to deformed offspring, people wanted to know the identities of the substances that were being used nearby to see if these might be the cause. Citizens were no longer willing to rely on the word of government or industry that a particular substance was safe. Thus, information provision, which had once seemed inapplicable to environmental regulation, came once again to seem both appropriate and desirable.

From surveys and informal talks with people who have experienced problems they associate with exposure to hazardous chemicals, we know the kinds of questions that citizens have asked about exposures to chemicals in the environment.[7] According to a survey of citizens of New Jersey and Massachusetts who had filed right-to-know requests under their respective state laws, people asked for the following kinds of information in addition to the chemical inventories or health-effects data they had received: (1) information about facilities, including reports of government inspections and permits and names of contact people; (2) information about particular chemicals, including storage and disposal techniques, chemical processes that use the substance, and routes of exposure for members of the community; (3) information about the procedures of the law, including which agencies to contact and how to get a complaint considered; and (4) other substantive information, including how to monitor discharges, sources for additional information, and where to find doctors knowledgeable about chemical exposures.

Of course, different people have somewhat different questions. For purposes of analysis, concerned citizens may be divided roughly into two groups: neighbors of facilities, who, like the citizen in the opening paragraphs of this chapter, are concerned about short-term but intense exposures resulting from accidents; and those, perhaps spread over a larger area, who are concerned about lower-level exposures over a longer period resulting from daily emissions or disposal of chemicals into air, water, or ground.

Citizens in the vicinity of an accident who are exposed to significant amounts of a chemical over a relatively short period want to know the answers to these questions:

1. To what substance(s) have I been exposed?
2. What are the health effects of such an exposure?
3. What can we do to prevent accidents in the future?

As part of the solution to preventing future accidents, citizens also want to know:

4. What hazardous substances are present in my community and in what amounts?

People exposed to chemicals as the result of an accident must immediately be told how to identify the symptoms of exposure and how to minimize exposure. After the incident is over, they want to know whether there will be any long-term health effects. They also want to know the name of the substance involved in order to be able to obtain information independent of the industry or government source that is giving information related to the accident. Citizens are skeptical of information provided by parties they believe to have a vested interest in a particular outcome; they want basic information that will enable them to do some checking on their own. In order to prevent further accidents, citizens and government officials need to know what substances are present in the community. Not only may they then prepare appropriate emergency plans, but they may also be able to work with facilities to ensure that substances are properly stored and disposed of.

Citizens who think they may be suffering from long-term low-level exposures to hazardous chemicals have similar concerns: They want to know about health effects, immediate palliative measures, and long-term preventive measures. Their strongest concern is expressed in the question "Am I exposed to any hazardous substances in the environment and do they have any health effects on me or my family?" It is easier to answer this big question if it is broken into a series of questions that are narrower in scope:

1. What hazardous substances are present in my community and in what amounts?
2. Are these substances being released into the environment? Have I been exposed?
3. If hazardous substances are released into the environment, by what route and at what level might I be exposed?
4. Do these exposures affect my health or that of my family? Alternatively, if I have a symptom, what substances might be causing it?

In addition to obtaining these basic facts, many people go on to ask deeper questions about the meaning of the information and what they might do about it:

5. Are the exposures acceptable in light of other considerations?
6. If they are not acceptable, are there any ways these exposures can be reduced?
7. If emissions can be reduced, should we ask the facility to do this? How can we persuade them?

This list of questions ranges from the purely factual--What materials are stored at facilities in the community?--to the evaluative--Are the risks offset by the benefits?--to the political--What kinds of actions can we take? Are all the questions really appropriate to RTK? The language of rights is central to political culture in the United States, and Americans take their rights very seriously. What is the right to know about hazardous chemicals in our communities? Is it merely a right to obtain data that used to be unavailable; does it include a right to the supplementary information needed to interpret that data; does it extend to a right to undertake action on the basis of the information? In short, what kind of policy is community RTK, and what roles does it entail for government, industry, and citizen? The limits of our newest right will finally be decided in legislatures, courts, and in the demands of the public for information and action concerning hazardous materials. In the next section, I outline a range of choices--the kinds of RTK that we might have.

What Is the Right to Know?

In the first two sections of this chapter, I argued that as people began to become concerned about environmental exposures to hazardous chemicals, they realized that they could obtain little or no information about such exposures. Right to know was a response to this juxtaposition of events.

Logically, then, the most basic purpose of RTK is to ensure that interested people can find out what chemicals are "out there." As we have seen, industry had little incentive to provide such information; it took governmental action to ensure that the data became available. (In Chapter 2, I discuss in more detail exactly which data the present law requires to be disclosed.) Having ensured that the data are available, the government has fulfilled its duty. The burden is on the citizen to acquire, understand, and act upon the information as he or she sees fit. This form of RTK is very similar to the theory underlying food labeling as practiced in the United States: The government requires manufacturers to list ingredients but leaves it to consumers to determine whether the risks of any of the ingredients are unacceptable to them.

Policies that emphasize information provision may also serve as indirect incentives to undertake self-regulation. Thus, facilities that must report emissions to the environment or the fact that they store extremely volatile and hazardous chemicals might prefer to reduce the emissions or change the substances they use rather than make public information that could damage their reputations. It is possible that RTK is less important for the information that citizens may obtain than for its effects in actually reducing the risks to which citizens are exposed. There are many people who believe that data about chemicals are too complicated for most citizens to understand; for these people, the indirect effects of disclosure are the most important. The information can also prove directly useful to government regulators in determining the need for additional regulations that would protect the health and safety of citizens. Thus, the role of government in this kind of RTK is stronger than merely ensuring that information is available to citizens; it must also act on their behalf if self-regulation is not forthcoming or sufficient.

Information informs decisions. Some people believe that the true purpose of RTK is to allow citizens to make better decisions about hazardous materials in the community. This purpose requires not only that information be available but that it be understandable and appropriate. Thus, government may have to help citizens interpret or manipulate the data they obtain in order to make it germane to community decisions, not just to ensure its availability. The larger role of government does not necessarily lead to a reduced role for citizens; on the contrary, because the purpose is to allow citizens to make better decisions, there is a great burden on citizens to evaluate information and actually make choices rather than leaving them to government or industry.

Once citizens are involved in decisionmaking, they may change the balance of power, tipping it away from the "big" institutions-- industry and government--and toward "the people." By ensuring access to information in this view, government empowers people first to understand, then to demand changes in the effects environmental pollutants have on their lives. The idea of information as power has preoccupied democratic theorists down to our own time; RTK as applied to hazardous materials is only its most recent manifestation. Although in one sense the role of government is limited to providing the information, a more realistic description of this kind of RTK recognizes that government must also create or support institutions for participation and decisionmaking that will help citizens make use of their new information.

Table 1-6 summarizes these four kinds of RTK. The differences among them stem not only from differing notions of what citizens need to know about hazardous materials in their communities but also from differing ideas about the role of government in American life and about the proper balance of power between citizens and large institutions that have access to technical expertise. These issues will remain implicit throughout much of the discussion that follows and will be considered again in the concluding chapter.

Forewarned by this brief discussion, the reader will see different elements of these kinds of RTK in the laws and activities described throughout the study. The attitudes and actions of citizens, industry, and government reflect different conceptions of RTK; the same people may act as if RTK should be or is something different under different circumstances. Which is the real RTK? All the types have validity; all serve an important social purpose. Which of them should be the

TABLE 1-6 Tentative Typology of Rights to Know

Type	Purpose	Governmental Role
Basic	Ensure that citizens can find out about chemicals.	Ensure data are created and available.
Risk Reduction	Reduce risks from chemicals, preferably through voluntary industry action but also by government if necessary.	Regulators use information to create new standards or enforce existing ones if industry fails to police itself.
Better Decision-making	Allow citizens to participate in making decisions about appropriate levels of hazardous materials in the community.	Provide citizens with analyzed data, methods for manipulating and interpreting data.
Alter Balance of Power	Empower citizens with respect to big government, industry.	Provide citizens with analyzed data, means of participating.

kind of RTK toward which the polity strives? Each reader may have a different answer to this question. In Chapter 10, I shall try to justify my own answer, which is that a desirable form of RTK comes very close to being a kind of informed consent. Before that, however, we shall see the various kinds of RTK in practice--in the laws that now give Americans the right to know, in the implementation of those laws, and in the problems for RTK that are raised by our institutions and the state of knowledge itself.

Notes

1. James Wilson of Virginia said, "The people have a right to know what their agents are doing or have done, and it should not be the option of the legislature to conceal their proceedings." Quoted in David M. O'Brien, *The Public's Right to Know: The Supreme Court and the First Amendment* (New York: Praeger Publishers, 1981), p. 38. He was arguing for a constitutional provision

that both houses of Congress should keep records; such a provision is found in Article II, section 5, clause 3. The term "right to know" came to public attention in modern times on January 22, 1945. Kent Cooper, the executive director of Associated Press, told an audience that he believed that "citizens are entitled to have access to news, fully and accurately presented. There cannot be political freedom in one country, or in the world, without respect for ˋthe right to know.'" Editorial, *New York Times*, January 23, 1945, p. 18.

2. See Hugh D. Crone, *Chemicals and Society: A Guide to the New Chemical Age* (Cambridge: Cambridge University Press, 1986), pp. 7-9.

3. United States International Trade Commission, *Synthetic Organic Chemicals: United States Production and Sales 1985*, (Washington, D.C.: USITC, September 1986), p. 5.

4. National Public Opinion Survey, sponsored by Resources for the Future and reported in "The Polls: Environmental Protection," *Public Opinion Quarterly*, Winter 1980; and "Public Opinion on Environmental Issues," Roper Organization and Cantril Research, Inc., 1980. The 1988 Roper Poll is reported in Citizen's Clearinghouse for Hazardous Wastes, Inc., *Newsletter* 19 (July 1988), p. 6. (Percentage of respondents ranking other problems serious or very serious were: worker exposure to toxics, 89 percent; industrial accident pollution, 88 percent, genetic alteration damage, 66 percent.)

5. The Appendix describes this survey in more detail.

6. U.S. Council on Environmental Quality, *Environmental Quality: The Fifteenth Annual Report of the Council on Environmental Quality* (Washington, D.C.: Government Printing Office, 1986), pp. 13, 82.

7. In addition to the New Jersey/Massachusetts survey reported in the Appendix, see Campbell Communications, Inc., "EPA Title III Needs Assessment Project: 1988 General Public Focus Groups, Summary of Findings," Summer 1988, p. 19.

2 / Gaining the Right to Know

The methyl isocyanate gas that was accidentally released on December 3, 1984, from a pesticide manufacturing plant in Bhopal in central India killed more than 2,000 people and injured more than 100,000. The Bhopal incident raised questions about the possibility of similar accidents in the United States, especially about preparedness at the local level for chemical emergencies and about the kinds of information available to local officials and residents. As soon as Congress convened in January 1985, bills were introduced that would provide local officials and citizens with enough information about hazardous chemicals in their neighborhoods to allow sound emergency planning. The Emergency Planning and Community Right-to-Know Act was finally passed on October 17, 1986; despite the legislative delay, its passage was still clearly tied to Bhopal.

The gaps in our information about the hazardous chemicals around us (and about other risks as well) stem from two major causes: lack of data and difficulty in obtaining existing data. The new act addressed both these problems--first, by creating new reporting requirements that would call forth previously unavailable data and, second, by ensuring that citizens would have access to that data.

Part of my argument in this book is that the law as passed in 1986 embodies primarily the basic, data-provision type of RTK. It does not require all the kinds of supplementary data people need and does not provide for the support activities needed to aid citizens in turning data into information. The antecedents of the law help explain this focus. In the first and second sections of this chapter, I discuss worker right to know and the political history of the 1986 act. In the third section, I describe the provisions of the act in some detail, and in the last section, I give a preliminary assessment of the statute by describing the extent to which it answers the questions listed in Chapter 1. In Chapter 3, this discussion is amplified by a look at right-to-know programs in two states--one whose program precedes passage of the 1986 act and one whose program was developed primarily in response to the new law.

Information for Workers

In the mid-1970s, the term "right to know," which had earlier been used to refer to freedom of the press and to citizen access to information about government activities, was appropriated by the labor movement. Employee right to know referred especially to information about substances in the workplace that pose long-term hazards to health and to information about each worker's exposure to such substances. The federal Hazard Communication Standard (HCS) that resulted from workers' demands for the right to know plays a central role in the 1986 Community Right-to-Know Act as well.

In some ways, it is surprising that employees were forced to assert this right as late as the fourth quarter of the twentieth century. Even in the early part of the century, when collective bargaining was regarded as an impediment to the individual's right to negotiate a contract with an employer, it was understood that employees need to know about the risks of the job if they are to obtain an appropriate wage. As the risks best understood at the time consisted of such obvious dangers as cutting of fingers by sharp machinery, government intervention did not seem to be required to ensure that workers understood job risks.

The distinction between short-term risks, such as those posed by sharp machinery, and long-term risks is very important in understanding the development of government regulation of occupational risk. Information about short-term risks is relatively cheap to acquire and is easy to understand; employers have an incentive to provide it to workers because the employers themselves bear a large portion of the costs associated with short-term hazards, in the form of lost workdays and increased workers' compensation premiums resulting from a bad safety record. Employees have an equally strong incentive to attend to information about short-term risks, as they immediately bear the full unpleasantness of ignoring such risks, including costs of recovery not covered by workers' compensation.

Long-term risks--or, as they have come to be called under Title III, delayed risks--have very different characteristics. Information about them is often difficult to obtain and difficult to understand. Not only is the cost of the information higher for both employers and employees, but the benefits are lower for both parties: Lost workdays or reduced productivity of workers happen many years later, perhaps when the worker is in someone else's employ; workers find that wearing protective equipment or otherwise reducing the likelihood of exposure is difficult and unpleasant; and they know that there is only a chance that they will incur the delayed bad effects. Moreover, employers find it easier to hide delayed risks than short-term risks from workers, and workers who are poorly informed do not demand compensation.

By 1970, when the Occupational Safety and Health Act (OSH) was passed, workers had become very concerned about delayed health effects from workplace exposure. The OSH Act was especially intended to respond to these concerns. The law established the National Institute for Occupational Safety and Health (NIOSH), a research body to develop and recommend standards based on its scientific studies of workplace exposure. It also established a regulatory agency, the Occupational Safety and Health Administration (OSHA) and gave it the power to set standards for exposure to substances that pose long-term hazards.

Unfortunately, OSHA proceeded very slowly.[1] Aware that the twenty-odd standards the agency had managed to promulgate constituted but a drop in the bucket in view of the 60,000 chemicals used in the workplace,[2] workers began to seek other means of regulating exposure to hazardous substances. Information provision was a likely strategy, building as it did upon existing laws and industry practice. In 1975, occupational safety and health groups in the Philadelphia area initiated a national right-to-know campaign; they obtained thousands of signatures on a petition to OSHA to promulgate a federal standard and made the term "right to know" common parlance in the labor movement.[3] In 1976, PHILAPOSH, the Philadelphia Area Project on Occupational Safety and Health, with assistance from Ralph Nader's Health Research Group, formally petitioned OSHA for regulations requiring employers to inform employees about health risks.

In response to these demands and industry's general opposition to them, OSHA developed a three-part regulatory strategy: (1) Ensure employees access to records maintained by employers that document workers' exposures; (2) provide for identification and labeling of hazardous substances in the workplace; and (3) ensure that workers are trained and educated about proper use of these substances.[4]

Progress toward these goals was slow. In 1980, OSHA promulgated the Access to Employee Exposure and Medical Records Standard.[5] The standard grants workers the right to obtain copies of their own medical records from their employers; union representatives may also obtain records if individual workers have signed release forms. In addition, workers may obtain copies of industrial hygiene studies that have monitored chemicals in their work areas or areas where similar chemicals are used. In order to ensure that workers and unions can use these records to help establish that workplace exposure caused certain diseases, the records must be kept for thirty years.[6]

Although OSHA was known to be working on a right-to-know standard that would cover the second point of its three-point program, workers came to believe that they could achieve their goals more quickly at the state level. In 1979, Connecticut passed a law providing workers the right to information about twenty-one known carcinogens that might be found in their workplaces.[7] New York, Michigan, Maine, and California passed worker RTK laws in 1980, each covering different substances and setting different requirements for the format and nature of available information. They were followed by many other states and even localities: By 1984, there were seventeen state and sixteen municipal RTK laws; and by mid-1985, there were twenty-eight state laws.[8]

On January 16, 1981, as the Carter administration was drawing to a close, OSHA finally published its long-awaited Hazard Communication Standard. The standard was withdrawn almost immediately by the Reagan administration; in March 1982 a substitute proposal was published and the final rule was promulgated in November 1983. One of the most hotly debated aspects of the regulation was its coverage; as published, it affected only certain manufacturers. Standard Industrial Classification (SIC) codes group industry according to the kinds of products or services they provide; the OSHA standard covered SIC codes 20-39, which include manufacturers of most products ranging from food, textiles, and furniture to machinery, transportation equipment, and petroleum products, but exclude nonmanufacturing employers ranging from dry cleaners to construction contractors.

The standard requires the following of all covered manufacturers:

- assess the potential hazards of all materials used in the workplace and prepare a list of hazardous materials there;
- provide a written hazard communication program including Material Safety Data Sheets (MSDSs) if workers are found to be exposed to hazardous chemicals;
- make MSDSs and lists of hazardous chemicals available to employees at all times;
- provide a training program that ensures that employees are aware of the requirements of the standard, know how to recognize the hazardous materials in their workplaces, know what the hazards are, and know how to use the materials safely; and
- label containers, packages, and storage tanks with the identity of the substance and appropriate hazard warnings.[9]

In addition, chemical manufacturers must develop MSDSs for their products and include them with the first shipment of a hazardous chemical made to a customer who is a manufacturer in the covered SIC codes.

A regulation entailing such an important change could not fail to have its critics. Industry, although pleased with many of the concessions embodied in the final regulation, such as not having to label pipelines, still thought the regulation entailed some unreasonable costs. Workers were especially concerned about two features of the regulation: its definition of hazardous substances and its limited industrial coverage. Rather than trying to cope with an ever-changing list of chemicals used in the workplace and with an ever-changing state of knowledge about the hazards presented by those chemicals, OSHA decided to detail twenty-three hazard categories and require manufacturers to determine whether substances they were shipping fell into any of those categories. Some critics felt that this mechanism provided manufacturers with an incentive not to find whether their products were hazardous. By the time contrary information became available, many workers would have been exposed. A related problem concerned trade secrets--claims that information would be too valuable to potential competitors to be released. Trade secrets are discussed in Chapter 4.

The question of industrial coverage was resolved through the courts, in which two different issues were raised: preemption and extent of coverage. Many of the state right-to-know laws covered more than SIC codes 20-39. Industry hoped to show that the federal regulation preempted those state laws and applied uniformly throughout the nation. Although the court agreed that the OSHA Hazard Communication Standard preempted portions of state laws covering SIC codes 20-39, it allowed to stand those portions of state laws that covered nonmanufacturing sectors.[10] OSHA was, therefore, ordered to extend the HCS to other sectors or show more clearly why this was inappropriate.[11]

On August 24, 1987, OSHA promulgated proposed regulations extending the HCS to SIC codes 1-89, which cover all commercial establishments except those in the public sector.[12] After various delays occasioned by further court challenges, OSHA declared the standard effective on June 24, 1988, for all nonpublic businesses except the construction industry.[13] These developments not only extended the scope of employee RTK, but, as we shall see, also broadened community RTK, two sections of which are directly tied to the HCS.

Employees' right to know about hazards in their workplaces evolved slowly, from an assumption that they would be able to see risks unaided to government assurance that they would have access to information and training about unseen, long-term risks posed by low-level exposures to hazardous materials. By the 1970s, when OSHA began considering a standard for hazard communication, the right of workers to know was generally accepted. Employers might wish to limit that right with respect to trade secrets, but several factors made it almost self-evident that employees needed to know about the substances with which they were working. These factors included the intensity with which workers were exposed, the growing possibility of liability suits, and the increased level of knowledge about possible long-term hazards. But this logic did not seem nearly so self-evident to many concerning community right to know.

Winning the Right to Know[14]

The Bhopal incident may have provided the impetus for the federal community RTK law, but even before that accident some people had been seeking--and gaining--the right to know about chemicals present in their neighborhoods and communities. In 1979, the Philadelphia occupational safety coalition PHILAPOSH and the Environmental Cancer Prevention Center sponsored a conference on toxic substances in the workplace. In the course of the discussions, attendees asked why only workers should know about hazardous substances; all members of the community are exposed to the same risks, albeit at lower intensity, by permitted and accidental emissions, as residues on workers' clothes, and through the passage of vehicles transporting the materials. Thus was born community right to know.[15]

Although this right seemed to conference participants to be a logical extension of employee right to know, the right of citizens to know about hazardous materials stored and used in their communities is not so obvious. Workers are exposed to substances at high intensity. Workers bargain with employers about the conditions of employment; systematic denial of information about workplace hazards would jeopardize their abilities to bargain appropriately. But community RTK requires private bodies to provide information to assist citizens in public decisionmaking, a conceptual step that was more difficult to accept.

In Philadelphia and other places where community RTK was broached, opponents tended to raise three major arguments: Citizens already have the right to know; RTK entails unnecessary paperwork for industry; and local laws would encourage industry to relocate to areas without such costly legislation.[16] These arguments raised cost issues without mentioning offsetting benefits and also avoided raising an essential (if politically unstimulating) question: Is ensuring the availability of information about environmental pollution a useful and therefore appropriate governmental function? Aside from the cost arguments, right to know was difficult to oppose; as the president of the Philadelphia Chamber of Commerce said, "It sounds like you are standing up for cancer."[17]

In 1981 Philadelphia passed the nation's first right-to-know law that covered both workers and the community. (Philadelphia's law actually consists of two separate ordinances, one each amending the Air Management Code and the Fire Code.) Several California cities, including Santa Monica, Vallejo, and Sacramento, soon followed, passing only community RTK laws as California already had worker RTK. In 1982, Cincinnati, like Philadelphia a city with a high cancer fatality rate, passed its law. More and more states and localities passed RTK laws that extended to the public, and each law was slightly different. Like the federal law to come, passage of the laws was often spurred by an accidental release or some emergency; emergency response was, therefore, an important element of local ordinances. The more important differences included the substances covered, threshold amounts covered, particular industries covered, means for making the information public, the kinds of information industry was required to submit, and exemptions from the law for trade secrets.[18]

The focus on community RTK moved to the federal level in 1985. Within three months of the Bhopal incident, three bills had been introduced in Congress that included various provisions relating to public access to information about hazardous materials and to improving response to emergencies involving them. Several more were introduced throughout the summer. Each contained slightly different provisions or embodied a slightly different approach to the problem.

As so often happens in Congress, issues only partly related became joined. Prior to Bhopal, public and especially media interest in hazardous materials had generally been focused on hazardous wastes, as the surveys reported in Chapter 1 indicated. One important hazardous waste law is the Comprehensive Environmental Response, Compensation, and Liability Act of 1980 (CERCLA), often called "superfund" because among other provisions, it established a fund for cleaning up abandoned waste sites. CERCLA was scheduled to expire on October 1, 1985; both opponents and proponents hoped to use the reauthorization process to change the law. Nine different congressional committees claimed jurisdiction over superfund bills.[19] During the mark-up of a comprehensive superfund amendment in the

Senate Environmental and Public Works Committee, Senator Frank Lautenberg of New Jersey proposed and the committee adopted a "materials balance" amendment.[20] The amendment, which drew upon the experience of the New Jersey industrial survey, required facilities that manufacture or store more than certain threshold amounts of the more than 700 chemicals listed as hazardous in the CERCLA regulations to account for the disposition of all of the substance--in manufacture, emissions into air and water, disposal, and so on. As New Jersey also had a strong community right-to-know program that required disclosure of data acquired in the successor to the first industrial survey, one effect of the Lautenburg amendment was to link community right-to-know legislation with superfund reauthorization. When the complexity and expense of superfund and the politics of the many congressional committees delayed passage of superfund reauthorization until October 1986, RTK was also delayed.

The various RTK bills embodied either or both of two distinct purposes: (1) to improve emergency planning and response and (2) to create new data about hazardous materials at facilities. Although these two activities are interrelated--both planning for and response to emergencies depends in large measure on knowing what hazardous materials are present in the community and where--they entail rather different kinds of information and information management. Bills concerning emergency response, the most obvious response to the Bhopal incident, often incorporated a new interest in emergency planning, which was in turn stimulated by the Chemical Manufacturers Association (CMA) Community Awareness and Emergency Response (CAER) program. The CAER program, a private response to Bhopal, encouraged member industries to work with local officials and citizens in their communities to develop appropriate emergency response plans and educate people about these plans. By the end of 1986, the program covered about 320 communities. One important part of the plans is to ensure that emergency responders know what substances are stored, where, and what kinds of precautions should be taken if an accident or fire occurs.

Proposals to create new data (and give citizens access to them) tended to draw on local legislation and on the emergency response bills without explicitly considering what citizens might wish or need to know. In general, they simply extended the emergency response requirements, such as covered chemicals and amounts, by making the data available to the public. Many supplemented or supplanted this information by requiring industry to submit Material Safety Data Sheets, used by OSHA in the HCS as one source of health effects information. A subset of public information was reflected in the "industrial survey" or "materials balance" approach, which provides an estimate of how much of any substance is entering the air, water, or ground.

Cutting across these two purposes were a set of issues or requirements.[21] The first issue concerned the specific chemicals to be covered. CERCLA includes a list of 717 substances hazardous to people or the environment. Other bills referred to those chemicals for which the OSHA Hazard Communication Standard requires an MSDS according to the twenty-three hazard categories. Still others referred to the lists of chemicals in the RTK laws of New Jersey or Maryland, which were in turn based on a variety of criteria and sources.

Because of the Bhopal incident, Congress was particularly concerned with toxics in air. Dissatisfied with the efforts of the Environmental Protection Agency (EPA) under section 112 of the Clean Air Act, which focused on substances posing long-term low-level exposures quite different from Bhopal's acute exposure, three members of Congress introduced bills listing from 25 to 85 substances that must be regulated. EPA, however, was developing its own response to Bhopal: the Chemical Emergency Preparedness Program (CEPP). Based on the assumption that most acutely toxic exposures would arise from a point source that could be identified and regulated locally, CEPP was designed to further the agency's continuing effort to delegate responsibilities for environmental protection to states and localities. The program provided guidance for designing voluntary response programs for air toxics emergencies. EPA identified 402 chemicals that may cause severe irreversible health effects following a single short-term exposure.[22] An additional 26 "other" chemicals were listed as being of concern because they are manufactured in large amounts and pose health hazards; among them are cumene, ethylene oxide, and vinyl acetate, all of which are among the 50 chemicals manufactured in largest quantity in the United States.[23] In July 1985, Senator Lautenberg introduced another amendment that referred to these 400-odd substances as "extremely hazardous chemicals."

A related issue of concern was the amount of each chemical that would trigger regulation. Because risk is a function of the number of people exposed as well as the hazardousness of each chemical, Congress was reluctant to impose the costs of regulation on facilities that store or manufacture very small amounts of chemicals, perhaps believing that small amounts are inherently less likely to affect many people. Several of the bills identified threshold amounts below which facilities would not be subject to reporting requirements, but these amounts differed as there was little scientific basis upon which to determine appropriate thresholds. This problem stems less from the lack of a scientific basis for relating injury to exposure than from the lack of a theoretical basis for relating exposure to amounts produced, stored, or used.

Although participants differed widely on these issues, right to know was generally treated as a sacrosanct concept: Who could disagree that local officials should be able to prevent or respond to Bhopal-like incidents? Although industry had at first opposed the notion of community right to know, the proliferation of state and local community RTK laws created a desire for consistent federal regulation, just as it had with worker RTK. The adverse public reaction to the Bhopal incident reinforced the conviction of many industry representatives that a uniform federal law was not only inevitable but desirable. Environmental groups, which were active in all phases of the superfund reauthorization, supported right to know as a matter of principle but were especially interested in the industrial survey provisions that could help identify sources of environmental pollution.

By the end of 1985, each house had passed a superfund reauthorization bill, although the two bills differed significantly. When Congress returned in 1986, two conference committees were appointed, so complex were the unresolved issues; in June, one committee was further subdivided according to issues. On July 25, 1986, conferees announced that they had agreed upon the right-to-know issues. After further feuding over tax problems, the conferees presented a complete report that passed the Senate on October 3 and the House on October 8. On October 17, 1986, President Reagan signed the bill, called the Superfund Amendments and Reauthorization Act (SARA). The Emergency Planning and Community Right-to-Know Act was embodied in Title III of SARA.

What Do We Have a Right to Know?

The conference committee achieved consensus on Title III of SARA in large part by simply combining requirements of the two different bills. As a result, the law as passed was complicated, specifying five reporting requirements, four recipients of reports, three different groups of covered facilities, three lists of chemicals, and two sets of threshold quantities. Table 2-1 summarizes the reporting provisions, and Table 2-2 lists the statutory deadlines for all activities.

Emergency Planning and Notification

Title III may be divided into four parts, two for emergencies, one for community RTK, and one containing the industrial survey. Sections 301-303 concern emergency planning. According to the law, governors of states designate State Emergency Response Commissions, which in turn designate local planning districts and Local Emergency Planning Committees (LEPCs). The law specifies the composition of LEPCs, dividing members into five required categories:

- state and local elected officials
- law enforcement, civil defense, fire fighting, first aid, health, local environmental, hospital, and transportation personnel
- broadcast and print media
- community groups
- owners and operators of facilities subject to the requirements of Title III[24]

LEPC chairpeople and the SERCs (State Emergency Response Commissions) who approve LEPC membership have interpreted these guidelines in different ways. Some believe that five people, one from each major category in the law, constitute an adequate LEPC, whereas others believe that there must be many more, representing subcategories of these groups. The more than 3,000 LEPCs contain a varied number of members ranging from five to more than sixty.

The LEPC is treated as a government body by the law: It must establish rules, give public notice of its activities, and establish procedures for handling public requests for information. Its primary statutory task is to develop an emergency response plan by October 17, 1988. Section 303 requires that the plan focus especially, but not exclusively, on the 406 "extremely hazardous chemicals." Most of these, of course, are the original airborne toxics identified for the CEPP that grew out of the Bhopal incident; four were added by EPA based on Title III's additional hazardous criteria: toxicity, reactivity, volatility, dispersability, combustibility, and flammability.[25] The law specifies that several elements be included in the plan, including on-site and off-site emergency response procedures and a training program for emergency responders.[26] Underpinning the plan is information to be gathered by the LEPCs:

TABLE 2-1 Title III Reporting Requirements

Section	Facility	List	Quantities	Form	Submitted to:				Frequency	Deadline
					Fire Dept.	LEPC	SERC	EPA		
302 (emerg. planning)	all	1	threshold planning (TPQ)			x			once 5/17/87	notify changes-- ongoing
304 (emerg. release)	all	1,3	reportable (RQ)			x	x		if accidental release of listed substance	
311 (right to know)	OSHA	2, 1	threshold	list/ MSDS	x	x	x		once	10/17/87a
312 (right to know)	OSHA	2, 1	threshold	Tier 1 Tier 2	x	x	x		annual	first due 3/1/88a
313 (toxic chem. release)	manu- facturing	4	threshold				x	x	annual	first due 7/1/88

a Facilities newly covered because of the expansion of the OSHA Hazard Communication Standard were to comply in November 1988.

Lists:

1= 402 extremely hazardous chemicals--52 Fed. Reg. 13387 (April 22, 1987).
2= Substances covered by OSHA HCS 29 CFR 1910.1200 (c).
3= CERCLA 302.4 [40 CFR 302, Table 302.4 and para. 302.5 (b)].
4= Maryland-New Jersey list--52 Fed. Reg. 21152 (June 4, 1987).

Facilities:

OSHA=facilities covered by OSHA HCS. See 52 Fed. Reg. 31852 (August 24, 1987).
Manufacturing=facilities in SIC codes 20-39.

Quantities:

302 TPQ--in 52 Fed. Reg. 13387 (April 22, 1987).
304 RQ--see references for lists 1 and 3.
311--in 52 Fed. Reg. 38365 (October 19, 1987) for list 1 chemicals, 500 pounds or the TPQ; for others, 10,000 pounds in 1987; zero pounds in 1988 and thereafter for chemicals for which an MSDS has not yet been submitted.
312--in 52 Fed. Reg. 38365 (October 19, 1987) for list 1 chemicals, 500 pounds or the TPQ; for others, 10,000 pounds in 1988 and 1989; zero pounds in 1990 and thereafter.
313--in 53 Fed. Reg. 4526 (February 16, 1988): for chemicals manufactured or processed at the facility--75,000 pounds in 1987; 50,000 pounds in 1988; 25,000 pounds in 1989 and thereafter. For chemicals "otherwise used" at the facility, 10,000 pounds.

- identification of facilities storing or using the extremely hazardous substances and of routes by which these substances are transported;
- development of methods for determining occurrence of a release and probable affected area and population;
- description of available emergency equipment and facilities, both public and private.

Although facilities are also expected to identify themselves under the reporting sections of the law, the other activities are mentioned only in this section. Any information that is provided to the LEPC under this or any other section of the law becomes accessible to the public.

The emergency notification provisions in section 304 cover both the extremely hazardous substances and substances covered by CERCLA. When more than the "reportable quantity" of one of these chemicals is released, the facility must notify some local body immediately with the identity of the chemical, health effects, and

TABLE 2-2 Statutory Deadlines in Title III

1987	
April 17	State governors must appoint SERCs
May 17	Facilities subject to section 302 planning must notify SERC
July 17	SERC must designate Emergency Planning Districts
August 17	SERC must appoint members of LEPCs
September 17	Facilities notify LEPC of selection of facility representative
October 17	Section 311 reports due
1988	
March 1	Facilities must submit first section 312 reports
April 17	Final report on emergency systems study due to Congress
July 1	First section 313 reports due
October 17	LEPCs complete emergency plan
1991	
June 30	Report to Congress on section 313 information
October 17	EPA mass balance study due

precautions and must later notify both the LEPC and the SERC in writing giving response actions.

The emergency planning provisions of Title III are not directly intended to increase the community's right to know, although data submitted under the community RTK sections of the law will be used for planning and emergency response. Additional information-gathering activities, such as identifying transportation routes and determining populations likely to be affected by releases, will add significantly to citizens' abilities to assess risk in their communities--if these activities are completed. As part of the compromise between the two houses needed to pass Title III, Congress appropriated no money for right to know. Although training funds for emergency response were available through another program, few localities have the funds or personnel to do the kinds of technical analysis envisioned in the law.

Both the lack of funding and the technical nature of many of the activities needed to conduct emergency planning at the local level mean that industry must play an important role. Congress recognized this in two provisions of the law, placing representatives of affected facilities on LEPCs, thus requiring private participation, and by deriving many of the emergency planning provisions from the CMA's CAER program, a voluntary industry effort to develop appropriate emergency plans. If regulated industry is the sole source of technical expertise concerning affected populations, health effects of chemicals, and other important information, however, citizens may feel skeptical that they are being adequately protected. Congress apparently did not consider the abilities of local governments nor the implications of giving private industry such a large role.

Inventory Reports

Sections 311 and 312 are called the "community right-to-know" provisions of Title III. They apply to facilities that are covered by the OSHA HCS; although such facilities were limited to manufacturers when SARA was passed in 1986, by July 1988 the extension of OSHA also extended the applicability of sections 311 and 312 to all commercial businesses except the construction industry. Section 311 requires a one-time-only report to be sent to the LEPC, SERC, and local fire department; it offers covered facilities two options: to submit a list of chemicals, grouped by hazard category, or to submit the MSDSs for each covered chemical--that is, each chemical covered by the OSHA HCS--present in excess of certain threshold quantities that are phased in over three years. The list or set of MSDSs was to be submitted by

October 17, 1987. Although this was a one-time-only report, facilities must update the submissions when there are changes in the chemicals they handle or in the health information available on already-submitted MSDSs.

Section 312 requires submission of an annual inventory report to the same three entities: SERC, LEPC, and fire department. The law also provides two options for the inventory report. "Tier 1" reports allow facilities to provide aggregate information according to OSHA hazard category rather than providing information about specific chemicals. Tier 1 reports include an estimate of the maximum amount of chemicals in a hazard category present in a facility at any one time, an estimate of the average daily amount present, and the general location of these chemicals. Tier 2 reports, which may be requested by any of the recipients, provide similar information but include chemical identities, description of the way in which each chemical is stored, the location of each chemical, and an indication of whether the submitter elects to withhold location information from the public.

Although called the "right-to-know" sections of the law, the inclusion of fire departments in the set of report recipients indicates that emergency response is also an important goal. By providing two different forms in which each of the two reports may be provided, however, Congress may have impeded both right to know and emergency response. For example, if fire departments receive MSDSs for each chemical stored or used by each of several hundred facilities, they will have thousands of documents to file and store. Obtaining the correct document quickly enough to respond to an emergency will be a serious problem. (MSDSs are discussed further in Chapter 6.)

Similar problems of storage and retrieval will confront LEPCs and SERCs, to which citizens will turn when hoping to exercise the right to know. Some states, faced with the possibility of receiving hundreds of thousands of MSDSs, have said that they will only accept lists of chemicals to fulfill facilities' requirements under Section 311. Many localities and especially fire departments have decided to do the same. The advantage is the reduced cost of storage and retrieval of information; the possible disadvantage is the absence of contextual information about the risks presented by any substance or about appropriate measures for containing those risks. This disadvantage may be overcome by access to this information in reference books or standardized collections of MSDSs that many emergency responders already own.

The reporting options under Section 312 raise similar concerns. Respondents choosing the Tier 1 format were to allocate chemicals among more than twenty risk categories mentioned in the OSHA HCS.

Many chemicals fit in more than one category; double-counting will, therefore, make the estimates of amounts meaningless. Citizens may well be alarmed by what appear to be vast quantities of stored hazardous chemicals. Even though the number of hazard categories was subsequently reduced to five, the problems of double-counting and obscuring true amounts remain. The new hazard categories, moreover, are so broad that they are not useful for emergency responders.

To avoid this problem and associated difficulties of adding together quantities of chemicals that have in common only a hazard category, many facilities prefer using the Tier 2 format. On the assumption that precise locations of specific substances are of use primarily to emergency responders, Congress determined that facility owners could request that this information be kept hidden from the public. This places a burden on receiving governmental entities to store information in such a way that citizens making RTK requests can have access to quantities and identities of chemicals but not to the location information provided on the same form.

The state and local committees must make Tier 1 and Tier 2 information available to the public if it is in their possession. If it is not, the committee must request the information and then make it available within forty-five days. The exception is requests concerning chemicals stored in quantities of less than 10,000 pounds. To obtain this information, the requestor must submit a general statement of need along with his request, and the SERC or LEPC then determines whether to forward the request to the facility. Once the committee determines that it will request information, it cannot subsequently be withheld from the public, however.

In short, the information available to citizens through sections 311 and 312, the so-called right-to-know provisions of Title III, consists at best of a list of chemicals, amounts, and methods of storage (Tier 2) along with a Material Safety Data Sheet of unknown quality describing health effects, safety measures, and physical and chemical properties of the substance. At worst, the citizen knows only the names of chemicals present (from the set of MSDSs) or how many pounds of all the chemicals presenting a particular hazard are stored or used in a location.

Section 313 provides for the "mass balance," or toxic chemical release, report. This is the portion of the law derived most closely from the New Jersey industrial survey. Its purpose is to gather data on releases and disposal of covered chemicals--data that, as we have seen in Chapter 1, is generally unavailable. Under section 313, EPA must gather information about waste treatment and disposal methods,

36

(Important: Type or print; read instructions before completing form.)

(This space for EPA use only.)

EPA FORM **R**
PART III. CHEMICAL SPECIFIC INFORMATION

---

1. CHEMICAL IDENTITY

1.1 ☐ Trade Secret (Provide a generic name in 1.4 below. Attach substantiation form to this submission.)

1.2 CAS # ☐☐☐☐☐☐ - ☐☐ - ☐ (Use leading zeros if CAS number does not fill space provided.)

1.3 Chemical or Chemical Category Name

1.4 Generic Chemical Name (Complete only if 1.1 is checked.)

MIXTURE COMPONENT IDENTITY (Do not complete this section if you have completed Section 1.)

2. Generic Chemical Name Provided by Supplier (Limit the name to a maximum of 70 characters (e.g., numbers, letters, spaces, punctuation))

---

3. ACTIVITIES AND USES OF THE CHEMICAL AT THE FACILITY (Check all that apply.)

3.1 Manufacture:
a. ☐ Produce
b. ☐ Import
c. ☐ For on-site use/processing
d. ☐ For sale/distribution
e. ☐ As a byproduct
f. ☐ As an impurity

3.2 Process:
a. ☐ As a reactant
b. ☐ As a formulation component
c. ☐ As an article component
d. ☐ Repackaging only

3.3 Otherwise Used:
a. ☐ As a chemical processing aid
b. ☐ As a manufacturing aid
c. ☐ Ancillary or other use

---

4. MAXIMUM AMOUNT OF THE CHEMICAL ON SITE AT ANY TIME DURING THE CALENDAR YEAR

☐☐ (enter code)

---

5. RELEASES OF THE CHEMICAL TO THE ENVIRONMENT

You may report releases of less than 1.000 lbs. by checking ranges under A.1.		A. Total Release (lbs/yr)					B. Basis of Estimate (enter code)	
		A.1 Reporting Ranges			A.2 Enter Estimate			
		0	1-499	500-999				
5.1 Fugitive or non-point air emissions	5.1a						5.1b ☐	
5.2 Stack or point air emissions	5.2a						5.2b ☐	
5.3 Discharges to water 5.3.1 ☐ (Enter letter code from Part I Section 3.10 for stream(s).)	5.3.1a						5.3.1b ☐	C. % From Stormwater 5.3.1c
5.3.2 ☐	5.3.2a						5.3.2b ☐	5.3.2c
5.3.3 ☐	5.3.3a						5.3.3b ☐	5.3.3c
5.4 Underground injection	5.4a						5.4b ☐	
5.5 Releases to land 5.5.1 ☐☐☐ (enter code)	5.5.1a						5.5.1b ☐	
5.5.2 ☐☐☐ (enter code)	5.5.2a						5.5.2b ☐	
5.5.3 ☐☐☐ (enter code)	5.5.3a						5.5.3b ☐	

☐ (Check if additional information is provided on Part IV-Supplemental information.)

EPA Form 9350-1(1-88)

FIGURE 2-1 One page of the section 313 reporting form

efficiency of methods for each waste stream, and the quantity of the chemical entering each environmental medium annually, in addition to repetitious information such as an estimate of the maximum amount of the chemical present at the facility. Figure 2-1 reproduces one page of the five-page reporting form used to collect this information. The National Academy of Sciences will conduct a mass balance study using data similar to that required by section 313 from states that already required such information to be submitted. EPA and designated state agencies, but not the LEPCs, are designated recipients of Section 313 reports.

EPA is required to make section 313 data from available in a computerized database--an issue discussed in more detail in Chapter 5. Citizens also have an unusual opportunity to petition to add chemicals to or delete them from the list of covered toxic chemicals, which is different from any of the other lists in Title III. Often called the "New Jersey/Maryland" list, it comprises chemicals covered by the industrial surveys of those two states. Certain critics believe that the list contains some substances that are no longer widely used by industry and omits some important substances that are now more widely used, reducing the efficacy of section 313 as a tool for research or RTK.[27] Further details of Title III's provisions are included in later chapters. But even this brief overview shows how complex the law is. Disregarding the content and format of the information, the adequacy of which is considered in Chapters 6 and 9, one might still argue that Title III has the potential for impeding rather than promoting right to know because it specifies so many different reports, covers so many different facilities and chemicals, and fails to take into account the difficulties states and localities will have in managing the reported data. In short, the very structure of the law may create difficulties in fulfilling its purpose.

A Preliminary Assessment of Title III

The list presented in Chapter 1 suggests the kinds of questions citizens may have about hazardous materials in their communities. One way of predicting whether Title III even has a chance of fulfilling its goals is to assess the extent to which the law can answer these questions. The three questions most closely associated with short-term exposures are:

What are the health effects of an exposure I have experienced? Title III makes health-effects information available through MSDSs and through the requirement that officials of facilities that experience chemical accidents provide local agencies with information about the health effects. Citizens may have to take the initiative to retrieve this information, however, as Title III does not provide that facilities or agencies must publicize the information. Citizens might find it helpful, for example, if in addition to being told about appropriate methods for treating immediate symptoms, doctors were apprised of any possible delayed effects of acute exposures and could inform their patients.

What can we do to prevent accidents in the future? The emergency planning provisions in Title III are the law's answer to this question. To the extent that the LEPC works directly with facilities to identify problem spots and correct them, it will work. It is possible, however, for a plan to be developed that meets the requirements of the law but does little to reduce risk. Title III gives LEPCs the power to ask facilities for supplementary information, including scenarios involving spills of their most hazardous chemicals under unfavorable conditions of wind or weather. These analyses may constitute another important source of data upon which to build an accident prevention plan.

What hazardous substances are present in my community and in what amounts? The reporting requirements of Title III do answer this question in large part. Among the chemicals citizens will not know about are those stored or used below the threshold reporting requirements, those stored at facilities not covered by the law, those stored at facilities too confused or uninformed to report, or those covered by the trade secret exemptions. Moreover, citizens will not know quantities stored if a facility files both a sheaf of MSDSs under section 311 and a Tier 1 report under section 312, as neither requires relating quantities to specific chemicals. In addition, different facilities may use different names for the same chemical.

The third question involving short-term exposures is also relevant to citizens' concerns about longer-term exposures. Other questions citizens might have about possible long-term effects from exposures to chemicals in the environment are:

Are these substances being released into the environment? Have I been exposed? Two provisions of Title III help answer this question: the section 304 requirement that accidental releases of the extremely hazardous substances over a certain threshold amount be reported and the section 313 requirement that manufacturing facilities report all their "routine" emissions of the 300 or so chemicals on the section 313 list. Limitations on the section 313 data include the fact that they cover only certain SIC codes and that facilities do not have to create new information to fulfill the reporting requirement, a problem that is discussed further in Chapter 6. Another limitation in the short run is the reliance LEPCs must place on state agencies or EPA to make the data available at the local level.

If hazardous substances are released into the environment, by what route and at what level might I be exposed? Section 313 data will show the routes by which a citizen might be exposed, since facilities report whether they have emitted each substance into air, water, or ground. But the data do not consider the "environmental fate" of these substances: Some materials placed in landfills may leach into groundwater; some in water may volatilize into the air. MSDSs, which Congress adopted as the primary source of information about individual chemicals in Title III, were intended for workers and seldom discuss routes of community exposure. Levels of exposure differ among individuals but depend in part on the concentration in the air or water. Emissions data do not give any indication at all about concentrations, which must be measured separately (and at considerable cost).

Do these exposures affect my health or that of my family? If I have a symptom, what substances might be causing it? Although Title III makes provision for giving citizens general information about known health effects of substances through MSDSs, it does not ensure that citizens can answer this question. First, as noted, MSDSs usually concern workers, whose exposures are more intense than those in the community. Second, actual exposure levels are needed in order to determine whether a health effect is likely. Individuals respond very differently to exposures, other exposures may enhance or deter adverse effects from a particular substance, symptoms are often vague (fatigue, red eyes), causation is often difficult to establish, and many doctors are unfamiliar with environmental health risks. Answering the second half of this question requires thumbing through many MSDSs hoping to see a reference to the symptom of concern. Title III does not make direct provision for getting at the information "backwards." The same would apply to citizens hoping to identify a chemical present at a facility because they know what it manufactures or because they have detected an odor or color in the water.

Are the exposures acceptable in light of other considerations? This question assumes that a primary purpose of Title III is allowing people to make sensible decisions about hazardous materials in their communities. Not all substances pose equal hazards; not all the substances get out into the environment. Facilities that store, use, and manufacture hazardous materials give people jobs, and the substances contribute to the manufacture of products that people enjoy. We know that people are more willing to put up with risks that they choose than with ones that they do not know about or have no choice about. One advantage of Title III is that it lays the basis for all members of the community to be informed participants in deciding about risks and balancing them against benefits. However, the law does not provide specific ways for citizens to participate in decisionmaking or even to learn about balancing risks and benefits.

If they are not acceptable, are there any ways these exposures can be reduced? Title III does not make specific provision for citizens to acquire information about waste reduction, alternative production technologies, and other methods for reducing community exposures to hazardous substances, although of course it does not prevent people from obtaining this information. More important, it does not ensure that citizens know that such techniques are even possible, nor, again, does it establish methods specifically intended to bring together citizens and industry to achieve these goals.

If emissions can be reduced, should we ask facilities to do this? How may we persuade them? Title III was certainly not intended to give citizens the answers to these questions. Once information is available, citizens must develop their own plans for action. Decisions such as these are ultimately based on economic and engineering considerations as well as on citizens' desires, and citizens must be prepared to master these topics in some detail as well.

A preliminary assessment of Title III based only on its ability to answer a particular set of citizens' questions is mixed. On the one hand, Title III makes available data that has seldom been public before-- data about private facilities' chemical inventories, storage practices, transportation routes, and "hazard analyses," as well as the emissions inventories for manufacturing facilities. On the other hand, it is not strong on providing information about health effects or on providing data that will help people decide whether risks from hazardous materials are acceptable.

The questions themselves embody a rather activist conception of RTK. To the extent that Congress had a more limited view of the right to know, the mixed assessment may be unfair. If, for example, Congress intended only that people be able to obtain the chemical inventories and emissions inventories--that people simply have access to data-- then Title III might be adjudged very successful. But even the limited history of the law presented here suggests that this was not the full extent of legislative goals, as almost from the outset members of Congress focused on emergency planning and response as an integral part of RTK. I will suggest in Chapter 5, moreover, that the sheer quantity of data means that people cannot know or even obtain access to data in any meaningful sense without further assistance.

It is more likely that Congress intended the law as part of its ongoing effort to reduce the risks citizens face. That view of RTK would be more consistent with legislators' concern about emergency planning as well as with the components of the law that prescribe stronger penalties for violations of section 304 reporting requirements than for violations of the other reporting requirements.[28]   Section 313 reports also serve as a potential aid to regulators in enforcing other pollution and risk-reduction laws.

The list of questions, especially those concerning longer-term exposures to chemicals present at low levels in the environment, largely embodies the "better-decisions" view of RTK. At least some participants in the fight for RTK have held this view--those, for example, who urged that LEPCs should be able to ask facilities for supplementary information concerning transportation routes and worst-case accident scenarios. The penalty provisions also appear to support this view of RTK.

The hope that RTK might change the balance of power in communities may also have been a goal for at least some legislators or participants. Congress required that citizens be members of LEPCs in part to ensure that decisionmaking could not remain the domain of an elite and that there would be channels for getting the information available under Title III out into the community. The ability of citizens to petition to include new substances on the section 313 list also formalizes a stronger role in regulation for citizens than they usually have.

Readers may disagree that one or more of the list of questions offered here really represents citizens' concerns. These questions have, however, served well in highlighting both the strengths and limitations of the federal statute that for most Americans defines community right to know. In the remainder of this book, I assess the law from the more practical standpoint of implementation, rather than focusing only on its relationship to goals that, in retrospect, may only be imputed to Congress and the other actors. That assessment begins in Chapter 3 with a discussion of the RTK programs in two states that were differently affected by the passage of Title III.

Notes

1. Among the myriad critiques of OSHA, one that best explains some of the reasons for the delay is John Mendeloff, *The Dilemma of Toxics Substance Regulation: How Overregulation Causes Underregulation* (Cambridge, Mass.: MIT Press, 1988).

2. In 1974 OSHA established a standards advisory committee on product labeling and in 1975 NIOSH recommended to the secretary of labor

that he promulgate a standard requiring that hazardous substances in the workplace be labeled, but apparently these measures did not satisfy workers' concerns. The NIOSH request is cited in Nelson A. Clare, "Hazardous Chemicals in the Workplace: The Employer's Obligation to Inform Employees and the Community," October 1988, p. 8.

3. Ken Silver, "The RTK Story: No Easy Victories," *Exposure*, March/April 1983, p. 4, quoting Caron Chess. According to the same story, the Philadelphia groups undertook the campaign with a grant from the Youth Project, a national social change foundation.

4. Testimony of Vicky Heza, United Paperworkers, in U.S. Congress, House, Committee on Education and Labor, Subcommittee on Health and Safety, Hearings on OSHA Oversight--Worker Health and Safety in the Manufacture and Use of Toxic and Hazardous Substances, 99th Cong. 1st sess. (May 1, 1985), p. 96.

5. 29 CFR (Code of Federal Regulations) 1910.20 (1987).

6. The standard also gave employees access to Material Safety Data Sheets (MSDSs) if the employer had them--a point that has become moot since the promulgation of the Hazard Communication Standard.

7. Unfortunately, the carcinogens named in the law were rarely used in industry. Rebecca Doty, "The Connecticut Story," in Caron Chess, *Winning the Right to Know: A Handbook for Toxics Activists* (Philadelphia: Delaware Valley Toxics Coalition, 1984), p. 81. (The law was revised and expanded in 1981 and 1982.)

8. Complete counts differ from source to source; these figures are from Ilise L. Feitshans, "Hazardous Substances in the Workplace: How Much Does the Employee Have the `Right to Know'?" *Detroit College of Law Review 1985*, Fall 1985, pp. 695-696.

9. These duties were outlined in the original HCS, which was published in 48 Fed. Reg. 53279 ff (November 25, 1983) and codified in 29 CFR 1910.1200. For the 1983 version of the standard required labels to be used on containers of hazardous materials in the workplace to apprise employees of all hazards to which they are exposed, see 29 CFR 1910.1200 (f)(4) (1984). The new version, promulgated in 1987, calls for the more limited duty described in the last entry of this list: to provide only an appropriate hazard warning. This is 52 CFR 1910.1200 (f)(5) in versions of 1988 and later.

10. In *New Jersey State Chamber of Commerce* v. *Hughey*, 600 F. Supp. 606 (Dist. N.J. January 3, 1985), Judge Dickinson Debevoise held that the Hazard Communication Standard is a "standard" rather than a "regulation," thereby invoking the preemption provisions of the OSH Act (29 U.S.C. 667b), and that the preemption provisions do not apply to nonmanufacturing sectors. He also held that the preemption provisions did apply both to the worker and to the community RTK portions of New Jersey's law for the manufacturing sector. However, in *United Steelworkers of America* v. *Auchter*, 763 F 2d 728 (May 24, 1985), a suit that combined several challenges to the OSHA Hazard Communication Standard, the court held that the preemption provisions applied only to worker parts of state right-to-know laws as well as only to the manufacturing sector. This finding was repeated on October 10, 1985, when the court heard an appeal

of *New Jersey State Chamber of Commerce* and reversed a portion of the district court's ruling on community right to know, directing the district court to determine whether enforcing the environmental hazard (community RTK) portion would interfere with accomplishing the purpose of the worker portion. The court also held that limiting the standard to the manufacturing sector "ignores the high level of exposure in specific job settings outside" that sector and that OSHA had not sufficiently justified this limitation (although in its original decision to limit the coverage of the HCS, the agency had cited statistics showing that the manufacturing sector employed 32 percent of workers but accounted for more than half the reported cases of illness caused by chemical exposure), 48 Fed. Reg. 53285 (November 25, 1983).

11. *United Steelworkers of America* v. *Auchter.* On May 29, 1987, the Court of Appeals for the Third Circuit issued an order requiring OSHA either to extend the HCS to all workers or to justify its decision not to extend the standard. *United Steelworkers of America* v. *Pendergrass*, 83-3554, 3rd. Cir., finally decided in a combined suit, *Associated Builders and Contractors, Inc.* v. *Brock*, 862 F. 2d 63 (1988).

12. 52 Fed. Reg. 31852. The effective date was to be May 23, 1988.

13. See Clare, "Hazardous Chemicals in the Workplace," for a good summary of these events, which included the granting of a stay by the same court that had ruled in *United Steelworkers* and a clarification by that court that the stay applied only to construction employers. 53 Fed. Reg. 27679 (July 22, 1988) making August 1 the effective date.

14. The title of this section is borrowed from and used in honor of Caron Chess, author, on behalf of the Delaware Valley Toxics Coalition, of *Winning the Right to Know.*

15. The same thought was occurring around the nation, although it was less well documented and bore less immediate fruit. Texas workers and their advocates also recognized the implications and need for RTK outside the workplace. Interview with Steve Frishman, formerly of the Texas Environmental Coalition, Houston, Texas, November 14, 1988.

16. Chess, *Winning the Right to Know*, pp. 39-41 describes these arguments.

17. Chess, *Winning the Right to Know*, p. 38, quoting the *Philadelphia Inquirer.*

19. Summaries of some of these early laws can be found in Susan Sherry and Regina Purin, *Community Right to Know: Hazardous Materials Disclosure Information Systems: A Handbook for Local Communities and Their Officials,* (Sacramento: Golden Empire Health Systems Agency, January 1983). Also see Chess, *Winning the Right to Know*, pp. 27-35.

19. A clear chronological account of the complexities of the reauthorization process can be found in Bureau of National Affairs, Inc., *Environment Reporter* 17, no. 42 (February 13, 1987), part 2, "Superfund II: A New Mandate," pp. 100-114.

20. Interview with James Aidala, Congressional Research Service, August 4, 1987.

21. For a similar discussion of issues, see James V. Aidala et al., "After Bhopal: Preventing and Responding to Chemical Emergencies," Washington, D.C.: Congressional Research Service, July 9, 1985, pp. 17-23.

22. Environmental Protection Agency, *Chemical Emergency Preparedness Program: Interim Guidance*, November 1985. Toxicity criteria on p. 6-3. EPA enjoins localities to consider other hazardous features such as flammability when developing a plan.

23. *Chemical and Engineering News*, June 8, 1987, p. 27.

24. SARA paragraph 301(c).

25. SARA 302 (a)(4); four substances added at 52 Fed. Reg. 13397 (April 22, 1987). Other substances continually being added and deleted to refine coverage.

26. The National Response Team (NRT), created under the National Contingency Plan 40 CFR 300 and composed of fourteen federal agencies with responsibilities for emergencies, is directed to assist LEPCs by publishing a guidance document on emergency response planning. The document, *The Hazardous Materials Planning Guide*, or NRT-1, includes material from the CEPP interim guidance as well as from the Federal Emergency Management Agency's (FEMA) *Planning Guide and Checklist for Hazardous Materials Contingency Plans*, which was widely known as FEMA-10.

27. Interview with member of New Jersey RTK staff, May 12, 1987, and with environmentalists, May 13, 1987. Both sources have requested anonymity for this attribution.

28. Section 325 describes penalties. Most reporting violations may be penalized by as much as $25,000, with each day of noncompliance constituting a separate violation--section 311 violations are limited to $10,000. But section 304 violations may rise to $75,000 per day for second or subsequent violations and may also be subject to criminal penalties, which reporting violations under sections 311, 312, and 313 are not. Criminal penalties are possible for trade secret violations.

3 / Implementing Right to Know: New Jersey and Texas

With the exception of section 313, Title III delegates the responsibility for ensuring the right to know to state and local governments. Citizens' abilities to exercise this right will depend on what those governments do. In this chapter, I describe programs in two states: New Jersey, whose RTK program predated Title III and provided the model for many parts of it, and Texas, whose unfunded community RTK program had to be greatly expanded as a result of Title III. The problems and successes of these two programs provide insights into the broader question of what and how people need to know.

Right to Know in New Jersey

Although New Jersey's right-to-know law, which includes both workers and community, was not passed until 1983, it is worthy of special consideration because it strongly influenced the federal RTK legislation. My analysis focuses on three phases of the program: the industrial survey prior to passage of the state law; administrative actions in implementing the law; and changes following the passage of Title III.

The Industrial Survey

The Industrial Survey Project was begun in 1979 by the Office of Science and Research of the New Jersey Department of Environmental Protection (DEP). DEP, among other responsibilities, grants permits to those disposing pollutants into the air or water; according to the procedures in use before 1979, applicants would simply describe the amount and physical characteristics of the substance proposed to be emitted. As they were processing permits, DEP staff began to wonder about the substances that were being permitted--"What is this stuff that is so acid? What are they using it for? Why is there so much of it?" Thus the idea of the industrial survey was born.[1] The purpose of the industrial survey was to establish a database that would include toxic substances stored, used, and disposed in New Jersey along with their amounts and locations. This database would, in turn, be used to identify areas or population groups that were most likely to experience an increased risk of disease from chemical exposure and to determine ways of reducing that exposure.

The first step was to decide which chemicals were to be included in the survey; the resulting list included substances that met any of three major criteria: evidence of chronic health effect, evidence of production in commercial quantities in the United States, presence on EPA's Priority Pollutant list. A list of 155 chemicals was compiled for this exercise. No minimum amounts were set, so any use of the 155 chemicals had to be reported with the exception of limited uses in laboratories or impurities of low concentration.

The survey was sent to 15,000 facilities in New Jersey, including all manufacturing facilities and some others. Facility managers were asked to fill out one form for each covered substance, telling how much was used, how much released into various media, and what waste disposal technologies were used; they were also asked for locations of old disposal sites--a question included almost by chance that proved very valuable in subsequent superfund activities.

Of the 155 substances on the list, 43 were reported as not in use by any facility.[2] This has taught New Jersey as well as other states and, ultimately, EPA to include large numbers of substances in their lists. Of the remaining substances, the survey found greatest production and use of aromatic hydrocarbons, halogenated alkanes, phenols, and phthalates. Respondents to the survey described the disposal of more than 6.75 million pounds of the selected substances annually in water, 250,000 pounds of which went directly to surface water and the rest into treatment facilities. The survey also received reports of more than 40 million pounds of stack emissions into air and about two million pounds of fugitive emissions. Some of the results of the first industrial survey summarized in Table 3-1.

The industrial survey taught several important lessons, both positive and negative, that were put to good use when the federal right-to-know law came to be drafted. First, there were serious problems in locating all the appropriate respondents. Placing the burden on companies to know that they have the responsibility to report alleviates this problem; that approach is embodied in the RTK laws of both New Jersey and the federal government. (Conversely, depending on industry initiative probably reduces the rate of compliance, especially for small facilities.) A second problem

TABLE 3-1 Selected Results of New Jersey Industrial Survey (pounds in t[housands], m[illions], b[illions])

Chemical Group	Amount Discharged	Maximum Inventory	Stack Emissions	Water Discharge
Halogenated alkanes and alkenes	20m-102m	24m-101m	6.9m	32t
Phenols	600T-2m	11m-52m	97t	16t
Halogenated aromatics	1 m-5m	2m-12m	215t	26t
Phthalates	155m-610m	6m-13m	133t	5t
Ethers, epoxides, aldehydes, anhydrides	110m-550m	4m-16m	560t	50t
Imines, nitriles, hydrazines	100a	210t-1m	2t	10a
Nitroso compounds	50t-100t	50t-100t	0	300a
Amides and amino compounds	3m-15m	2m-7m	6t	1t
Pesticides	5m-10m	2m-12m	1t	0
Aromatic hydrocarbons	710m-2b	81m-251m	32m	19t
Inorganics	2m-7m	24m-118m	298t	109t
Nitro compounds	60m-160m	2m-7m	28t	36t
Dyes	631t-1m	234t-845t	101a	10a
Miscellaneous	10m-50m	5m-10m	50t	600a

a Absolute amount.

Source: New Jersey Department of Environmental Protection, *New Jersey Industrial Survey Final Report* (Trenton, 1986), pp. 12, 15, 20, and 24.

concerned the quality of the reported data; some companies made low estimates (or failed to respond to the survey), and there was not adequate staff to verify all reports. The importance of adequate technical staffing and funding for a reporting program became very clear. A third problem concerned the capacity and ease of use of the database that held the survey results. In Chapter 5, data management problems are considered in more detail.

Despite these problems, the survey was of immediate use. The question about disposal practices allowed New Jersey to identify abandoned hazardous waste disposal sites; the disposal data are used for routine monitoring of facilities with air and water permits and for identifying the sources of certain unpermitted contaminants. Results have been used to help develop the state's air toxics program and for other research efforts. Local emergency response personnel requested data from their areas to plan for appropriate responses to potential accidents. Finally, the public interest group INFORM used the survey data to choose facilities for an important study of ways that chemical facilities can lessen their waste streams.[3] The close parallels of section 313 of Title III with the New Jersey industrial survey suggest that section 313 data will be useful for many of the same kinds of tasks.

Meanwhile, activists fresh from victory in Philadelphia, other environmentalists, and representatives of New Jersey's strong labor movement, their collective will emboldened by such events as a large chemical fire in Elizabeth and the problems of the asbestos workers in Manville,[4] decided to seek a state right-to-know law. In the fall of 1982, coalition members donned moon suits (protective clothing worn by chemical workers) and poured out 55-gallon drums of petitions before Governor Thomas H. Kean, who was running for reelection. To show his support, the governor himself donned a moon suit.

On August 29, 1983, Governor Kean signed the Worker and Community Right-to-Know Act, which became effective in August 1984. The law guarantees citizens' access to the chemical identity of hazardous substances in workplaces or communities and provides information about the kinds of hazards posed by different substances. It requires that employees be trained to handle the substances and ensures that containers are labeled with the chemical name of their contents. It also establishes means of funding the RTK programs administered by the New Jersey Departments of Labor, Health (DOH), Environmental Protection, and Treasury through fees collected from employers.

Implementation of RTK

Because proponents' energies were devoted to getting the law passed, the final version, like Title III, was a congeries of provisions reflecting existing administrative divisions rather than a plan for a unified program.[5] The law effectively created two programs--a worker RTK program in the Department of Health, emphasizing training, and a community RTK program in DEP based on the industrial survey. Because industry had wanted to delimit the scope of each part of the program clearly, the law required each agency to develop different lists of chemicals that would be considered hazardous for different purposes. In implementation, these multiple lists generated multiple reporting forms, engendering additional work for industry and agencies.

DOH was required to develop two hazardous substance lists: (1) a workplace hazardous substance list composed at a minimum of DEP's list, seven substances named in the law itself, OSHA's "Z" list of hazardous chemicals (so called because it appears in Tables Z1 through Z3 in the relevant OSHA regulations), and other substances included in other well-known lists; and (2) a special list of particularly dangerous substances hazardous to health for which no claims of trade secrecy would be allowed. DOH was also required to develop a workplace survey to assist employers in reporting substances in their facilities found on either of the two lists (the survey to be distributed by the Department of Labor) and also to develop fact sheets for the substances listed.

The first workplace hazardous substance list comprised 2,051 substances, including several hundred that pose special health hazards. By 1987, more than 2,870 substances were listed, including approximately 135 substances that are optional to report and a large number of generic substance names. The special health-hazard substance list contains substances with the following properties: carcinogen, mutagen, teratogen, flammable, reactive, and corrosive. DEP's list of environmentally hazardous substances included 153 chemicals, of which 97 came from the selected substances list of the earlier industrial survey.

The complex reporting implicit in three different lists of chemicals was exacerbated by other requirements of the law and by the agencies' implementation strategies. For example, in October 1984, DOH mailed affected employers the first annual Workplace Survey, consisting of six different forms, including two computer-coding forms to be filled out with a number 2 pencil for machine reading of information written on the other forms. The complexity and apparent redundancy of the reports angered many respondents and gave RTK a reputation for government heavy-handedness that has plagued Title III.

DEP's industrial survey also required reporting forms, which of necessity overlapped in part the DOH forms. In order to avoid engendering public anger by seeking information from facilities for which the information was irrelevant, and in order to focus the agency's limited resources on facilities in which problems were likely to arise, DEP decided to conduct the environmental survey in two parts: Part 1, for all covered facilities, and Part 2, a longer and more detailed form for those whose replies to Part 1 suggested that further questioning would be appropriate. The long form, which is the survey specified in the law, must be filed only for the list of environmentally hazardous substances; it is similar to the reporting form for section 313 of Title III.

Finally, DEP created a new form particularly designed to assist emergency responders. The DOH survey asks only for names of substances; emergency responders need quantities stored as well. Emergency responders also need to know about more kinds of chemicals than are covered in the environmental survey, but they need to know less information about them--primarily, locations, quantities, and storage methods. Since the state RTK law does not specifically mention a survey for emergency services, however, DEP envisioned a possible challenge by industry and decided to make the new survey separate from the clearly legitimate environmental survey. DEP also felt that a different list of chemicals would be more appropriate for the needs of emergency responders and, for this purpose, adopted the U. S. Department of Transportation (DOT) Optional Materials Table.[6]

Although the differences in reporting requirements may be explained by their divergent purposes, the ill will among covered industries that was created by their complexity contributed in part to the legal challenge against the law. It was New Jersey's law that was in contention when the U.S. District Court ruled that state RTK laws--both worker and community--did not apply to employers already affected by the OSHA HCS. Although the portion of the ruling that applied to community RTK was subsequently overturned, the legal proceedings slowed and complicated implementation of the state's law.[7]

In the early stages, right to know in New Jersey really consisted of two separate programs, one in DOH and one in DEP. Under pressure from constituents, the two departments began working more closely together, especially on a joint survey. Rather than receiving six forms from DOH and two or three from DEP, in 1987 employers received one two-page form that takes the place of most of the earlier surveys, requesting mostly identification information and a list of hazardous substances with inventory ranges to be provided by single-digit codes.

DOH's worker RTK program focused most strongly on information and training for workers. The department developed a program to assist employers in developing appropriate training materials and finding adequate trainers. The law also required DOH to prepare fact sheets on the materials listed on the workplace list and to transmit them to employers as they file workplace surveys. The fact sheets serve purposes similar to that of the MSDSs required by OSHA but differ significantly in form. They are designed as folders, with the first and last (outside) pages containing the most often used information in plain English, including a hazard summary, workplace exposure limits, how to determine if you are being exposed, ways of reducing exposure, and a summary of emergency information such as first aid and what to do for spills. Intermediate pages provide more detailed information on the same topics. Figure 3-1 shows four pages of the six-page fact sheet for benzene; missing pages include a list of definitions that are standard to all fact sheets and some additional chemical-specific information. Of the 2,055 substances on DOH's list that are chemicals, fact sheets were available or in preparation for all but about 400 in March 1987.[8] EPA adopted the New Jersey fact sheets for use in public education in conjunction with Title III section 313 emissions data.

DOH included a questionnaire with its July 1986 mailing of fact sheets. Participation was voluntary; 234 people responded (out of some ten thousand facilities in all SIC codes but manufacturing that received the mailing). Table 3-2 provides a summary of the answers of the few respondents. Although the survey is hardly representative, it does suggest that right to know can change both employee and employer work habits. Chapter 9 includes further discussion of useful formats for presenting information.

Because Title III closely resembles certain parts of New Jersey's law, it is worth examining the latter's effectiveness. Between the passage of the New Jersey RTK law and September 1987, about 180 people had directly requested information from either DEP or DOH; many more made requests to their employers and local agencies. In the following year, the number of people requesting community RTK information from DEP approximately tripled.[9]

I conducted a mail survey of the 180 people who had requested information in the earlier period. New Jersey would not release the names of these people in order to maintain their confidentiality, so DEP mailed the surveys for me. Respondents were provided an opportunity to give their first names and telephone numbers for a more detailed telephone survey. The overall response rate was 42 percent. Since I was especially interested in community RTK, I was surprised to find that nearly half the respondents were people who had learned about RTK and made requests for information as part of their jobs; that is, they were safety engineers, lawyers, public officials, or facility operators who needed to know about the program in order to comply, rather than citizens concerned about nearby facilities. Most people who asked for information sought several different kinds: more than 70 percent asked for fact sheets, 50 percent for a workplace survey, 33 percent for environmental surveys, 25 percent for the emergency services information survey, and 13 percent for information about all the facilities in an area.

I had assumed that people would ask for information

New Jersey Department of Health
HAZARDOUS SUBSTANCE FACT SHEET

Common Name: **BENZENE**

CAS Number:	71-43-2	
DOT Number:	UN 1114	

RTK Substance number: 0197
Date: 1/31/88

HAZARD SUMMARY
* Benzene can affect you when breathed in and by passing through your skin.
* Benzene is a CARCINOGEN--HANDLE WITH EXTREME CAUTION.
* Exposure can cause you to become dizzy and lightheaded. Higher levels can cause convulsions and death.
* Exposure can irritate the nose and throat and may cause an upset stomach and vomiting.
* Benzene can cause an irregular heart beat that can lead to death.
* Prolonged exposure can cause fatal damage to the blood (aplastic anemia).
* Benzene is a FLAMMABLE LIQUID and a FIRE HAZARD.

IDENTIFICATION
Benzene is a colorless liquid with a pleasant odor. It is used mainly in making other chemicals, as a solvent, and is found in gasoline.

REASON FOR CITATION
* Benzene is on the Hazardous Substance List because it is regulated by OSHA and cited by ACGIH, DOT, NIOSH, IARC, NTP, CAG, DEP, NFPA and EPA.
* It is on the Special Health Hazard Substance List because it is a CARCINOGEN, a MUTAGEN and is FLAMMABLE.
* Definitions are provided on page 5.

HOW TO DETERMINE IF YOU ARE BEING EXPOSED
* Exposure to hazardous substances should be routinely evaluated. This may include collecting air samples. Under OSHA 1910.20, you have a legal right to obtain copies of sampling results from your employer. If you think you are experiencing any work-related health problems, see a doctor trained to recognize occupational diseases. Take this Fact Sheet with you.

* ODOR THRESHOLD = 12.0 ppm.
* The odor threshold only serves as a warning of exposure. Not smelling it does not mean you are not being exposed.

WORKPLACE EXPOSURE LIMITS
OSHA: The legal airborne permissible exposure limit (PEL) is 1 ppm averaged over an 8-hour workshift, and 5 ppm which should not be exceeded in any 10 minute period.

ACGIH: The recommended airborne exposure limit is 10 ppm averaged over an 8-hour workshift.

NIOSH: The recommended airborne exposure limit is 1.0 ppm, which should not be exceeded during any 60 minute period.

* Benzene is a CANCER-CAUSING AGENT in humans. There may be no safe level of exposure to a carcinogen, so all contact should be reduced to the lowest possible level.
* The above exposure limits are for air levels only. Skin contact may also cause overexposure.

WAYS OF REDUCING EXPOSURE
* A regulated, marked area should be established where Benzene is handled, used, or stored.
* Wear protective work clothing.
* Wash thoroughly immediately after exposure to Benzene and at the end of the workshift.
* Post hazard and warning information in the work area. In addition, as part of an ongoing education and training effort, communicate all information on the health and safety hazards of Benzene to potentially exposed workers.

FIGURE 3-1 Four pages of a New Jersey fact sheet

This Fact Sheet is a summary source of information of all potential and most severe health hazards that may result from exposure. Duration of exposure, concentration of the substance and other factors will affect your susceptibility to any of the potential effects described below.

HEALTH HAZARD INFORMATION

Acute Health Effects

The following acute (short-term) health effects may occur immediately or shortly after exposure to Benzene:

* Exposure can cause symptoms of dizziness, lightheadedness, headaches, and vomiting. Convulsions and coma, or sudden death from irregular heart beat, may follow high exposures.
* Exposure can also irritate the eyes, nose, and throat.

Chronic Health Effects

The following chronic (long-term) health effects can occur at some time after exposure to Benzene and can last for months or years:

Cancer Hazard

* Benzene is a CARCINOGEN in humans. It has been shown to cause leukemia.
* Many scientists believe there is no safe level of exposure to a carcinogen.

Reproductive Hazard

* There is limited evidence that Benzene is a teratogen in animals. Until further testing has been done, it should be treated as a possible teratogen in humans.

Other Long-Term Effects

* Repeated exposure can damage the blood-forming organs causing a condition called aplastic anemia. This can cause death.
* Long-term exposure may cause drying and scaling of the skin.

MEDICAL TESTING

Before beginning employment and at regular times after that, the following are recommended:

* Complete blood count.
* Urinary *Phenol* (a test to see if Benzene is in the body).

Any evaluation should include a careful history of past and present symptoms with an exam. Medical tests that look for damage already done are not a substitute for controlling exposure.

Request copies of your medical testing. You have a legal right to this information under OSHA 1910.20.

WORKPLACE CONTROLS AND PRACTICES

Unless a less toxic chemical can be substituted for a hazardous substance, ENGINEERING CONTROLS are the most effective way of reducing exposure. The best protection is to enclose operations and/or provide local exhaust ventilation at the site of chemical release. Isolating operations can also reduce exposure. Using respirators or protective equipment is less effective than the controls mentioned above, but is sometimes necessary.

In evaluating the controls present in your workplace, consider: (1) how hazardous the substance is, (2) how much of the substance is released into the workplace and (3) whether harmful skin or eye contact could occur. Special controls should be in place for highly toxic chemicals or when significant skin, eye, or breathing exposures are possible.

In addition, the following controls are recommended:

* Where possible, automatically pump liquid Benzene from drums or other storage containers to process containers.
* Specific engineering controls are recommended for this chemical by NIOSH. Refer to the NIOSH criteria documents on *Benzene # 74-137 and "Refined Petroleum Solvents" # 77-192*.

54

Good **WORK PRACTICES** can help to reduce hazardous exposures. The following work practices are recommended:

* Workers whose clothing has been contaminated by **Benzene** should change into clean clothing promptly.
* Do not take contaminated work clothes home. Family members could be exposed.
* Contaminated work clothes should be laundered by individuals who have been informed of the hazards of exposure to **Benzene**.
* If there is the possibility of skin exposure, emergency shower facilities should be provided.
* On skin contact with **Benzene**, immediately wash or shower to remove the chemical.
* Do not eat, smoke, or drink where Benzene is handled, processed, or stored, since the chemical can be swallowed. Wash hands carefully before eating or smoking.

PERSONAL PROTECTIVE EQUIPMENT

WORKPLACE CONTROLS ARE BETTER THAN PERSONAL PROTECTIVE EQUIPMENT. However, for some jobs (such as outside work, confined space entry, jobs done only once in a while, or jobs done while workplace controls are being installed), personal protective equipment may be appropriate.

The following recommendations are only guidelines and may not apply to every situation.

Clothing
* Avoid skin contact with Benzene. Wear solvent-resistant gloves and clothing. Safety equipment suppliers/ manufacturers can provide recommendations on the most protective glove/clothing material for your operation.
* All protective clothing (suits, gloves, footwear, headgear) should be clean, available each day, and put on before work.
* ACGIH recommends *VITON* gloves for short periods of protection.

Eye Protection
* Eye protection is included in the recommended respiratory protection.

Respiratory Protection
IMPROPER USE OF RESPIRATORS IS DANGEROUS. Such equipment should only be used if the employer has a written program that takes into account workplace conditions, requirements for worker training, respirator fit testing and medical exams, as described in OSHA 1910.134.

* At <u>any</u> exposure level, use a MSHA/NIOSH approved supplied-air respirator with a full facepiece operated in the positive pressure mode or with a full facepiece, hood, or helmet in the continuous flow mode, or use a MSHA/NIOSH approved self-contained breathing apparatus with a full facepiece operated in pressure-demand or other positive pressure mode.

HANDLING AND STORAGE

* Prior to working with Benzene you should be trained on its proper handling and storage.
* **Benzene** must be stored to avoid contact with OXIDIZERS (such as PERMANGANATES, NITRATES, PEROXIDES, CHLORATES, and PERCHLORATES), since violent reactions occur.
* Store in tightly closed containers in a cool well-ventilated area away from HEAT.
* Sources of ignition such as smoking and open flames are prohibited where Benzene is handled, used, or stored.
* Metal containers involving the transfer of 5 gallons or more of Benzene should be grounded and bonded. Drums must be equipped with self-closing valves, pressure vacuum bungs, and flame arresters.
* Wherever Benzene is used, handled, manufactured, or stored, use explosion-proof electrical equipment and fittings.

QUESTIONS AND ANSWERS

Q: If I have acute health effects, will I later get chronic health effects?
A: Not always. Most chronic (long-term) effects result from repeated exposures to a chemical.

FIGURE 3-1 New Jersey fact sheet *continued*

>>>>>>>>>>>>>>>>>> E M E R G E N C Y   I N F O R M A T I O N <<<<<<<<<<<<<<<<<

Common Name: **BENZENE**
DOT Number: UN 1114
DOT Emergency Guide code: 27
CAS Number: 71-43-2

NJ DOH Hazard rating	
FLAMMABILITY	3
REACTIVITY	0
CARCINOGEN	
CONTAINERS MAY EXPLODE IN FIRE	
POISONOUS GAS IS PRODUCED IN FIRE	

Hazard Rating Key: 0=minimal; 1=slight; 2=moderate; 3=serious; 4=severe

FIRE HAZARDS

* **Benzene** is a FLAMMABLE LIQUID.
* Use dry chemical, CO_2, or foam extinguishers. Water can be used to keep fire-exposed containers cool.
* POISONOUS GAS IS PRODUCED IN FIRE.
* CONTAINERS MAY EXPLODE IN FIRE.
* The vapor is heavier than air and may travel a distance to cause a fire or explosion far from the source.
* If employees are expected to fight fires, they must be trained and equipped as stated in OSHA 1910.156.

SPILLS AND EMERGENCIES

If **Benzene** is spilled or leaked, take the following steps:

* Restrict persons not wearing protective equipment from area of spill or leak until clean-up is complete.
* Remove all ignition sources.
* Ventilate area of spill or leak.
* Absorb liquids in vermiculite, dry sand, earth, or a similar material and deposit in sealed containers.
* Keep **Benzene** out of a confined space, such as a sewer, because of the possibility of an explosion, unless the sewer is designed to prevent the build-up of explosive concentrations.
* It may be necessary to contain and dispose of **Benzene** as a HAZARDOUS WASTE. Contact the NJ Department of Environmental Protection (DEP) or your regional office of the federal Environmental Protection Agency (EPA) for specific recommendations.

FOR LARGE SPILLS AND FIRES immediately call your fire department. You can request emergency information from the following:

CHEMTREC: (800) 424-9300
NJDEP HOTLINE: (609) 292-7172

HANDLING AND STORAGE (See page 3)

FIRST AID

In NJ, POISON INFORMATION 1-800-962-1253

Eye Contact
* Immediately flush with large amounts of water for at least 15 minutes, occasionally lifting upper and lower lids.

Skin Contact
* Quickly remove contaminated clothing. Immediately wash area with large amounts of soap and water. Seek medical attention.

Breathing
* Remove the person from exposure.
* Begin rescue breathing if breathing has stopped and CPR if heart action has stopped.

PHYSICAL DATA

Vapor Pressure: 75 mmHg at 68°F (20°C)
Flash Point: 12°F (-11°C)
Water Solubility: Slightly soluble

OTHER COMMONLY USED NAMES

Chemical Name: Benzene
Other Names and Formulations: Benzol; Coal Naphtha; Phenyl Hydride

---

Not intended to be copied and sold for commercial purposes.

NEW JERSEY DEPARTMENT OF HEALTH
Right to Know Program
CN 368, Trenton, NJ 08625-0368
(609) 984-2202

TABLE 3-2 Results of Informal Survey of Fact Sheet Users

	Yes	No	No Answer
A. Understanding of HS fact sheets			
1. In general, do you understand the information on the fact sheets?	232	2	0
2. In general, do your employees understand the information on the fact sheet?	216	9	9
3. Is the information provided useful?	197	21	16
Which two sections are the most useful?			
Hazard summary	50		
Health hazard information	28		
Ways of reducing exposure	25		
Emergency information	24		
Workplace controls + procedures	20		
First aid	20		
4. Were you aware of the health effects before?	146	79	9
B. Use at the facility			
5. Have you used the fact sheet in the RTK training program?	154	70	10
6. Have employees requested fact sheets?	47	181	6
7. Has there been an incident at your facility in which the fact sheets were used as a resource?	9[a]	222	3
8. Have you improved work practices (e.g., local ventilation) as a result of recommendations in the fact sheet?	114[b]	113	7
9. Have employee work habits changed?	104[c]	110	20
10. Should any changes be made to the fact sheets?	42[d]	164	28

[a] Example: Acetone splashed into eye--used quick-flushing information.

[b] Examples: Changed storage procedures; added labels.

[c] Examples: Using protective gear; no longer using xylene to wash hands.

[d] Example: List trade names, common names, not just generics (e.g., say sulphuric acid, not hydrogen sulphate).

Source: Compiled from questionnaires supplied by New Jersey Department of Health.

sequentially, initial information spurring additional interest, but people seemed to ask for several items at once. This may be attributed in part to the fact that they were professionals and could predict what data they would need; another explanation that many of the telephone respondents provided was that it was so hard to find out which agency would provide data that once they found it they asked for everything. People generally expressed satisfaction with the information: 67 percent found it understandable and useful, and 60 percent received all they asked for. Table 3-3 presents a summary of a few of the results of the survey of New Jersey citizens who had made right-to-know requests (for comparison, a related survey of Massachusetts citizens is also reported). Additional information about the survey is provided in Appendix B.

An increase in the number of people making RTK requests in 1988 over the number who had made requests prior to the survey suggests that a certain amount of time must pass before citizens learn that an RTK program exists and how to take advantage of it. DEP is continuing to expand its citizen outreach efforts in order to ensure that New Jersey residents know they have the right to know.

One reason that the New Jersey program has been successful in gathering and, to a lesser extent, disseminating information is that the law provided for automatic funding, through a $2 per employee fee assessed against every employer in the state. Of the money collected, which averages about $1 million per year, 15 percent goes to the Department of Labor, 30 percent to DEP, 40 percent to DOH, and 15 percent to designated agents at the county level. Most of the designated local RTK authorities are county health departments, which receive funds ranging from $15,000 to $35,000 in return for providing an outreach program, including a newsletter and phone calls and visits to employers to help them implement worker RTK programs. DOH, which administers the local programs, also encouraged local agencies to use

TABLE 3-3   Characteristics of Information Received by Citizens (percent of total respondents[a])

	Understandable		Received All		Useful	
	N.J.	Mass.	N.J.	Mass.	N.J.	Mass.
Yes	66	61	61	67	69	33
Only part of it	23	17	20	8	17	--
No	01	17	15	33	04	17

[a] Totals do not add up to 100 because of missing answers and rounding.

some of their funds to purchase computers, which are linked directly to DOH by modem and are used by the department not only for RTK but for implementing other health programs.[10]

By 1987, New Jersey was operating an RTK program that was generally regarded as the nation's strongest. Reporting burdens on affected facilities had been reduced, data was computerized (and plans were under way to merge the data from DOH and DEP), fact sheets were widely available, training programs were in place for most employees, and an assured source of revenue was available for all components of the program. Criticism of the program focused on failures to publicize it both to employees and to the public, problems in interpreting the information about health risks provided by the two departments, lack of enforcement, and some continued difficulties in coordination between DOH and DEP.

Title III

By late 1987, the programs were again in flux. First, DOH had to prepare for the diminution of its program that would result from the increased coverage of the OSHA HCS in 1988. Its program would be limited to the 400,000 public employees in the state. Second, DEP especially had to work with EPA to determine how its existing program would be affected by Title III.

Among the problems New Jersey confronted are the following:

1. Chemical lists: New Jersey's unified chemical list does not match exactly any of the Title III lists, nor does the state law mention the OSHA HCS, whose criteria determine hazardousness for sections 311 and 312 of Title III. New Jersey believes that providing a list of covered substances, rather than requiring industry to identify hazards, increases compliance. In November 1988, observers were predicting that New Jersey's response to the federal law will have two parts: first, an amendment to the state RTK law to include a reference to the OSHA HCS; and second, the use of existing data to create a complete list of substances actually in use in New Jersey that are hazardous enough to merit reporting.[11]

2. Thresholds: With a minor exception, New Jersey's law neither specified nor precluded any thresholds or reporting quantities;[12] DOH chose to have no thresholds because it was concerned about health effects, and DEP omitted thresholds to be consistent. Federal law specifies threshold reporting quantities, and industry is urging DEP, which will implement Title III, to adopt some kind of threshholds as well. Although these are unlikely to be as high as 500 pounds, a

common Title III threshold, an amended New Jersey law will probably specify some minimum reporting quantity. This does not resolve the question of thresholds for the reporting periods before the state law is amended, nor does it resolve the question of which threshold to use for a substance for which more than one applies.

3. Timing: New Jersey's law requires the survey every other year; federal law requires annual reports. New Jersey places the burden on DEP to provide industry with the forms, lists, and help for the state survey; DEP will continue to conduct the biannual survey as before. EPA requires industry to take the initiative to report annually; in alternate years, DEP will make forms available and remind industry of its obligation but will not provide the full-scale support that characterizes its own survey.

4. Coverage: Before the broadening of the OSHA HCS in summer 1988, New Jersey law covered more facilities than federal law. After the deadline, federal law covered more facilities than state law. Which survey to send to whom and when, given the different state and federal reporting deadlines, constituted a serious problem for DEP.

5. Emergency response: Although DEP had created the Emergency Services Information Survey, New Jersey's emergency response program was really located in the state police department. That department decided to use the 567 municipalities with police departments for emergency planning under Title III; added to the 21 county lead agencies already responsible for RTK, this created 588 LEPCs in New Jersey. Coordinating among them and especially between the lead agencies and municipal police departments was difficult.

The weight of tradition, even a tradition only a few years old, may impede New Jersey's ability to comply with Title III requirements. Ironically, the complex structure of New Jersey's program that makes compliance with Title III difficult also accounts in part for the still more complex structure of the federal RTK program, since the architects of Title III modeled much of their program on New Jersey's. Nevertheless, the state program has many features that will facilitate meeting requirements of the federal program: a history, however mixed, of local participation in RTK implementation, the continued ability to fund state and local programs, and a tradition of using computers at both levels. Strong demand from citizens and strong staffing of the state RTK programs are likely to ensure that New Jersey's citizens can exercise the right to know easily and effectively.

Right to Know in Texas

Texas faced a very different problem from that of New Jersey. Its employee RTK law, which provided for public access to the reports filed, had never been funded by the legislature. Thus, parts of the program had to be constructed to meet the very rapid deadlines of Title III. On the other hand, Texas had in place a very strong emergency planning program, of which hazardous materials constituted a small part, and a very active privately sponsored community awareness program initiated after Bhopal. Because Texas produces more chemicals than any other state in the United States, its residents, especially those in the southeast near Houston, have long been aware of both the benefits and the hazards associated with these substances.

Its size and location also ensure that Texas is subject to a variety of natural disasters ranging from floods to hurricanes. The Division of Emergency Management (DEM) was created as a unit of the Governor's Office within the Texas Department of Public Safety. Under the Texas Disaster Act of 1975, DEM is required to promulgate standards and requirements for local and interjurisdictional emergency management plans. Texas has been very active in assisting localities to write emergency plans; some 870 local planning units (out of about 1,420) already have comprehensive emergency plans covering fire, flood, tornado, and other hazards. Hazardous-materials emergencies constitute one component of these plans. DEM works closely with the Federal Emergency Management Agency (FEMA), which helps to fund local planning and training efforts and in 1987 and 1988 provided some training funds to all the states to assist in planning required under Title III. DEM is also the coordinating member of the Texas State Emergency Management Council, which was established by executive order to oversee emergency response. The council is comprised of representatives of twenty-six state agencies and the Red Cross; appropriate members are convened for different kinds of emergencies. Because it oversees emergency planning in Texas, DEM assumed responsibility for coordinating the state's program to implement Title III. The State Emergency Management Council was designated to act as the SERC.[13]

In order to avoid interfering in the vagaries of state administration, Title III refers only to a single state body, the SERC. Texas's existing emergency management council was purely a coordinating body, however, without the ability to promulgate rules or take other actions. Therefore, the SERC also had no ability to promulgate rules; it had no staff other than DEM employees, no budget, and no space. In order to meet even the minimum requirements of Title

III, member agencies thus had to agree to take on (with no additional funding) responsibilities that were congruent with their existing duties.

In Texas, these responsibilities are dispersed among several agencies. The Texas Water Commission is the state's lead agency for hazardous waste activities, regulates discharges into water, and coordinates spill response; it provides a member of the Regional Response Team. The Texas Air Control Board regulates air emissions. The Texas Department of Health (TDH) has responsibility for implementing Texas's Hazard Communication Act (HCA), the state's employee right-to-know law. The Department of Agriculture regulates pesticides in every aspect, and the Railroad Commission regulates pipelines and certain aspects of underground injection wells. Finally, the Department of Public Safety houses the Division of Emergency Management and sponsors spill-response training.

The issue of delegating authority for implementing particular parts of Title III continued to absorb the attention of the agency representatives throughout the spring of 1987. At the June 24 meeting, members decided that TDH would be responsible for receiving reports submitted under sections 303, 311, and 312, and that TDH would establish a format for the reports. On July 7, the Texas Board of Health published a proposed rule describing the kinds of reports that it would receive. The rule made four important changes:

• It established a filing fee of $25 for each list. The power to collect a fee had been granted as a rider to the state appropriation bill passed the same month. From the first meeting of the Emergency Response Council, funds for the program had been a major concern; Texas's poor economic situation virtually precluded legislative appropriations for new programs. Even the existing state Hazard Communication Act had received no appropriations for implementation, and its entire staff consisted of one half-time professional. As approximately 50,000 facilities were expected to file lists, even a small filing fee would provide a significant fund for implementing both the federal and the state right-to-know laws. This effect was increased because section 312 reports have to be submitted separately and therefore entail a separate filing fee.

• It prohibited facilities from filing Material Safety Data Sheets to fulfill any reporting requirements under Title III or the state law. Without funds to implement the Texas HCA, the Health Department could not even computerize the 2,000-odd lists of chemicals submitted (out of about 50,000 nominally covered by the law); rather, the lists were stored in boxes with a computerized guide to the approximate storage location.[14] The department would obviously have been overwhelmed if each covered facility submitted a separate multipage MSDS for each chemical on site. It chose, therefore, to prohibit one of the section 311 filing options.

•It allowed the department to specify a format for filing required lists. By 1988, facilities in Texas might have to file three different forms--one for the Texas HCA, one for OSHA, and one for section 311 of Title III--all providing nearly duplicate lists of chemicals. Although some of the definitions in Texas law differed from those in federal law--especially concerning threshold reporting amounts--the HCA staff designed a reporting format that would allow each chemical to be listed only once. The requirement of Title III that chemicals be listed in groups by hazard category would be met by simply designating the hazard category on the line for each chemical. The format for section 312 Tier 2 reports would be the one specified by EPA.

•It required that reporting facilities meet the more stringent of federal or state threshold requirements. Texas HCA specified 500 pounds or 55-gallon drum as the threshold reporting requirement. EPA's rules under section 311 of Title III specify limits decreasing from 10,000 pounds to 0 pounds over three years, except for the "extremely hazardous substances," for which the threshold limit would be 1 pound.[15] By specifying that the reporting facility is responsible for meeting the most stringent threshold, and by providing a form that works for all three reporting requirements, the TDH maximized simplicity and flexibility.

The other issue confronting the SERC was the designation of Emergency Planning Districts (EPDs) before the July 17 deadline. During early SERC meetings, this issue was raised as a potential problem. Counties have other responsibilities for emergency planning and response, and thus seemed logical units for EPDs, but Texas has 254 counties--which would make a large number of bodies for the SERC to coordinate. In some areas, most notably around Houston, the center of a multicounty concentration of petrochemical plants, the county seemed an inappropriately large region. The SERC chose to designate counties as EPDs but offered them three options that would provide flexibility in actual planning areas. There could be a single, countywide LEPC; a single committee with subcommittees representing subsections of the county; or two or more independent committees representing various subsections of the county. County judges, chief executive officers of Texas counties, were informed of this choice in a letter that also provided a list of the kinds of individuals to be named to the LEPC and other guidance.

By August 17, the statutory deadline for EPDs to name their LEPCs, 48 counties had submitted their committee lists to the SERC, and 7 had requested an extension of time. Title III had specified that by May 17 facilities covered by the emergency planning provisions should so notify the SERC. Only approximately 2,000 facilities had complied, instead of the expected 50,000. Of the counties with registered facilities, 34 had established LEPCs and 117 had not by August 17; 14 counties without any registered facilities had established LEPCs. Most of the counties chose to establish a single committee, but about fifteen chose subcommittees, and a few chose multiple committees. Harris County (including Houston), with the highest concentration of petrochemical facilities in the state, decided to establish 32 LEPCs, corresponding in many cases to existing CAER planning units.[16]

The SERC, which must approve the LEPCs, decided that it could not exercise any reasonable judgment about particular individuals who were unfamiliar to it and determined to approve all the committee lists submitted. Some reservations were expressed about the composition of some committees: For example, some counties failed to designate a hospital representative; as these counties did not have hospitals, this lack is understandable. The SERC suggested that clinic personnel be designated instead. Two counties submitted identical lists of people, intending to make their plan together; this was deemed sensible. Finally, some counties designated Chamber of Commerce representatives or staff people of multicounty agencies as their "community group" members. Some reservations were expressed about the appropriateness of this procedure, but no action was taken.[17]

As the autumn went by, DEM continued to press counties to establish LEPCs, finally threatening to designate committee members from Austin if local officials refused to fulfill their duties. The SERC finally had to appoint LEPCs in nearly 20 percent of the counties in January 1988. In spring 1988, the Texas Water Commission agreed to receive section 313 reports that would be filed in July; although it was unable to computerize them at the outset, the agency created a system of file cards that gave citizens access to reports for particular facilities within a few minutes of requesting them. Other issues that continued to concern the SERC were training for emergency responders and LEPC members, relationships with EPA, and availability of funds. By November 1988, the Department of Health had received only $87,500 from filing fees, although it had expected to collect three times as much.[18]

The Texas program could be characterized as an effort to comply with Title III by taking as few new actions as possible. Lack of resources and a strong existing emergency planning program contributed to that attitude and also contributed to a creative solution to the dilemma created by multiple overlapping reporting requirements between state and federal laws. Thus, the "minimalist" approach to implementation does not necessary mean that citizens will have their right-to-know undermined.

Like the New Jersey program, the Texas program suffered from the outset because of confusion arising from multiple agencies with jurisdictions over parts of the program. Also like New Jersey, Texas was faced with the need to revise its state worker RTK law when the coverage of federal OSHA was expanded. Agency rivalries slowed initial implementation and could surface as a problem later. Texas also created at least an interim funding mechanism, although it is neither so reliable nor so munificent as New Jersey's. Texas differs from New Jersey in its lack of emphasis (to date) on computerization; the unified reporting form is intended to facilitate computerization later, but the state has not begun to consider assisting localities in managing the masses of data that Title III will generate.

Implementation in the Counties

As the account of appointing the LEPCs may suggest, Texas's 254 counties differ considerably, ranging in population from more than 10 million to less than 10,000 people. Brewster County in west Texas has an area larger than Connecticut and Rhode Island together. Some counties contain small "silicon valleys," whereas others obtain the bulk of their revenues from hunting and fishing licenses. These differences were reflected in the ways in which the counties implemented Title III.

In November 1987, a research team conducted field visits to eleven counties, where they interviewed a variety of public officials, emergency responders, and LEPC members. The counties were selected on the basis of geographic location, population size, and apparent risk from hazardous materials; some were chosen because of their participation in the chemical-industry-sponsored CAER program. Interviewees were asked about implementation of Title III and about emergency response. In April 1988, one member of the project team conducted a telephone survey of thirty-six LEPC chairpeople in counties not included in the earlier field survey; results of the survey are reported in Chapters 4 and 7. However, many of the respondents made additional informal comments on Title III after answering the questionnaire; these informal comments clearly complement and reinforce the findings from the field survey.

Although the counties differ so widely, interviewees expressed many common concerns. First, respondents in every county were concerned about the lack of funding for implementing Title III. County officials mentioned both the lack of resources for emergency response training and the need for resources to collect, compile, and store the MSDSs or chemical lists from the local industries. Counties do not have enough money for either computer facilities or personnel to operate the computers, yet they feel that they cannot manage the data without such assistance.

Many of the county officials expressed concern or dissatisfaction over what they perceived to be the patchwork of state statutes regarding hazardous materials. Some were frustrated by what they believed to be a lack of interest on the part of the state in helping them to understand what is expected of them and to aid in the preparation of a hazardous materials plan. Others felt resentful of Title III, as many already had what they considered to be good hazardous materials plans. This feeling was echoed by one of the LEPC chairpeople in the telephone interview, who said that since the community in which an incident occurred would have to respond, requiring the entire county to develop a joint plan was a waste of time. Another said that ultimately the fire chief was in charge and that it would be his plan that would be implemented, not the LEPC's.

Counties that had CAER programs seemed to be at a considerable initial advantage in meeting the planning requirement under section 303. Many of them already had hazardous materials response plans, and the plans were more likely to include industry response to emergencies. In Brazoria County, for example, the plan was developed by industry and is tested weekly through computer simulation. Areas with CAER programs tend to have received financial support from the industry, including, in some cases, funds for the purchase of computers to aid in planning. Citizens in CAER counties are more likely than citizens in counties starting emergency planning without CAER plans to complain that the LEPCs are dominated by industry or that they have trouble getting their views heard, however, suggesting a possible tradeoff between efficiency in planning and equity in access.

Although all the counties in the field survey have at least one annual training exercise for emergency responders, counties with CAER programs also tend to have more training time, either because industry pays for the firefighters to be sent to national or state programs or because industry loans the fire departments equipment for training. Large cities that have hazardous materials units provide additional training for their own staff. One county noted that it could not meet the training requirements implicit in Title III because its fire department is composed entirely of volunteers, who would have to sacrifice their paychecks to go to training sessions that are always held outside of the county. "They don't know how we live," that chairman said. These LEPCs are unsure that they will be able to fulfill their responsibilities without people, resources, or funds.

Another concern of county officials is the LEPCs' lack of power to enforce the collection of MSDSs or chemical lists. Although they were hopeful that Title III would improve emergency response by identifying locations of chemicals present even in the smaller "mom-and-pop" shops, they were also concerned that these smaller facilities would fail to comply with the Title III regulations through ignorance. In the telephone survey of LEPC chairpeople, which was conducted after the facilities' chemical inventory reports were due, several of the respondents noted their surprise at learning from the initial reports how many varied businesses use hazardous materials. This only heightened concern about unwitting noncompliance.

The field survey was conducted in November 1987, before counties had had a chance to begin implementing Title III. Respondents were most aware of and interested in the emergency planning and response portions of the law, in part because the CAER program already focused on those issues. They were worried about acquiring the resources necessary to implement all portions of the law, especially those that depend on acquisition and management of the extensive records required by the law--emergency planning and community right to know. The telephone survey in April found little change in the kinds of concerns expressed. Because it did not ask about implementation or about emergency response or planning, we have no comparison with the earlier survey on these issues. However, officials, especially in smaller counties, seemed still to be overwhelmed by the complexity of the law and the new institutions it has been creating.

The most important finding of both surveys is that a two-class system of counties is emerging. One class has the infrastructure for emergency response and planning, either because it includes a large city that had an emergency response unit or because it includes one or more major facilities that support emergency planning and response, either informally or through the privately sponsored CAER program. These counties have trouble mobilizing additional resources but will manage to meet all their obligations under the law.

The second class of counties, in contrast, does not have either the resources or, in many instances, the motivation to comply. When all the emergency response personnel are volunteers, when there are few or no facilities that manufacture or use significant amounts of hazardous chemicals, when the economy is precarious or worse--under these conditions, counties have trouble fulfilling the intent of the law.

The results of the surveys of Title III implementation in Texas are consistent with those of a survey of states that EPA conducted early in 1988. That survey formed the basis of an EPA "white paper," which in turn outlined suggestions for agency Title III programs for 1990 and beyond. In the forty-two states EPA surveyed, 3,555 LEPCs were to have been formed and 2,162 were functioning. Impediments to LEPCs' operations were reported to include lack of funding, lack of awareness of the law, and a general lack of incentive and direction. States estimated that between 5 and 70 percent of facilities had complied with the reporting requirement under section 302, and between 8 and 85 percent had complied with sections 311 and 312. In several states, as many as 80 percent of the facilities had supplied MSDSs under section 311.[19] These data suggest that states could use some EPA assistance in implementation.

Implementing Right to Know

New Jersey's experience refines our understanding of some of the problems inherent in the specific provisions of Title III; more important, it gives us insight into the operation of an RTK program. Perhaps the primary lesson to be learned from the New Jersey experience is that it is easier for public agencies to mobilize rapidly to do some tasks, such as collecting data, than to do others, such as public outreach. DEP has collected industrial survey data; DOH has created hundreds of fact sheets and has also offered agencies some assistance in creating required training programs. Citizens still complain about the scope of the training programs and access to DEP data, however. Localities, where outreach programs must be focused, have difficulty in conducting such programs even when funded.

The experience so far in Texas confirms this analysis. Without funding, agencies can only do the kinds of tasks they are already set up to do. TDH will collect data required by Title III; it has also taken steps to minimize the reporting burden on affected industry--steps that will ease as well the agency's task in managing the data. Localities were usually apprised of their duties, but agencies were unable to assist them in fulfilling these tasks.

These brief descriptions of activities in two states suggest that there are many facets to implementing a right-to-know program, including assigning roles to many people and institutions, managing the data, making the data available, and then deciding what, if anything, to do with the data. The combination of these activities at the federal, state, and local levels will determine what RTK means in the United States. In the five chapters of Part 2, I examine these different facets of RTK, drawing on the experiences of Texas, New Jersey, and other states, as well as on evidence drawn from the implemention of other laws and information policies.

Notes

1. New Jersey Department of Environmental Protection, Office of Science and Research, *New Jersey Industrial Survey: Final Report*, Trenton, August 1986, p. 1; interview with Ed Stevenson, Office of Science and Research, Trenton, May 12, 1987. According to others familiar with the program, Stevenson is the "father of the industrial survey." The following three paragraphs draw very heavily on the Final Report.

2. One explanation for this is that the list purposely included outmoded substances whose disposal locations DEP wanted to know. Another explanation is that industry was systematically avoiding several of the EPA Priority Pollutants because scientific tests for pollutants focused especially on those substances. It was reported that substitutes that would avoid the test screen had been devised, although the substitutes were not necessarily less toxic than the avoided substances. Interview with former member of DEP staff, who in turn received this information from a trusted industry source. Both names have been withheld by request.

3. David J. Sarokin, Warren R. Muir, Catherine G. Miller, and Sebastian R. Sperber, *Cutting Chemical Wastes* (New York: INFORM, 1985).

4. These events mentioned in a note from Garrett Keating.

5. Interviews. Trenton, N. J. and Washington, D. C. May 1987.

6. 49 CFR 172.102 is the DOT list. For DEP decision, see 16 N.J.R. 648 (April 2, 1984).

7. *New Jersey State Chamber of Commerce* v. *Hughey*, 600 F. Supp. 606 (D. N.J., Jan. 3, 1985). *United Steelworkers of American* v. *Auchter*, 763 F 2d 728 (May 24, 1985).

8. New Jersey Department of Health, "Status of Fact Sheets," March 1987.

9. Telephone interview with Barbara Sargeant, New Jersey DEP, November 10, 1988.

10. Interview with Kathleen O'Leary, chief of occupational health, New Jersey Department of Health, May 12, 1987.

11. Telephone interview with Barbara Sargeant, N. J. DEP, October 8, 1987.

12. New Jersey Administrative Code, Title 8, Chapter 8:59-10.1.

13. Executive Order WPC-87-6a, *Texas Register*, April 28, 1987, p. 1424.

14. Interview with William Elliott, Occupational Health Program, Texas Department of Health, January 8, 1987. I used the word "stored" in the text because "filed" would have misrepresented the orderliness of the procedure.

15. Proposed 52 Fed. Reg. 26357 (July 14, 1987); final 52 Fed. Reg. 38322 (October 15, 1987). Most observers believe that the 0-pound threshold will be replaced by a 500-pound or 55-gallon-drum limit, making Title III regulations very similar to Texas law.

16. List submitted to August 20, 1987, Texas SERC meeting by Division of Emergency Management.

17. August 20, 1987, SERC meeting.

18. The astute reader will remember the $25 fee and the 250,000 reports and wonder whether my arithmetic is in error. The Texas Department of Health did not expect all the covered facilities to file at first, but it also did not expect facilities to consolidate reports. In one case, a firm filed 495 chemical lists under one $25 filing fee. Interview with William Elliott, Texas Department of Health, November 30, 1988.

19. EPA, "Summary Questionnaire," no author, February, 1988, xerox copy. (Results of the questionnaire distributed to states to gather information for the "white paper.")

PART 2
Aspects of Right to Know

We don't have the knowledge to make decisions about which way it should be done or which way it should not be done. But what we do know is we feel like we are being jammed something down our throat. . . . Give us the opportunity to know what is going on. Let's get rid of the fear.

---Citizen testifying at a public hearing
on a superfund site

4 / Institutional Factors

Laws that embody public policies are made by legislatures, but the policies must be effected within and by institutions, including private industry, membership organizations, and the courts, as well as the government agencies given the immediate responsibility for implementation. The provisions of SARA (Superfund Amendments and Reauthorization Act) Title III ensure that these institutions play a particularly strong role in implementing the law, which explicitly mentions public agencies at three levels of government, embodies both public information and emergency response goals, and ensures that a variety of interests are incorporated into the planning process. In my discussions of Texas and New Jersey, I suggested that these requirements sometimes conflict with the existing institutional arrangements, which may in turn slow achievement of the goals of right to know even when the actors agree upon the goals. To the extent that actors and organizations differ in their definitions of RTK, institutions may act deliberately to limit implementation of certain aspects of the law embodying that right.

In this chapter, I consider several aspects of institutional arrangements that most strongly affect RTK, beginning with a brief discussion of the effects of the federal structure of U.S. government and of certain professional concerns that affected the immediate implementation of Title III. This discussion is followed by a consideration of bureaucratic and procedural impediments to exercising the right to know. Two legal constraints may also impede the availability or access to information--trade secrets and liability.

Federalism

Federalism is both the strength of U.S. democracy and the source of many of its problems. One of the strengths and purposes of having a federal government is to provide a forum that supersedes states and localities, where minority groups of all kinds may not be able to affect public policy: It is at the federal level that many important social changes have received their first governmental imprimatur, including many areas of civil rights, medicare and medicaid, and social security. Another benefit of having a federal government is to ensure uniformity among the states; at least some proponents of a federal RTK law were representatives of affected industries who did not want to have to comply with fifty different kinds of state reporting requirements and with local requirements as well. Although some uniformity may be desirable, federalism also provides the flexibility to allow programs to be tailored to the very diverse needs of different states and localities. Indeed, observers have noted a recent resurgence of innovative policy initiatives at the state level to respond to special state needs.[1]

However, federalism entails some problems as well, especially in coordinating among the levels. In this section, I will consider three such problems. First, in cases like Title III's, in which a federal law places most of the burden for implementation on the states and localities, the lower levels of government may not have the same goals as Congress or the federal agency. Thus, federal purposes may be lost or weakened. This eventuality is especially likely when, as is also the case for Title III, the federal government is not providing the lower levels with any money for implementation. Second, lower levels of government may have similar goals but may feel resentful of federal interference; this, too, is more likely when no funds are provided. Finally, and in many ways most important, state or even local laws are likely to conflict with the new federal law. We know that this is a problem for implementation of Title III as one reason for industry's support of Title III was to circumvent the myriad state and local community RTK laws.

Even when a program is federally funded, as Title III was not for at least its first three years, other levels of government may not feel that the goals of the federal law are appropriate for them. A small survey of Texas LEPC chairpeople was conducted in March and April 1988 (see the Appendix for a description of the survey); nearly 40 percent (14 of 35) of the LEPC chairpeople surveyed disagreed with the statement "The LEPC should publicize right-to-know provisions," and 18 out of 35 agreed with the statement "Keeping Title III information is a burden for local government." Combined with their general belief that citizens cannot understand Title III information (21 of 32), this means that many LEPC chairpeople may not feel a strong incentive to expend a lot of effort on the RTK portions of Title III. One chairman specifically stated that LEPCs do not have to publicize the right-to-know provisions; instead, he said, "people should take responsibility for themselves." Similar attitudes have been reported for other states.[2]

The multiple purposes of Title III, in effect, allow lower levels of government to choose to emphasize those purposes that are consonant with their own. In many instances, emergency response has come to dominate RTK at these lower levels of government. SERCs and LEPCs are dominated by emergency response personnel rather than by citizens or environmental personnel. Twenty-two states have designated the emergency management or public safety department as head of the SERC, and in another eight states such a department head serves as cochair. Only eleven states have designated a department of the environment to head the SERC; the remainder have recruited other departments, such as health, or private individuals.[3] One reason for this is that many states, like Texas, already had emergency management councils, which were adapted to the requirements of Title III.

A similar situation prevailed at the local level, as most localities have fire departments and many have emergency response divisions as well. Professional staff of these agencies were already involved in emergency response and, often, emergency planning and were able to seize whatever opportunities Title III offered for their departments. Unfortunately, the quasi-military organizations associated with emergency response, which depend upon strict hierarchies to achieve orderly and accurate actions under duress, are not much used to public outreach. Furthermore, the Community Awareness and Emergency Response program sponsored by the Chemical Manufacturers Association had also emphasized emergency response; in the cases in which CAER committees were converted into LEPCs, emergency response continued to dominate local concerns.

Many if not most LEPCs delayed consideration of RTK issues. Although a majority (21 of 35) of Texas LEPC chairpeople surveyed agreed that LEPCs should publicize right-to-know provisions, only eight out of the eighteen LEPCs in the survey that had met said that they had discussed right to know and community access. Note that half the LEPCs surveyed had not even met seven months after they were to have been created and seven months before the emergency plan was due, another indicator of lack of interest in Title III's goals.

Independent of their interest (or lack of it) in particular federal goals, state and local officials are often resentful of what they regard as an intrusive, inappropriate, or cold federal government. These attitudes and problems emerged in most states after Title III was passed. Considering a request for a list of certain industries from EPA, one member of the Texas SERC received the approval of his colleagues by remarking, "EPA is always asking us for information and help, but they never give us any. Let's not go to any special effort to comply with their request for information." Later, when the EPA regional office asked the SERC to send within a week or two a "State Implementation Memo," listing areas of the state as priorities for EPA training or assistance, members felt that, in the words of one, "They really don't understand us. If we rank a county high, implying that the risk from hazardous materials in the area is high, the state legislator from that county will jump down our throats asking how we came up with the ranking. To do ranking that would stand up to such scrutiny would take us more staff and time than we have."[4] Other states adopted a stance of doing as little as possible to comply with the letter but not the spirit of the law. Four states, including Georgia and, until July 1988, Minnesota, created statewide LEPCs that will certainly not be in very close touch with either the facilities or the citizens.

Title III's distribution of responsibilities among three levels of government has in some cases allowed all of them in turn to disavow responsibility. EPA, for example, is required to computerize the section 313 emissions reports, although the SERCs are also designated to receive them. Many states are waiting for EPA to provide the data in electronic form, choosing to keep the data in hard copy only in order to reduce costs. EPA expected to provide the electronic data early in 1989; until that time, citizens did not necessarily know where to turn. Those who called one state's Department of Natural Resources were told to call the EPA regional office, but staff there also disavowed knowledge of or responsibility for providing access to any Title III data.[5]

Perhaps the most serious problem associated with federalism is the existence of conflicting laws at the different levels.   More than twenty five states and numerous localities had community right-to-know laws in effect when Title III was passed.[6] The problems created by multilevel government are illustrated again by emergency planning in Texas. Under the state emergency planning act, designated planning areas file emergency plans. These areas are usually municipalities but may also be unincorporated areas of counties. There are 1,421 such planning areas in the state. Title III requires LEPCs (which are usually countywide units in Texas) to file plans for responding to hazardous materials emergencies with the SERC. This created a contradiction, because the state law expects smaller planning units to create multihazard plans. Could the LEPCs file plans? With what official body? What would happen to the plans, inasmuch as they came from units not recognized by state law?[7] These questions could be resolved with some creativity; for example, LEPCs could pull together the hazardous materials portions of all state emergency planning areas in their counties and submit them to the SERC. Not only would such action provide some incentive for coordination across the smaller planning units, but it would reduce the amount of new work the LEPCs have to do. People who were inimical to the federal law or to federal intervention in state matters, however, kept this problem festering for months.

New Jersey, with its very strong state RTK program, faced somewhat different problems. Most troubling among these for a time was the question of what to do about the reporting forms. New Jersey was unwilling (and unable under its law) to give up certain questions it wanted to ask facilities; it also wanted to continue using its own forms with which facilities were familiar. During talks with New Jersey staff, EPA was adamant that the questionnaires should be consistent with the EPA-prescribed format.[8] But in fact, when EPA finally issued the regulations, they included a statement that states and localities were free to adopt their own forms or require additional information so long as they contained all the required information.[9]

Many states responded to the problems raised by conflicting requirements by altering their own laws. Amending the legislation also afforded these states the opportunity to impose fees for filing Title III forms, thus creating some funding for the program, and to enable state and local officials to take responsibility for enforcing the (state version of the) law. This meant that certain enforcement actions would no longer have to be filed only in a federal court. Among the states that had passed such legislation by May 1988 were Louisiana, Kentucky, Missouri, Ohio, and Wisconsin.[10]

Preemption is another means of overcoming some of the problems created by conflicting federal and state laws. When federal law preempts state or local law, it overrides conflicting provisions. Many environmental laws contain a provision that allows state or local standards to remain if they are more stringent than federal standards; these laws are intended to ensure that states achieve at least some minimum performance. Others preempt completely; these create uniform standards throughout the country.

There are advantages and disadvantages to each pattern. In the case of worker RTK, employers with facilities in more than one state became concerned with the difficulty of complying with the diverse requirements and began to work with OSHA to institute a nationwide Hazard Communication Standard. Thus, they filed suit to overturn New Jersey's law; as noted in Chapter 2, the court held that the employee portions were preempted but not the community RTK portions (Title III had not yet been passed). Even when Congress expresses the wish to preempt, actual preemption is often decided in court based on congressional intent to supersede, a "dominant federal interest," or a conflict between the two laws so strong that compliance with one precludes compliance with the other.[11]

In contrast to laws that indicate congressional preference for preemption, Title III explicitly notes that it does not supersede state law.[12] With the court battle over the OSHA HCS recent in their memories, environmental groups and other supporters of Title III were presumably reluctant to allow preemption of existing state programs that might better serve RTK by covering more substances, imposing lower reporting thresholds, or requiring reporting of more detailed information. Nonpreemption was, in part, responsible for the difficulties experienced by New Jersey, Massachusetts, and other states with strong existing programs. A number of localities had adopted ordinances similar to one in effect in Santa Clara County, California, which includes some very low reporting thresholds and relatively broad coverage of mixtures.[13] Fire departments charged with enforcing these ordinances were generally reluctant to give them up, arguing that however well designed Title III was for emergency planning or RTK, firefighters needed to know about much smaller quantities. Preemption or voluntary alteration of these ordinances would reduce the purview of enforcing agencies; in Austin, Texas, for example, about 1,500 facilities were covered under the local ordinance, and only about 250 under Title III.[14]

Failure to preempt has affected implementation of Title III. Because the law does not preempt, state laws have determined whether the LEPC should be treated as a federal, state, or local agency. The attorney general of Kentucky ruled that the state could not fulfill the federal requirement to include elected state and local officials on LEPCs because it would "place them in the executive branch" and thereby violate the separation of powers clause (keeping executive, legislative, and judicial functions apart) of the state constitution.[15]

Federalism is supposed, among other benefits, to ensure that policies and programs are tailored to the very diverse needs of different states and communities--a goal certainly germane to RTK, as citizens of different areas may have very different levels of tolerance for the risks imposed by hazardous materials. However, jurisdictions may simply ignore federal directives if their values are not congruent, especially if the federal government is not providing funds whose availability is dependent upon meeting certain program goals. This means that a minority of constituents who do agree with the federal goal are less able to exercise their rights. Any tendencies to undermine federal programs because of disagreement with their substance are exacerbated by distrust or dislike of the "feds" by almost all lower levels of government; when the lower level already has comparable legislation, hostility to the higher level is likely to be enhanced. Conversely, activities such as enforcement and planning that require detailed knowledge of local situations are virtually impossible without cooperation from state and local officials. As with all other federal policies, the trick lies in developing a balance between central direction and local implementation.

Bureaucratic and Procedural Impediments

Even if the problems of federalism did not arise, Title III would still face institutional barriers to its implementation arising from bureaucratic procedures, often created by agency rivalries or concern about protecting programs. These impediments, not always of the agencies' making, can inhibit RTK as effectively as if created on purpose.

Agency rivalry has been a particular problem for RTK and for Title III because the multiple purposes of the law virtually mandated interagency cooperation. Chapter 3 presented in detail the differences among the New Jersey Departments of Health, Environmental Protection, and Labor in implementing the state law and among the Texas Department of Health, Air Control Board, Water Commission, Railroad Commission, and Department of Public Safety on the SERC. New Jersey gave oversight of Title III programs to yet a fourth agency, its Department of Public Safety, which is an emergency responder. DPS designated as LEPCs its familiar units--local fire departments, of which there are more than 500 in New Jersey.

In several states, agency rivalry was exacerbated by the proposed expansion of the OSHA HCS to all commercial facilities. Because the court had held in 1985 that the OSHA HCS did preempt state employee laws that regulated the same industries, uncertainty about the extent and timing of the OSHA expansion prevailed throughout the first eighteen months of Title III implementation. Localities and states could not be sure even of the number of facilities from which they would have to receive reports because the OSHA HCS defined the extent of coverage for sections 311 and 312 of Title III.

Federal preemption of state right-to-know laws had the potential for leaving some agencies, often health departments with primary responsibility for worker health, with little to do under the remaining, nonpreempted parts of the community RTK laws. In New Jersey, for example, the Department of Health, which realized that its large RTK program would have to be contracted to cover only public employees when OSHA coverage expanded, began to emphasize the importance of its fact sheets for community RTK--an argument given support when EPA selected the fact sheets as the chemical information format of choice for supplementing the section 313 emissions data. In contrast, the Texas Department of Health was not unhappy about the contraction of its statutory responsibilities; the program had never been adequately funded and the half-time staff person had sufficient alternative tasks.

When the federal deus ex machina created the SERCs and LEPCs and required them to perform functions that were already being performed in part by existing agencies, it virtually ensured that there would be rivalries among agencies. To make matters worse, the SERCs especially were not given any particular powers by the federal law, although state legislation could enhance their standing. Even when four of the Texas agencies in the SERC wanted to cooperate by publishing a brief overview of all of their spill-reporting requirements, they were inhibited from doing so by the fact that no agency could approve for insertion into the *Texas Register*, which serves as the formal record of agency actions, the procedures of another agency. Even to insert what amounted to a nontechnical statement of their own procedures--already approved and previously published as regulations in the *Texas Register*--the agencies had to receive formal approval from their legal departments, their executive directors, and their commissioners (agency policymakers appointed by the governor). Thus, a six-page overview of spill procedures that would enhance emergency response capability in the state took several months to make public.[16] Similarly, the staff of the Texas Fire Commission on Personnel Standards, which had expertise that would be of considerable use to the subcommittee of the SERC concerned about training emergency responders, was required to go before their commissioners to get permission to participate as informal members of the subcommittee, delaying their involvement by several weeks.

Just as the powers of the SERC are not made clear in the federal legislation (the many states that have passed state laws have largely overcome this problem), the extent of LEPCs' powers is also not clear. One LEPC that was coordinating emergency response for several smaller jurisdictions had a gentleman's agreement with facilities not to enter plant grounds until a formal request was made during an emergency. The LEPC was criticized by citizens for failing to enter a facility when an emergency occurred, even though the LEPC chairman, the emergency response coordinator, believed that plant personnel were responding adequately. In another case, an LEPC was persuaded by some citizens who wanted a waste disposal facility to be denied a permit under another law, the Resource Conservation and Recovery Act, to say that the required emergency plan was not adequate to merit a permit. Are LEPCs able to undertake these additional responsibilities? Ought they to do so?

Another set of bureaucratic impediments to RTK began to surface when LEPCs and SERCs started to establish procedures for public access to Title III reports. Most states and some localities have an Open Records Act, which provides procedures for citizen access to public records as well as procedures for protecting certain records from public view because they contain confidential business information or trade secrets. Often such laws require that a request for information be made in writing; this allows an agency to keep track of requests and ensure that they have been fulfilled. Most states also have a Freedom of Information Act (FOIA), which, like its federal counterpart, ensures that citizens can obtain access to a variety of government records, again usually upon written request specifying the particular documents desired.

Agencies that began to keep Title III records often treated them the same way they treated other government records. By requiring citizens to request documents in writing, however, these agencies were undermining one of the essential features of right to know. RTK assumes that the citizen has the right to see any of the documents created under the law, even to browse among them just to see whether any interesting patterns or facts emerge. FOIA, in contrast, forces inquirers to know just which document they want and sometimes to justify the request. Agencies are justifiably concerned about the amount of staff time that might be entailed in locating and copying vast quantities of data that citizens request; citizens are justifiably concerned that they are not able to exercise the right to know.

In a survey I conducted of citizens in New Jersey and Massachusetts, (see the Appendix for details), a common complaint concerned procedures for obtaining information under RTK. Many written and all telephone responses mentioned the amount of effort required to obtain information, including how hard it was to reach appropriate agency personnel, how long it took to obtain replies, inconsistency of information provided by different state agencies, and the unhelpfulness of local health departments. In New Jersey, some respondents mentioned the need for the data to be available more hours of the day--perhaps in the public library. People had difficulty reconstructing the order in which events surrounding their RTK requests had occurred because each request had entailed so many telephone calls, letters, and meetings with agency personnel. One man told me that for several months he had two full-time jobs, his usual one and the late afternoon and evening job of locating, acquiring, and understanding RTK data he wanted. Other researchers have received the same complaints.[17]

The multiple overlapping reporting requirements built into Title III may also make exercise of RTK more difficult. The differences among the groups of facilities subject to different parts of the law, the different lists of chemicals, and the different reporting dates all combine to reduce the likelihood that any particular facility will be in full compliance with all aspects of the law. This is especially true for small facilities and those that use rather than manufacture chemicals. The multiple reporting requirements also make it difficult for citizens to find and collate all the reports from a particular facility. These built-in deterrents to effective RTK can be reduced by amending the legislation; some may also be reduced by taking advantage of the alternatives Title III provides. Many states and LEPCs, for example, have required facilities to file a chemical list rather than MSDSs under section 311. Not only does this reduce the pages of paper that an agency must manage, but it also avoids the difficulties that may arise from having substantively different MSDSs for the same chemical. Similarly, some states and LEPCs have required facilities to file only Tier 2 reports, inasmuch as the Tier 1 reports lump together very different chemicals and double count some as well. The law could easily be amended to remove these duplicative chemical inventory reports by requiring only the Tier 2 report and allowing LEPCs the option of requesting MSDSs for unfamiliar substances.

Differences in goals may affect relationships not only between but within institutions. It is often the case, for example, that the goals of the professional staff are not congruent with the goals of the more political personnel at the top of an agency's hierarchy. It is also important to remember that most large private corporations are affected by the same kinds of bureaucratic problems that the public is likely to see in government agencies. Facility managers, for example, used to have almost absolute power within their facilities; now, their expertise concerning both the facility and the local political situation within which it operates is often subordinated to decisions by accounting and other middle managers in the corporation's home office. Several facility managers complained to me that their ability to work with citizens--for example, to reduce emissions or work on input substitution--was seriously impeded by distant corporate staff who placed short-term profits ahead of long-term cost reductions through waste minimization and the gaining of community support.

Bureaucratic procedures are often unjustly criticized. At their best, they ensure that all citizens who are alike in some relevant respect are treated equally, and they ensure that citizens (or their attorneys) can know how to exercise their rights or how to obtain benefits to which they are entitled. At their worst, however, these procedures may undermine common sense and inhibit rather than promote the exercise of individual rights. The temptation for agencies to continue acting as they always have is especially important in RTK, because RTK makes directly accessible to citizens, with the government acting only as manager, environmental regulatory information that had previously been primarily governmental.

Trade Secrets

A potentially important limitation on citizens' access to data is the concept of trade secrets. Many statutes allow industry to declare certain information as secret so that potential competitors will not be given access to the information merely because a government agency has obtained it in pursuit of its regulatory duties. However, many environmental and health groups believe that industries sometimes declare information as trade secret in order to prevent the public from learning about risks rather than to prevent competitors from learning about the content or process for manufacture.

Before I discuss the substance of trade secret or other "confidential business information" exemptions from disclosure, it should be noted that the question of access to information is also burdened by the problems of conflicting statutory provisions at different levels of government and of multiple overlapping statutes at the same level. For example, most state open records acts specify procedures by which citizens may obtain access to records held by governments. Are Title III records held by a state agency also subject to state requirements? Freedom of information acts and procedures may also differ. "Confidential business information" is a related category of information that may be treated in a manner that differs from trade secrets and that differs from state to state.

The approach to trade secrets in Title III derives from three considerations: first, that RTK is impeded if too much information is declared to be confidential; second, that chemical identity, which is central to RTK because it allows citizens to obtain health-effects and other supplementary information about a product, may legitimately need to be kept confidential; and third, that the experiences of states such as Massachusetts and West Virginia, where information is inspected beforehand by government staff to determine whether it should really be confidential, could be applied on the federal level.

New Jersey had overcome problems in reconciling trade secrets with public access to information during the industrial survey by asking businesses who claimed trade secrets to submit two survey forms, one including the secret material and the other without it.

The trade secret provisions of Title III are among the most limiting of any federal statute. Although each section that specifies a report also provides for trade secrets, the law limits the data that may be so designated to the specific chemical identity, including any specific identifiers such as the CAS (Chemical Abstract Service) number. (Submitters may also ask that detailed location information provided to the LEPC under section 312 be kept confidential.) Moreover, even that information must meet four criteria: (1) The submitter must not have disclosed the information to anyone other than an LEPC or other governmental regulatory body and must have taken reasonable precautions to keep the information confidential; (2) the information must not be required to be disclosed or made public under any other federal or state law; (3) disclosure of the information must be likely to cause substantial harm to the competitive position of the submitter; and (4) the chemical identity must not be readily discoverable through reverse engineering. In addition, Title III differs from other environmental laws providing trade secret protection in ensuring that people requesting information will know precisely how the response has been affected by trade secrets; under other laws, the requester has no idea how much data are not being provided.

EPA's proposed regulations implementing the trade secret provisions broadened these restrictions in an important way. EPA argued that the detailed data requested under Title III might allow cross-referencing of information in such a way as to compromise trade secrets even when the chemical identity is not revealed. "For this reason," the agency wrote, "EPA believes that the statute allows trade secrecy claims for chemical identity to be made for the *linkage* between chemical identity and other information reported on Title III submissions (e.g., specific process information and special handling procedures), in addition to [standard claims described in the statute]."[18]

The importance of this approach became clear almost immediately. Title III requires EPA to identify the adverse health and environmental effects associated with each chemical reported under section 313 whose identity is claimed trade secret and to ensure that this information is available in the electronic database, at the same time ensuring that the data do not compromise the trade secret status of the chemical identity by providing a unique identifier.[19] EPA approached this problem by developing a matrix that compares the

309 chemicals in the section 313 list against the ten health and environmental effects mentioned in section 313(d).[20] Nearly seventy chemicals exhibited unique toxicity patterns that would allow knowledgeable people to determine the specific chemical identity from health-effects information alone. EPA began to reduce the number of health-effects categories in an attempt to develop a set of categories in which no chemical exhibited a unique pattern. To reach this point, EPA found that it had to collapse the ten categories into four very general ones: carcinogenicity, acute toxicity, other human health effects, and environmental toxicity. EPA reported itself to be "surprised" at this result, stating that the agency believes that "Congress did not anticipate that its mandate to balance trade secret protection with the ready availability of effects information would lead to such a low degree of specificity for the effects information."[21] As a result of this finding, EPA allowed facilities to designate their own generic chemical names for specific substances they declare as trade secrets. Any inconsistencies in nomenclature that result might impede RTK.

The extent to which trade secrets are claimed will be the final determinant of the extent to which RTK is limited. Although the exact numbers are difficult to pin down, it appears that only about forty trade secret claims had been submitted to EPA through March 1989.[22] In the New Jersey industrial survey, only eighty facilities (about 6 percent of respondents) claimed trade secrets.[23] My interviews with many chemical manufacturers suggested that few would make substantial trade secret claims, although representatives from other industries were more concerned about this issue. Industry representatives seemed to be especially concerned about limiting public access to the detailed location maps because of concern about "terrorists" as well as industrial espionage. Thus, the right of the public to know may not be severely impeded by the trade secret provisions of Title III.

Liability

Liability, or, perhaps more important, the feeling of being liable, is another barrier to RTK. For hundreds of years, the courts have been a place in which individuals who feel they have been injured to an unacceptable degree have had opportunities to receive relief. Legal doctrines, like other theories of society, change over time. In the twentieth century, U.S. courts have gone from demanding very stringent evidence from plaintiffs to a doctrine of strict liability that makes producers responsible for injury even though they may have exercised reasonable care or could not have known about the possibility of injury (for example, because there was no scientific data).[24] In the 1970s and 1980s, the courts' increased application of strict liability to consumer products began to affect other related areas, especially those involving contraception, pregnancy, childbirth, and childhood vaccines, in which consumers found it easier to win large awards in personal injury litigation.[25] Joint and several liability, another new legal doctrine, which makes all producers or manufacturers of a product liable for a consumer injury caused by a product made by only one of them, have combined with the courts' more liberal standards of evidence concerning causality to make everyone who handles toxic or hazardous chemicals feel very vulnerable to liability suits. Government is also increasingly concerned about liability suits; average awards in municipal liability suits increased from $230,000 in 1982 to $2 million in 1985.[26]

Liability concerns have affected implementation of Title III in at least three ways. First, members of LEPCs were concerned that they might be sued if a person were injured during a chemical spill even though response personnel were following the plan developed by the LEPC.[27] Most governments protect employees who are sued as a result of actions taken in exercise of their stated duties; emergency response or health staff working on the LEPC as part of their regular job responsibilities would, therefore, be protected. Some industries also protect employees who are discharging their stated duties. Citizen members of LEPCs may be vulnerable to such suits, however. Title III's lack of clarity about the precise status of the LEPC only exacerbated the problem, since state laws (or local ones, if the laws suggested the LEPC was a local body) would be binding.[28] Many of the states that passed RTK laws subsequent to the passage of Title III used the opportunity to limit the liability of LEPC and SERC members.[29]

A related concern arose about liability that might be incurred by ranking facilities or areas according to their riskiness. Both the hazard analysis portion of the local emergency response plan and the implementation memo that EPA asked states to prepare to indicate how the agency should use its training monies required that priorities be designated based on potential risk. LEPC and SERC members in Texas at least expressed concern about these exercises, saying that they could be sued both by areas or facilities that disagreed with a "high-risk" designation and by citizens if a unit designated as lower in risk subsequently had an accident.

These two problems inhibit RTK because they limit the extent to which designated bodies implement Title III. Of less importance to the statute but of more importance for RTK in general is industry's concern about liability arising from dissemination of health-effects information. This topic is treated in Chapter 9.

Enforcement

Thus far the discussion has been focused on the ways in which interactions among institutions may purposely or, more likely, inadvertently create barriers to citizens' access to the information created by SARA Title III. Because access to information is a central component of all forms of RTK, the barriers must be considered by anyone interested in RTK. Many of the same problems arise in activities that are important for the more activist notions of RTK. One such activity is enforcement. In the notion of RTK that emphasizes risk reduction, enforcement would extend beyond ensuring that facilities had submitted reports to ensuring that the reports were accurate and then using the reports as a means to help enforce existing regulatory standards.

Federalism poses important barriers to enforcement. SARA Title III is a federal law, of course, but only people in the field would know that a facility exists that might need to file. Thus, enforcement even of filing requirements must depend on local personnel; if they find a violation, however, they must literally make a "federal case" out of it unless the state also has a chemical inventory reporting requirement. That filing requirements may be violated is suggested by the fact that only about 18,000 facilities filed about 70,000 section 313 forms for 1987, whereas EPA had expected about 30,000 facilities to file about 10 reports each.[30] Texas's low level of receipt of section 312 reports suggests that the problem is not limited to emissions data; even New Jersey estimated its compliance rate at around 50 percent after four years of experience with RTK. In December 1988, EPA fined twenty-five companies nearly $1.5 million for failing to file section 313 reports.[31]

Conflicting state or local requirements impede determination that violations have even occurred. Ensuring the accuracy of information is even more dependent upon local personnel but is likely to be low on the list of concerns of state or community-level enforcement agents, who have myriad duties under their own laws. States that have their own RTK laws have indicated that improvements in the quality of data submitted can best be achieved by having trained field staff work with facilities as they complete emission report forms.[32] This activity could not be conducted by federal personnel.

Some proponents of right to know hoped to use the chemical inventories as a means of checking on the completeness of the emissions reports and the emissions reports as a means of checking on compliance with effluent permits under federal and state clean air and clean water acts. Because EPA is receiving the emissions data, however, whereas state agencies and LEPCs receive the inventories, merging the data was initially very difficult. As we shall see in Chapter 5, EPA is computerizing the section 313 reports, which should make comparisons easier; EPA has also tried to require facilities to submit detailed and unambiguous identifiers to ease the task of merging data.[33] Comparing the section 313 emissions reports with permit requirements is much more difficult, requiring at a minimum that citizens request the permits and be able to understand them. In some states, permits must be requested by number, so that citizens must search through a list finding the name of the facility in which they are interested and matching it with the appropriate number. In many cases, at least a formal rule-making procedure will be needed to allow state agencies to collect other kinds of facility identification information or to make permit information available by facility name. Procedures that were established to facilitate particular tasks may not be as useful for the new demands of right to know.

Title III allows for some enforcement by citizens themselves, following the example of the Clear Air Act. Under the latter statute, citizens may file suit against facilities they believe are violating emissions standards after providing the relevant government agencies sixty days' notice in which to take some action themselves. By 1985, more than 214 private enforcement actions had been taken, although most were limited to filing the sixty-day-notice letters.[34] Citizens learning about Title III for the first time highlighted the importance of this kind of role; as one said, "[The law] sounds great, but who is actually going to these companies . . . to be sure they're reporting? Who's going to follow through to be sure it is accurate?"[35]

Should a complaint or case be filed for noncompliance with Title III, success depends upon many variables other than the strength of the case. Among the institutional factors that might affect this phase of enforcement are the past record of the facility, the cleverness of its lawyers, the amount of time that government lawyers can devote to the particular case, political implications of the case, and the predilections of the judge. Trade secret claims may also inhibit enforcement.

In short, enforcement is inhibited by the same kinds of institutional forces that affect the most fundamental activity of RTK-- access to data. Inconsistencies and jealousies among different levels of government and between agencies, bureaucratic procedures, and, because enforcement often relies upon the courts, inconsistencies or difficulties in coordination between the administrative and judicial branches of government all combine to make enforcement difficult.

Conclusion

Information provision and access is central to all notions of RTK. Yet achievement of even this seemingly simple goal is threatened by institutional impediments--in many cases, barriers erected by the very organizations charged with implementing the policy. To some extent the problems associated with federalism, interagency competition, and procedural and bureaucratic norms burden any new program. They are particular problems for right to know for three reasons. First, Title III placed unusual burdens on states and localities, created new agencies that purposely overlapped the functions of existing agencies, and forced diverse agencies to work together to fulfill its varied purposes. That is, Congress's zeal to give citizens the right to know was not matched by its care in anticipating and forestalling difficulties raised by the program's requirements. Second, precisely because it is an information program, RTK depends for its success on streamlined access procedures. Whereas service delivery programs may be evaluated according to the numbers of people served or the harms prevented, information programs must be evaluated largely on the basis of their procedures for ensuring public access. Thus, procedural barriers of the kind I have described are especially serious.

Third, even a "basic" RTK program is partly revolutionary, because it gives information, a valuable commodity, to groups who have not previously had it. Thus, RTK cannot help but threaten the status quo at least a little bit. Organizations are known to take strong measures to preserve themselves; the institutional barriers described here may be, in part, evidence of resistance to change. In short, the institutional impediments to information access that result from the normal workings of institutions have particularly serious implications for a program whose very essence is information access. Stronger definitions of RTK, especially those that call for citizen participation in decisionmaking, will also be affected by institutional barriers, including the absence of any clear arrangements for encouraging citizens and private industry to work together on community issues.

Notes

1. The Woodlands Conference on New State Roles: Environment, Resources and the Economy, The Woodlands Texas, November 13-16, 1988, reflects this new interest.

2. For Virginia, see W. David Conn, William L. Owens, and Richard C. Rich, "Interim Report on Phase 1," Memo to EPA, June 15, 1988, p. 2; also Campbell Communications, Inc., "Survey of York, Pennsylvania, Emergency Response Committee: Final Report," August 1988, p. 4. The former study will be referred to hereafter as "Interim Report."

3. Compiled by me from National Governors' Association, *The Emergency Planning and Community Right to Know Act: A State of State Actions* (Washington, D.C.: NGA, April 1988).

4. I was present at the SERC meetings at which these situations arose-- January 1988 and July 11, 1988, respectively. The former statement would not, of course, be found in the minutes.

5. Interview with the director of the state's Department of Natural Resources. The state is not Texas, New Jersey, nor Massachusetts.

6. Nancy M. Davis, "How Can States Use Information on Toxic Materials," in Thad L. Beyle, *State Government: CQ's Guide to Current Issues and Activities 1986-87* (Washington, D.C.: Congressional Quarterly, 1987), pp. 168-169, lists twenty states with community right-to-know laws in effect when the article was originally published in 1985; the source for the list is the Chemical Manufacturers Association. The Regulatory Impact Analysis lists twenty-eight states with community right-to-know laws as of March 1987, based on an EPA undated draft document, "Review and Analysis of State Community Right-to-Know Laws." ICF, Inc., "Regulatory Impact Analysis in Support of Final Rulemaking Under Section 313 of Title III of SARA," February 1988, pp. 5-17 (hereafter, RIA). Also see *Community Right-to-Know Manual* (Washington, D.C.: Thompson Publishing Co., October 1987). Provisions of each law differ somewhat from each other and from Title III.

7. See Memo from Robert A. Lansford, state coordinator, Division of Emergency Management, to Brian Berwick, Office of the Attorney General, State of Texas, February 29, 1988.

8. Telephone interview with Barbara Sergeant, Right-to-Know Program, New Jersey Department of Environmental Protection, April 28, 1988.

9. 52 Fed. Reg. 38371 (October 15, 1987).

10. *Community and Worker Right-to-Know News*, a biweekly reporter, includes a section on state laws. These were reported in the issues of April 8, 1988; April 22, 1988; May 8, 1988.

11. Theresa B. Simkus and Beverley S. Clark, "A Preemption Dilemma: An Analysis of State R-T-K Laws in Light of the Hazard Communication," *Temple Environmental Law and Technology Journal* 3 (1984):39.

12. Section 321 (a).

13. A similar model ordinance is found in Golden Empire Health Systems Agency, *Community Right to Know: Hazardous Materials Disclosure*

Information Systems: A Handbook for Local Communities and Their Officials (Sacramento: Golden Empire Health Systems Agency, January 1983).

14. Calculations provided by Steve Compton, director, Hazardous Waste Program, Austin Fire Department, at meeting of Travis County LEPC subcommittee on reporting, March 22, 1988.

15. See the discussion in Memo from Pat Weatherly, Assistant Regional Council, EPA Region VI, to Minnie Rojo, chief, Contingency Planning Section, September 1, 1988, p. 2. (Hereafter, Weatherly Memo.)

16. Meeting of the Texas SERC, July 11, 1988. The topic was also discussed at meetings in April and June.

17. EPA, Title III Needs Assessment Project, 1988 General Public Focus Groups, "Summary of Findings," (Fall 1988), p. 10.

18. 52 Fed. Reg. 38314 (October 15, 1987); emphasis added. See also the final regulations, 53 Fed. Reg. 28772 (July 29, 1988).

19. Electronic database in section 322(h)(2); remainder of sentence from U.S. Congress, House of Representatives, *Superfund Amendments and Reauthorization Act of 1986: Conference Report*, 99th Cong., 2d sess., Report 99-962, p. 306 .

20. See 53 Fed. Reg. 4520 (February 16, 1988), containing the final version of the form for section 313 reports, for the matrix and the following description of the results. The ten effects of section 313(d) are: immediate health hazard; cancer; teratogenic effect; serious or irreversible reproductive dysfunction, neurological disorder, heritable genetic mutations, or other chronic health effects; toxicity; persistence in the environment; and bioaccumulation. (Hereafter, Final 313 Rule.)

21. Final 313 Rule, p. 4520.

22. Telephone interview with John Fogarty, attorney, Office of Toxic Substances, EPA, March 8, 1989. Up to that date, the office had reviewed six claims and denied four. Only three of these claims have been through the entire two-step review process.

23. New Jersey Department of Environmental Protection, *New Jersey Industrial Survey Final Report*, (Trenton, August, 1986) p. 8. About 25 percent of these requests were ruled invalid. However, most of the facilities claiming confidential business information were large chemical manufacturers, some of whom were the only manufacturer or user of a particular substance.

24 On strict liability, see, for example, Richard A. Epstein, *Modern Products Liability Law* (Westport, Conn: Quorum Books, 1980).

25. Peter Huber, "Injury Litigation and Liability Insurance Dynamics," *Science* 238 (October 2, 1987):33.

26. Ibid., citing D. M. Farmer testimony at the hearings before the Subcommittee on Business, Trade, and Tourism for the Senate Committee on Commerce, Science, and Transportation, 99th Cong., 1st sess. (December 3, 1985), p. 147.

27. EPA, "Title III White Paper," Draft, February 25, 1988, p. 48. (Report prepared by the deputy regional administrators of EPA to review problems of implementing Title III at the regional and state levels and to present possible solutions.) This concern was explicitly expressed in letters from the Houston

and Dallas LEPCs to the Texas SERC, May 25, 1988, and October 12, 1988, respectively.

28. Weatherly Memo, p. 4.

29. Kentucky's law, reported in *Community and Worker Right-to-Know News* 2, no. 13 (April 8, 1988):4, enacts Title III into state law and, among other provisions, protects local committees from liability. Similar statutes from Maine, Ohio, and Missouri are reported in *Community and Worker Right-to-Know News* 2, no. 14 (April 22, 1988):14.

30. The filing numbers are found in James W. Rubin and William A. Butler, "Section 313 Data Access and the New Role of Citizen and Community Action," October 1988, p. 2, citing a conversation with Doug Sellars, project officer at the EPA Title III Reporting Center. The estimates are found in the abbreviated Regulatory Impact Analysis contained in the Final 313 Rule.

31. "25 Companies Face Fines on Emissions," *New York Times*, December 21, 1988, p. 14 (national edition).

32. EPA, "Title III White Paper," Draft, February 25, 1988, p. 37. (Report prepared by the deputy regional administrators of EPA to review problems of implementing Title III at the regional and state levels and to present possible solutions.)

33. EPA is also hoping to use other statutes such as the Toxic Substances Control Act (TSCA) to help identify noncompliers under Title III. See "Right-to-Know: Creative Methods May Be Required to Obtain Enforcement and Information," Current Report, *Toxic Law Reporter*, July 13, 1988, p. 219.

34. Barry Boyer and Errol Moidinger, "Privatizing Regulatory Enforcement: A Preliminary Assessment of Citizen Suits Under Federal Environmental Laws," *Buffalo Law Review* 34:833-864.

35. EPA, Title III Needs Assessment Project, 1988 General Public Focus Groups, "Summary of Findings," p. 35.

5 / Managing All the Data

How shall I ever find the grains of truth embedded in all this mass of paper?

--Virginia Woolf

In the past, government's primary duties in implementing information policies were to ensure that information, if unavailable, was created and then to ensure that the information was made accessible. To implement policies that called for labeling of products with information about risks, for example, agencies require manufacturers to conduct laboratory tests and submit the data, which are then used to develop appropriate warnings for labels. A label that reads "Smoking causes lung cancer, heart disease, emphysema, and may complicate pregnancy" represents a conclusion about risk based on many years of laboratory and human studies.

Right to know has in common with other information policies that government has a clear responsibility to collect the data and make it available to citizens. RTK differs from earlier information policies because it provides access not only to the summarized and analyzed--almost predigested--information found on product labels but also ensures that citizens have access to the raw data on which such conclusions are based. Unfortunately, the sheer quantity of the raw data may inhibit people's abilities to understand the information or, perhaps, even to find a particular item they seek out of millions of pieces of paper. Accounts of fire departments storing boxes of MSDSs under the firefighter's beds exemplify this problem.

When data overload threatens, computers are an obvious solution. Congress recognized this by requiring EPA to establish an electronic database for the section 313 emissions reports and make it available to citizens. Once computers are deployed to ensure access to information, however, the temptation is very strong to use their power in other ways. Thus, RTK may be extended beyond data access to include aggregation and analysis of the data. Tying different computer databases together allows still further extension of RTK by making more readily available supplementary information that would be germane to decisionmaking, such as health effects data. Did Congress recognize that requiring the use of computers allowed or even encouraged a strong form of RTK?

This chapter provides a review of the progress to date in computerization of Title III data. The discussion is divided into two parts: computerization of section 313 and computerization at the state and local levels. This division is motivated by the very different ways in which computerization has occurred at the federal and at the other levels of government, largely as a result, of course, of the different statutory treatments, as Congress did not require states and localities to computerize their data.

Computerization of Section 313

Title III contains the first statutory mandate for a public access database. Heretofore, agencies complying with freedom-of-information requests have been allowed to decide the form in which they would supply information; at least one agency challenged in court the applicant's contention that the information should be provided in electronic format, arguing that an electronic database is not a "record" as defined by the FOIA.[1] Although agencies are increasingly likely to make data available in electronic format--that is, on disk or tape--Congress avoided any ambiguity in the case of Title III.

One important reason for seeking data in its electronic form rather than in hard copy is the relative ease of access that computers provide. Masses of data can be searched quickly and accurately. Because EPA expected to receive about 318,000 reports,[2] each of which is five or more pages long, the utility of a database for searching should be obvious. The reader may envision a simple database by imagining a vast matrix in which the rows include all the information provided on a single report form, and the columns include each entry in a particular category; for Title III, the columns would include facility name, facility address, chemical name, and so on. The database allows the user to search either by row or by column; in addition, some relatively simple programming should allow the user to search according to the value in a particular column: chemical = benzene, for example.

Although reports are filed by facilities, and the electronic version should be retrievable by invoking the facility name, with very little additional effort the database can be designed to retrieve information about particular chemicals, geographical locations, disposal sites, or any other category of information requested. Thus, access to information is a flexible concept that computers expand greatly. Computers also contribute to access in a different way, because users no longer have to be physically in the same room with the data, as they do to read books or examine paper documents; instead, they may obtain it from any place that has a computer and a telecommunications device--provided the database is designed to be examined in this way. Congress's directive clearly called for that sort of access as well for the database containing the section 313 emissions data.

The most basic forms of computerization, therefore, expand RTK by qualitatively changing the form and manner in which the public has access to data. A related benefit arises from the computer's ability to allow users to aggregate and manipulate the data. For example, the user might wish to ask, "How many facilities in my county have reported under section 313?" or "How many of the facilities report emitting benzene to air and what is the total quantity emitted?" Aggregating the data provides answers to questions that individuals would otherwise have to obtain by looking through every single report and tabulating the responses. Computers thus reduce the cost of obtaining composite data almost to zero, especially in comparison with the cost of obtaining it by hand.

In addition to mere aggregation, computers also allow other manipulation of data, especially statistical or quasi-statistical manipulations that may provide answers to more complex questions such as "Are emissions proportional to quantity of final product manufactured, or do they increase at a lower or higher rate?" or "Are smaller facilities more likely to be involved in accidents?" The answers to these and other, similar questions are more directly relevant to formulation of sound public policy than the more descriptive data obtained from searching and aggregating the data.

People who believe that RTK goes beyond the right of access to data to include access to more meaningful information are particularly interested in the ease with which the database may be manipulated by amateurs, which raises a question about the extent to which government should be responsible for developing "user-friendly" software for the database. This issue is considered further in Chapter 8. In this section, I briefly describe the establishment of the database itself and then turn to two other issues that are central to the relationship between computers and access to information: the data incorporated into the database and the quality of the data.

Establishing the TRI Database

The staff charged with establishing the Toxic Release Inventory (TRI) database faced the same problem that confronts anyone developing a large database: The purposes of the users must be anticipated so that the database can be designed in advance to meet them. In EPA's case, this problem was compounded by the need to be consistent with the statutory mandate, meet the criteria for information collection and dissemination imposed on all federal agencies by the Office of Management and Budget (OMB),[3] and work with the computer resources already available within the agency, given the lack of funding for Title III activities.

Before the computer database can be designed, a decision must be made as to the information to be included within it. Thus, the first task facing EPA was to design the reporting form (Form R) on which facilities would report their emissions. The statute required the form to be published by June 1, 1987. The proposed format was published on June 4, 1987, and the final rule on February 14, 1988.[4] The following subsection details how EPA selected the data that the regulated community should report.

The second decision facing EPA concerned where the public access database should be. The agency determined early on that its own internal computer, physically located in Research Triangle, North Carolina, was unsuited to public access for at least two reasons: First, it is not "user-friendly," and second, it was intended primarily for use in such internal agency tasks as tracking compliance.[5] Three other alternatives were considered: use of a commercial bibliographic retrieval service, installing the TRI at the National Library of Medicine (NLM), or working through a nonprofit organization. After protracted consideration, in spring 1988, only months before the July 1 due date for section 313 reports, EPA decided to develop an interagency agreement with the National Library of Medicine. The parties were still considering the precise terms of the agreement well after July 1.

Because developing the database that exploited the full capabilities of the computer would take several months, and because there was increasing demand for immediate access to the emissions data, EPA established a public TRI Reading Room. The room provides access to hard copies of section 313 emissions forms, indexed by facility, city/state, and CAS number. The indices are in three-ring binders that are updated periodically. Once users identify the forms they would like to see, they fill out a simple request form for as many as ten at any one time. For at least the first several months, no capabilities for statistical analysis were available to the public in the room, and access was sure but slow. EPA was considering a larger role for the TRI Reading Room with more capability for answering user questions, perhaps including analysis of data.

Realizing that many citizens would not have access to computers at all, EPA also determined to make the data available through nonelectronic means. The agency decided to provide copies of filed forms at cost if a citizen calls or writes the agency and to distribute the TRI data on CD-ROM (compact disc/read only memory--a form of data storage) through government depository libraries. In addition, NLM will allow citizens to obtain information through its eight regional libraries.[6]

The TRI database was to become available to the public in May 1989. EPA was attempting to meet the statutory requirement as expeditiously as possible while ensuring that the database would be useful for many years. In the following subsections, I consider in more detail two of the decisions the agency made; other decisions are examined in Chapter 8.

Data Content

As noted, the first step in developing a database is deciding what information will be included. Examining the list of information Congress required to be included in the TRI--identification of the facility, the annual quantity of the toxic chemical entering each environmental medium, estimates of the maximum amounts present at the facility during the preceding calendar year, and the treatment method employed for each waste stream and its efficiency--EPA realized that the database might not be adequate to fulfill the purposes of the law. In particular, to fulfill the Congressional mandate "to inform the general public . . . , to assist research, [and] to aid in the development of regulations,"[7] EPA thought it would need additional information that would identify facilities and substances unambiguously and, more important, allow cross-referencing to existing data. Based on interviews with potential users inside and outside EPA, the agency developed a list of other data that might also be included on the emissions reporting form: the Dun and Bradstreet number of the reporting facility, CAS number to identify chemicals, division of reported emissions into controlled and uncontrolled, identification of off-site treatment facilities used by the reporting facility, indication of whether the off-site facility is controlled by the reporting entity, explanation of changes at the facility that have reduced emissions in the previous five years, identification numbers of existing environmental permits for the facility, and names of bodies of water receiving releases.[8]

In deciding whether to include each of these reporting elements, EPA had to balance utility for users against the costs to the reporters. One suggested change, for example, was to require reporting on the components of a waste stream rather than the aggregate stream. Thus, a facility would have had to report separately on each "of the numerous waters from various process points that are combined for treatment."[9] EPA rejected this change as unduly complex and burdensome for industry and not especially helpful for users. Conversely, the agency accepted a proposal to ask facilities to report their latitudes and longitudes, information that is useful for computerized geographic information systems.[10] Of the other possible additional data listed in the previous paragraph, the final report form (Form R) includes all but the division into controlled and uncontrolled releases, although uncontrolled (accidental) releases must, of course, still be reported under section 304.[11]

In addition to making facility identification more unambiguous, EPA included some of the supplementary data on Form R for the express purpose of improving the links among the TRI database and other agency databases. For many years EPA and other regulatory agencies have been collecting data in fulfillment of their statutory duties. As computers became available, the sheer quantity of information they were managing compelled them to computerize. Often, however, different programs even within the same agency developed separate databases; for example, EPA's Permit Compliance System, which contains data collected under the Clean Water Act, stores data on reported quantities and concentrations of chemical discharges in a separate file from the unit-of-measurement data that are needed to interpret what the reported values mean.[12] Linking the available data would probably increase an agency's ability to fulfill its statutory mandates. A whole new program provided EPA with an opportunity to build a database that includes a wide variety of facility identifier; this increases the likelihood that at least one identifier will overlap with the identifier used in other databases.

By anticipating the desire to link existing databases, EPA implicitly adopted a form of right to know that goes beyond mere access to data. On the one hand, the agency may have been thinking about the benefits its own staff would obtain from the linked data; this would be consistent with the reduced-risk form of RTK. On the other hand, the agency may have been anticipating the desire of citizens for additional information to supplement the data provided under Title III. For example, a few citizens in the New Jersey survey indicated that they would like to know the conditions of a facility's permit in order to compare its reported emissions with the allowable quantities. A handbook issued in fall 1988 by the Kentucky Resources Council strongly emphasizes the use of permits to fill in gaps in the section 313 data and to allow citizens to monitor facilities more closely.[13] Ensuring that citizens can link TRI data to permit data would be consistent with the better-decisionmaking or balance-of-power forms of RTK.

In practice, most links among databases will be made on the internal EPA computer, to which SERCs and EPA staff but not citizens will have access; to accomplish even this will take some sophisticated programming. This limited access suggests that to the extent the agency has embraced a wider conception of RTK, it may focus on an increased role for regulators. However, EPA has made public a small computer program called "Roadmaps" that provides users with the names of the EPA databases accessible to the public in which particular kinds of information are available.[14] EPA's decision to locate the public version of the TRI database at the National Library of Medicine will also serve to aid citizens seeking supplementary information of a certain kind, as NLM already provides a wide range of public databases, including at least one that includes health effects, environmental fate, and manufacturing information for a wide range of chemicals.[15] These actions are consistent with an expanded role for citizens rather than for regulators in RTK.

Data Quality

RTK is hollow if the data that are available to the public are inaccurate. EPA was well aware of the concern about data quality from the outset, especially because Title III prohibited the agency from requiring facilities to create "new" data in order to fill out Form R. EPA developed methods for estimating emissions that would free facilities from making direct measurements but recognized that the complexity of these calculations and their novelty could compromise the quality of the data. In addition to these possible problems with the information submitted, databases built from regulatory reports always suffer from errors in data entry and transmission errors.

Data entry errors may occur as the form is compiled by the regulated facility or as EPA personnel type the data into the computer. Computers may be programmed to detect certain inconsistencies, either warning the typist to check his or accuracy or generating a letter to the reporting facility indicating the area of concern. The TRI system, for example, is designed to verify automatically whether the data are submitted in the correct format (numeric, for example), whether they fall into predetermined acceptable ranges, whether they are internally inconsistent, and whether any items are omitted.[16] Reports containing errors so severe that they would prevent the data from being useful will be rejected and returned with a computer generated error letter. Among these "fatal errors" are invalid or missing CAS numbers and missing facility identifiers.[17]

Transcription errors may be minimized if data are reported in electronic form. EPA recognized that many of the manufacturing facilities subject to section 313 requirements were already keeping similar data on computers. To reduce costs both for these facilities and for the agency itself, EPA established procedures for electronic submission of data. Transmission errors, which occur primarily when data are sent through telecommunications channels, will be detected by the same computer program that identifies transcription errors. EPA also minimized the likelihood of transmission errors by requiring facilities to submit data on disk or tape, although the decision was actually dictated by lack of funds and facilities for direct electronic submission.

Less obvious is that the computer may be used to detect low-quality data. As more data is gathered, the computer can be programmed to "learn" about emissions patterns from particular kinds of facilities; just as it detects simple data entry errors, eventually it will be able to detect logical errors as well. One company has developed an "expert system," or computer program embodying human expertise and logic, to assist in computing the emissions. This program already includes some logical checks on the consistency and accuracy of emissions estimates,[18] one of the most serious sources of likely error.

A rather different quality-related problem arises with respect to the dates of databases. Submitters will file data for the previous year any time from January to July 1, the statutory reporting date. If the data are entered into the large database as they are received, it will contain data from different years for different facilities. Data in related databases may be from other years or different reporting periods. Citizen users are unlikely to check these dates and may be using incomparable data to make comparisons. EPA proposes to ensure that the public-access database is updated annually, but this does not relieve the comparability problem with other databases. Computers could be programmed at least to warn users of this potential problem; at a minimum, the date of its last update should be readily apparent as the user enters the database.

The TRI Database and RTK

This brief discussion of a few of the decisions entailed in establishing the TRI database should suggest how central computers are to RTK. A right to spend thousands of hours reading through forms and hand-tabulating responses--an act that is itself subject to many transcription errors--is not a right many citizens would care to exercise. From the standpoint of data access alone, therefore, computers are a necessary component of RTK. Even at EPA, however, the process of creating a new database that is appropriate to the needs of users was slower than might have been hoped, delayed in many cases by the kinds of institutional barriers outlined in Chapter 4.

Once the data are computerized, however, the costs of additional activities such as aggregation and analysis are very small, especially if the database software is easy to use. Thus, it may be very difficult to distinguish between basic data-access RTK and more expanded forms that call for data analysis, although the question of whether the citizen or the government should manipulate the data remains unresolved.

The importance of the diminishing distinction between data acquisition and data analysis fostered by improved database software is highlighted by the response of agencies to freedom-of-information requests for information they already maintain in databases. Agencies argue that they do not have to respond to requests that would require significant programming, inasmuch as the statute only requires them to provide existing records, not analyze them. If agency databases are easy to use, however, resorting the contents may be a matter of only a few keystrokes, which is less work than photocopying paper documents--an activity all agree must be undertaken in response to FOIA requests. We do not yet have a clear understanding of the implications of electronic data storage and retrieval for freedom of information, just as we do not for RTK. Choices agencies make in each sphere will affect practices in the other.

Congress seems to have been at least partly aware of the implications of computerization for expanding the scope of RTK. The purposes it enumerated for the TRI database included not only informing the public but also assisting research and developing regulations. The latter of these purposes hints very broadly at the risk-reduction form of RTK, whereas the former seems to be quite consistent with the better-decisionmaking form. Because they can almost instantaneously retrieve or calculate, computers blur the difference between acquiring, storing, and disseminating data; in so doing, they have become a very potent force for strengthening both the form and the substance of what people have a right to know. The federal level, however, is in many ways the least important for RTK; as we shall see in the following section, computerization has proceeded more erratically at the state and local levels.

Computerization at the State and Local Levels

States and localities faced two major issues concerning computerization: how to fund it and what software to use. Few states and virtually no localities had any incentive to consider a third question---namely, the extent to which software compatibility is desirable and how it might be achieved. In this section, I briefly consider these questions and remind the reader of the ways in which computerization might serve the special needs of localities.

Software for RTK

Although virtually all states and most localities recognized the need for computerization, they had to make a variety of choices to implement that decision. The first was finding resources. Some states funded programs out of general revenues; more imposed filing fees for the reports to be received at the state level. Filing fees covered a wide range. Wisconsin imposed a one-time fee of $800 for section 302 notifications and a fee graduated from $100 to $300 for the other filings depending upon the number of chemicals listed, and Indiana imposed a flat fee of $50 for each section 312 submission.[19] Texas found that its fee did not generate enough revenue to fund its program, in part because of the failure of many covered facilities to file; TDH sought authority to raise the fees. New Jersey had a filing fee of $2 per employee with a minimum of $50. The expansion of the OSHA Hazard Communication Standard and the concomitant expansion of RTK, however, raised two concerns. First, many more small businesses would be covered; very small firms complained about the equity of the $50 minimum, arguing that a two-person firm, which could least afford the expense, had to pay more than ten times the rate per employee as did larger firms. Second, many firms that do not use hazardous substances would nevertheless be covered by the law and would have to submit the filing fee with the form indicating zero use. These problems could be resolved only through legislative action.[20]

The second question was determining what equipment and software to use. Because new funds were seldom available, states made use of the hardware and software already acquired for other programs.[21] This choice minimizes the need for new resources and speeds construction of databases, because staff do not have to learn new software. Unfortunately, it also turns the decision on its head, allowing the software to determine how the data will be treated rather than selecting equipment that will best meet specifications designed on the basis of the program's needs.

In response to Title III, a number of commercial firms developed report-generating software. An obvious market existed among facilities that had to file reports; chemical industry representatives report being "beseiged" by software vendors. The private sector was less successful in meeting any special needs of governments, however. Not only is the market smaller, but government software procurement decisions are notoriously slow. Moreover, until state and local right-to-know programs are funded, there is little incentive for the market to provide such software. Government agencies probably use a wider variety of hardware than is current within industry, since many agencies continue to rely on outdated mainframes. Many agencies would have to have software tailored to their particular machines, further cutting into the market for standard Title III software packages. Thus, most states have made use of existing database programs, trusting to staff to ensure that the databases were designed in ways responsive to user needs.

One unintended result of the absence of funding for Title III activities at the state (and local) levels, therefore, is the use of incompatible software by entities that might want to share data. Just as both EPA and the regulated community benefit from electronic submission of data, states and localities would both benefit not only from electronic submission of reports by facilities but also by having localities upload their electronic data to the states. This cannot occur without forethought in designing databases and software.

Implementing Computerization at the Local Level

In January 1988, EPA conducted a survey of states about implementation of sections 311 and 312. Eighteen respondents to the EPA survey thought that the agency should provide states with guidance on proven information systems in order to generate compatible systems nationwide.[22] The same number of respondents thought that EPA should help local agencies learn about local information management systems. There was also "considerable interest" in having EPA develop and provide software at no cost to states or localities.

EPA, itself without funds, did not respond specifically to this request. The agency did, however, work with the National Oceanographic and Atmospheric Administration (NOAA) to redesign a computer program that NOAA had created for emergency responders. CAMEO™, the Computer-Aided Management of Emergency Operations, contained response information and recommendations for more than 2,600 commonly transported chemicals and an air-dispersion model to assist in evaluating spills and releases; it was modified to include several databases and computational programs that allow emergency responders and planners to fulfill the requirements of Title III. It allows easy entry of facility floor plans with chemical storage locations, lists of facility contacts, and digitized maps of the planning area overlaid by plumes calculated from the air model; it also prints out reports and helps create qualitative risk assessments comparing the relative hazards of various chemicals found in a community.[23] CAMEO is implemented for a Macintosh computer to exploit its graphics and ease of use; unfortunately, many governments and many of the regulated community rely upon IBM-PCs or compatibles. CAMEO is available free.

Some states hoped to overcome the problems created by hardware and software incompatibility and the LEPCs' lack of resources by creating a database at the state level and making it available to LEPCs. There are several advantages to this approach: Filers have only one report to file; LEPCs may readily obtain the data already computerized; and states are more likely to be able to obtain access to important supplementary databases. SERCs, for example, will have access to the EPA section 313 database. Ohio was considering this approach and even intended to provide terminals to LEPCs, creating a statewide network.[24] All but one of the twenty-one respondents to EPA's state survey "agreed that there should be centralized data management" in response to the question 'Should states have one centralized data management operation that could serve State and Local needs?'"[25] Some respondents, however, wondered what might happen if an LEPC sued a state because it found that the state's system contains errors.

Some people think that EPA rather than the states should make available a database format for receiving information and user-friendly software for providing citizens with access to the data. Without directly supporting particular hardware, design specifications would assist local programmers and minimize the duplication of effort as 3,200 LEPCs hire contractors to design databases. The consistency achieved would assist filers, states receiving reports, and even the EPA itself. For example, TDH, which did not have resources to computerize the section 311 and 312 reports, developed a database for keeping track of the reports that had been filed using a common commercial database program. An officer in the EPA region that includes Texas had created a system for receiving reports using the same database program. Despite reliance on the same software, the two systems were different enough in structure that modifications to both had to be made in order for the programs to be compatible.[26] Federal specifications for databases for tracking reports, filing all the data, receiving section 313 reports, and answering user queries could overcome the problems associated with incompatible software and could also reduce programming time nationwide.

The user-unfriendliness of most generic database packages and the emphasis on generating rather than receiving reports that characterizes most of the specialized software suggest that RTK at the local and state levels may not be as well served by computerization as it could be. Given the lack of resources at the local level especially, computers could be deployed to reduce the need for staff response to individual citizen requests. In other words, immediate resource constraints suggest that states and localities adopt an approach in which very user-friendly software and easy access substitute for lack of staff.[27]

In the first two years of RTK, state and local governments focused more on meeting deadlines and mobilizing to identify facilities, set up LEPCs, and receive reports than they did on public outreach or RTK. Computerization, when it was possible, was often undertaken for data management by government rather than for data access by the public. States recognize the advantages of computerization, however, and virtually all expect eventually to computerize information obtained under sections 311 and 312; many have already done so.[28] Localities have been slower to assume this responsibility, in large part because they lack the computers, technical staff, and related resources. Even states that did not provide direct funding for a Title III program have infrastructure in existing regulatory agencies that most localities lack.

In these first years, hardware and software decisions were often driven by considerations of resources or politics rather than program need. Thus, in many cases, the attempt to overcome problems caused by too much data generated a problem of too much different and incompatible software. Even organizations that recognized the problem and tried to overcome it were inhibited by lack of resources--money for programmers, time to work with all the affected parties to select software and hardware, and organizational clout to impose decisions once they were made. In short, computers are not a panacea but are only tools that are no more effective than the organizations that use them.

Benefits of Computers for RTK

Despite their limitations, computers may, cleverly deployed, help to overcome some of the institutional barriers described in Chapter 4. In particular, computers might reduce costs of data collection and use for local agencies by tailoring information to the particular needs of the agency, again helping to overcome the difficulties raised by mountains of data.

Sections 311 and 312 of Title III have multiple purposes. Although they are jointly called the "right-to-know" sections of the law, the chemical inventories called for in both sections are intended (1) to assist the LEPCs in formulating a local emergency response plan; (2) to help emergency responders act appropriately if a spill occurs; and (3) to fulfill the public's right to know. Thus, at least three distinct categories of users for the data may be distinguished: emergency planners, emergency responders, and the public. At the state level, the data will also be used to expand and support existing environmental regulatory programs.

The three different users need three different subsets of the data reported under the law. Emergency responders, for example, want a database small enough to allow for extremely rapid access to the most important facts: what substances are stored in the area of the accident and any special characteristics of these (such as reactivity) or necessary equipment.[29] Emergency planners on the LEPC, on the other hand, need all the information that is provided in the section 311 and 312 reports, as well as some additional information not required by the forms but available by request, such as whether a facility owns some emergency response equipment or has staff trained in emergency response. Citizens may seek any of the reported information as well but do not have the right to see information that has been declared trade secret, including specific chemical identities and specific storage locations. Neither planners nor citizens would need the rapid access required by emergency responders, nor would detailed information about emergency response procedures and equipment be of use to these groups.

If each agency were to enter into its computer those portions of the data that were most needed, however, many of the benefits of computerization would be overwhelmed by the large costs of data entry. LEPCs that have decided to computerize have usually designated a single agency to receive the reports and enter all the data, which are automatically distributed to two or three different databases. The appropriate database is then sent to the agency for which it was created.

Not only can computers overcome the problems created by too much data and by the different information needs of the different users, they can also assist the regulated community in managing the data they must file. For example, section 311, 312, and 313 reports require much of the same facility identification material; a secretary could type that information only once, but it could be sent to three different files in the computer that would later be used to create the three separate reports. Many of the states and localities that already had RTK laws in effect require separate or additional information. For example, New Jersey requires for its chemical emissions reports the following information that is not required for any Title III reports: starting inventory; amount produced; quantity brought on site, consumed, and shipped; and final inventory. New Jersey also includes questions on waste minimization, which are optional on the section 313 report form.[30] To the extent that localities and states retain their own reporting requirements, computerization can further reduce the resources required to generate several similar but not identical reports.

Computers may also serve as mechanisms for disseminating expertise, an advantage that may accrue especially to small businesses among the regulated community. Following the expansion of coverage of the OSHA HCS, sections 311 and 312 began to affect many nonmanufacturing facilities, and regulated businesses found that they lacked the expertise to determine which of the substances and, especially, mixtures they use are reportable. A computer program that provides an interactive, questioning format combined with a database of covered chemicals could help businesses rapidly and accurately determine the extent of their reporting obligations. Computers dedicated to the RTK program and available in public places could provide the benefits of electronic reporting even to small facilities that do not own computers.

A related area of expertise that computers could help disseminate is identification of chemicals, an activity central to all the purposes of Title III. Not only might submitters make errors in transmitting the data, as discussed in connection with section 313 reports, but they are likely to identify the same substance with different names; conversely, citizens using the database may know only one of the many names of a substance.[31] Mixtures present the same kinds of problems, with the added difficulty that the components are often not known even to the final users. Pesticides, for example, often include so-called "inert" ingredients that have important chemical or human health effects despite their lack of insecticidal efficacy.

Computers could help overcome many of these difficulties. They can be programmed to recognize synonyms; one facility has "purple goo," a term used by workers to describe one of the substances they use, as an accepted identifier on the internal computerized chemical information system used by employees. The CAS identification numbers may be used to eliminate the need for data entry personnel to type difficult chemical names; alternatively, an alphabetical list of chemical names could be provided that the person need only highlight to place into the database. A computer programmed with the components and proportions of a mixture could also automatically calculate whether the amounts a facility stores contain more than the reportable quantities of the hazardous substance.

This system sounds utopian, and its development will surely be time-consuming and expensive. It would also have to be very large. Ohio is purportedly considering the possibility of maintaining a large database (on a mainframe computer) to which LEPCs may be tied through a telecommunications network, an approach that would make the information available to a wide audience without the need for many large computers. Florida has tried a similar approach to improve access to non-Title III records; not only has the state been able to respond to more public inquiries, but the information operation has shown a net profit from the small access charges for using the telecommunications network.[32] A system such as Ohio proposes would not, however, mark a major expansion of the idea of RTK, because even simple access to data depends so strongly on accurate identification of chemicals.

Once such a system is developed, it would be tempting to include a variety of supplementary data, including health effects, ambient physical state, and threshold reporting requirements, thus expanding and extending the notion of right to know beyond its minimum. Tying such a chemical information database to the chemical inventory reports, a relatively straightforward task for computer programmers, would further enrich the right to know, extending it beyond data about chemicals to the beginnings of information about the effects of such chemicals in the community's environment.

Conclusion

Citizens confronted with thousands of forms submitted under Title III would be forced to limit their data-collection efforts to one or a few facilities. With computers, however, right to know can take on a new meaning. Citizens can acquire information about all the facilities in an area, or can define their data searches by chemical or other delimiters. Computers, therefore, create a different kind of RTK, one in which citizens can "play" with the data and allow interesting patterns to emerge rather than having to know in advance what they seek. The ability to tie together databases adds further to citizens' abilities to turn data into information that may be used as a basis for decisionmaking.

Once the initial costs of data entry and software construction are overcome, therefore, computers strikingly reduce the cost of data. The condition for obtaining the cheap data, however, is that users know how to manipulate computers and have access to hardware, including modems or CD-ROM readers. These kinds of costs were unanticipated in Title III, and in fact have been poorly considered for virtually all information policies at all levels of government. RTK poses the questions most clearly, because the right to know is not universally distributed if exercising it requires a degree in computer science or permission to use the local university's computer equipment. On the other hand, Congress neither directed EPA to develop software that would ease citizen access to data nor did it provide EPA with funds to undertake such a task. Private groups are starting to fill in the gaps by developing software, providing hardware, and performing their own analyses of the data for citizen members.[33] The level of government activity in these areas is still in question; it will be decided as the interested parties define more clearly what form they believe RTK itself should take.

Notes

1. *SDV* v. *Mathews*, 542 F. 2d 1116 (9th Cir. 1976) held that agencies do not have to supply electronic data. In *Army Times Publishing Company* v. *Department of the Army*, Div. A. No. 87-2833, May 2, 1988, however, the court held that computerized records were not exempt from disclosure under FOIA as protected personnel records.

2. Based on ten reports (chemicals) from each of 31,800 facilities. See the Final Rule for Submission of Section 313 Reports, 53 Fed. Reg. 4520 (February 16, 1988). (Hereafter, Final 313 Rule.)

3. See OMB Circular A-130, 50 Fed. Reg. 52730 (December 24, 1985) for guidelines for management of federal information resources.

4. Proposed rule in 52 Fed. Reg. 21152; also see Final 313 Rule.

5. Telephone interview with Stephen Newburg-Rinn, Information Management Division, Office of Toxic Substances, EPA, June 7, 1988.

6. Interview with Jan Bearden, Office of Toxic Substances, EPA, May 25, 1988. On CD-ROM, see Vanessa Jo Grimm, "GPO Aims for On-Line Public Access," *Government Computer News*, September 12, 1988, p. 127.

7. U.S., Congress, House of Representatives, *Superfund Amendments and Reauthorization Act of 1986: Conference Report*, 99th Cong., 2d sess., Report 99-962, p. 299. (Hereafter, Conference Committee Report.)

8. "Attachment: Section 313 Background," Draft attached to a memorandum from John Viola, ICF Inc., to Debra Harper, Office of Toxic Substances, EPA, December 23, 1986: Memo and draft attachment included in ICF report. A justification for these data elements in linking databases is found in CRC Systems, Inc., "Overview of Requirements for the Toxic Chemical Release Inventory" (Prepared for Information Management Division, Office of Toxic Substances), November 6, 1987, pp. 3-15 and passim. (Hereafter, "Overview.")

9. Final 313 Rule, p. 4517.

10. Ibid., p. 4512.

11. Ibid., p. 4513, discusses in detail why EPA wants to include the 304 releases in the total (because these are otherwise not in the national database as they were only reported to states and localities) but should not require facilities to separate the two in the report (because of trade-secret considerations).

12. Greenpeace, *Mortality and Toxics Along the Mississippi River* (Washington, D.C.: Greenpeace, September 1988), p. 26.

13. Kentucky Resource Council, *Waking a Sleeping Giant: A Citizen's Guide to Toxic Chemical Releases Reported Under Section 313 of the Emergency Planning and Community Right-to-Know Act* (Frankfort, Ky.: KRC, September 1988), pp. 11, 16-17.

14. "Roadmaps" is a database of sources of information on the chemicals regulated under section 313. It includes federal regulations covering the chemical, states that have drinking water standards for that chemical, states that have information on ambient air concentrations of the chemical, state contacts for air and water information, and general sources of data, including EPA databases and documents. It may be searched by CAS number, substance name, hazard characteristics, or state. It runs on IBM-PCs and compatibles and is available from EPA.

15. The database is called "Toxnet." It is accessible through a variety of public access networks including Telenet and Dialog.

16. "Overview," pp. 4-8.

17. Among the most common errors of initial submitters are failure to sign each individual facility identification page; failure to submit separate facility identification pages for each chemical report, and use of chemical

names not in section 313. See "EPA Admits 95% Error Rate in Sec. 313 Forms so Far," *Community and Worker Right-to-Know News* 2, no. 16 (May 22, 1988):1,3.

18. Telephone interview with Bob Webodau, Engineering Services Division, E.I. DuPont Nemours, April 29, 1988. On the utility of expert systems for regulators and the regulated, see, for example, W. James Hadden, Jr., "Intelligent Advisory Systems for Hazardous Waste Permits," *Journal of Resource Management and Technology* (April 1988). On expert systems in general, see, for example (among a large literature), Donald A. Waterman, *A Guide to Expert Systems* (Reading, Mass.: Addison-Wesley, 1986).

19. Compiled from *Community Right-to-Know Manual* (Washington, D.C.: Thompson Publishing Company, October 1987).

20. Telephone interview with Barbara Sargeant, RTK Program, New Jersey Department of the Environment, November 10, 1988.

21. Statements by staff from Louisiana, Utah, and North Dakota at the EPA/FEMA Title III Information Management Workshop, Dallas, Texas, June 21-22, 1988, illustrate this trend.

22. EPA, "Summary Questionnaire," (February 1988) p. 37. (Results of the questionnaire distributed to states to gather information for the deputy regional administrators' White Paper.) At the Dallas meeting, states made this demand forcefully; EPA staff reported that similar demands had been made at other regional meetings.

23. "About CAMEO-II," pamphlet distributed by NOAA/Hazardous Materials Response Branch, 7600 Sand Point Way N.E., Seattle, Washington 98115.

24. U.S., Congress, Senate, Committee on Environment and Public Works, Subcommittee on Superfund and Environmental Oversight, Hearing on Implementation of Title III, Testimony of Sandy Buchanan, May 26, 1988.

25. EPA, "Summary Questionnaire," p. 40.

26. Information presented by Steve Mason, EPA Region VI and William Elliott, Texas Department of Health, at the EPA/FEMA Title III Information Management Workshop, Dallas, Texas, June 21-22, 1988.

27. We have developed some CAMEO-compatible software that fulfills this definition. For information, contact me at The LBJ School of Public Affairs, University of Texas, Austin, Texas 78713.

28. EPA, "Summary Questionnaire," p. 18.

29. Statement of Steve Compton, Hazardous Materials Division, Austin Fire Department, to the Information Committee of the Travis County LEPC, March 4, 1988, and April 8, 1988. Also see statement of Warren Isman, chairman, Hazardous Materials Committee, International Association of Fire Chiefs in U.S., Congress, Senate, "Community Right to Know Legislation and Its Regulatory and Paperwork Impact on Small Business," 99th Cong., 1st sess., June 18, 1985, p. 115.

30. *Community and Worker Right-to-Know News* 2, no. 15 (May 8, 1988):6.

31. CRC Systems, Inc., "Overview of Requirements for the Toxic Chemical Release Inventory" (Prepared for Information Management Division, Office of Toxic Substances), November 6, 1987, pp. 3-18, also notes

the importance of chemical identification to the Title III effort and the difficulty of making accurate identifications.

32. Reported in John Horrigan, "State Telecommunications Policy," a background paper prepared for the Woodlands Conference on New State Initiatives: Environment, Resources, and the Economy, The Woodlands, Texas, November 31, 1988.

33. For analyzed data, see Greenpeace, *Mortality and Toxics Along the Mississippi River*. Apple Computer, Inc., among others, receives requests from public interest groups for donations of hardware. The Right-to-Know Network, sponsored in part by the Bauman Family Foundation, will use these machines to develop a nationwide network of Title III activists.

6 / Imperfect Information

Any notion of RTK that goes beyond bare provision of data assumes that the information is intended to support and improve decisionmaking. No matter who makes the choices--whether regulators, industry, citizens, or all of them together--decisionmakers need scientific and technical information beyond the chemical lists and emissions inventories provided by Title III. What is the nature of the hazard that the chemical poses? Should the chemical be included in the list of regulated substances? If yes, does the hazard it poses arise under reported conditions of storage or use? When might a hazardous exposure occur?

Unfortunately, this supplementary information does not always exist. Environmental monitoring reports are often unavailable; air dispersion models are dependent upon such a wide variety of factors that even computers may not be able to obtain accurate results; scientists don't know much about the health effects caused by long exposure to substances at very low levels. Moreover, much of the information we do have about health effects is based on laboratory or epidemiological studies, the validity of which rests on inferring causation through statistical analysis of data. Laypeople are often skeptical of these results, in part because careful experts will seldom make the kinds of unequivocal statements about risk or safety that they would like to hear.

The absence of scientific and technical information and uncertainties about its meaning are important determinants of the regulatory process in the United States. Industry and government are often at odds over the appropriate level for an exposure standard, with each side offering expert testimony in support of its position. Long experience has brought general agreement that at least some aspects of these regulatory decisions are political rather than scientific; risk assessment, the scientific portion, is commonly distinguished from risk management, which includes nonscientific decisions about acceptable risk levels and policies for reducing risks.

Experiences in the regulatory arena with problems arising from scientific uncertainty have caused many experts to question the very premise of RTK. "What good does it do to provide citizens with access to chemical lists," they ask, "when there is no scientific evidence on which to base answers to their questions about the risks caused by these chemicals? All that Title III does is create unnecessary fears, especially since some regulated chemicals should not even be on the list of hazardous substances." People holding this view often believe that the central purpose of RTK should be to reduce risks, with decisionmaking left to experts who can bring sound judgment to bear on complex and uncertain technical data. Other people point to the realization that the uncertainties of the data allow or even require that decisions concerning risks have a political component. In that case, scientific and technical experts are no more competent than anyone else; RTK, therefore, must entail an element of citizen participation.

Depending upon the point of view, the absence or uncertainty of scientific and technical information may be regarded either as a limitation on RTK or as a further justification for citizens' full participation in decisionmaking about hazardous chemicals. As noted, the relationships between scientific evidence and regulatory decisionmaking have been widely explored. This chapter is an attempt to apply what we have learned to RTK.

Information Not Available

Title III focuses on one impediment to sound decisionmaking--absence of data. It attempts to rectify this problem by requiring facilities to report the hazardous chemicals that they store, use, and emit. But these data alone cannot provide the basis for decisions; supplementary information is needed. Not only does Title III not address this problem thoroughly, it virtually ignores the fact that much of the supplementary information is actually not available. Although most public attention has focused on lack of health-effects information, there are many other kinds of information that we also lack. As noted in Chapter 1, we lack comprehensive data about concentrations of particular substances in air and water; yet the data available under section 313 are almost meaningless without these measurements, since we can infer little about exposure from simple emissions data.[1]

Because emergency response focuses directly on short-term effects, it would seem to be less prone to problems relating to lack of knowledge. On the contrary, there are many things we do not know that would improve both planning and response. The Office of Technology Assessment has determined that along with human error, it is lack of knowledge, not equipment failure, that is the cause of most accidents and spills.[2] Another area of relative ignorance involves the way in which different materials behave during accidental releases. Experts have modeled dispersion of gases in air; these models range from relatively simple to quite complex, taking into account season and topography as well as obvious factors such as temperature and wind direction. CAMEO, the computer program described in Chapter 5, includes two dispersion models: the simple model, contained in the vulnerability assessment module, which outlines a plume that can be superposed on a map; and a separate dispersion model that uses a more sophisticated analysis and will even draw a plume on a map contained in the computer. Virtually all these models assume that each substance will disperse by virtue of turbulence in the atmosphere. We now know, however, that some substances create a "slumping, ground-hugging dense cloud, which displaces the atmospheric flow around it" rather than mixing with the surrounding air.[3] Guidebooks for evacuation often do not take this fact into account. Similarly, the evacuation distance for chlorine, a chemical commonly found in large quantities at water treatment plants and public swimming pools, is based on the assumption that no aerosol is formed during the release. Without experimental data, however, the validity of this assumption remains unexamined.[4]

EPA faced the problem of lack of knowledge when providing guidance to industry to calculate emissions for section 313 reports. Because the statute specifically stated that facilities were not required to conduct a lot of expensive tests to obtain the desired information, EPA developed some methods for estimating releases. The agency drew on available information, primarily a study of emissions from large petrochemical plants, to develop its estimation methods. The petrochemical plants use large pipes as much as three or more feet in diameter, with concomitantly large valves. EPA incorporated the leak factors from these pipes and valves into its estimation technique, even though many facilities use 2- or 3-inch pipes with valves the size of those in a home water faucet. Thus, in some cases, a facility calculated that its fugitive emissions (unintended losses from valves and leaks) were greater than the amount of chemical purchased from the supplier.[5] Many facilities that could afford to instituted direct monitoring in order to provide more accurate estimates; using these data, EPA will eventually be able to develop more sensitive and accurate estimation techniques.

In many other areas, information we would like to have before making any decisions is simply missing. Of these, the most obvious is information about health effects caused by long-term, low-level exposure to a particular chemical; a related gap in knowledge concerns the consequences of any kind of exposure that do not appear for many years--known as delayed, chronic, or long-term effects. Data about delayed health effects are amazingly skimpy. A study of information available for a sample of 675 chemicals found many serious gaps in the data; of the substances in the category "chemicals in commerce" (not including pesticides, drugs, cosmetics, or food additives), for not even one was sufficient information available to "permit a complete health-hazard assessment." Only the boiling point was available for between 40 and 70 percent of the substances, depending upon their category.[6] No toxicity information is available for nearly half of the food additives and more than three-fourths of nonfood or drug chemicals in commerce.[7]

Because laboratory tests to determine delayed health effects are so expensive and difficult and the numbers of chemicals for which they are missing so large, policymakers have spent considerable effort in determining ways to set priorities for obtaining information about the myriad substances for which it is lacking. In vitro, short-term tests, which are relatively low-cost because they test the effects of substances on cells rather than on whole animals, are now widely used by regulators trying to set priorities for the more expensive tests. Because in vitro tests actually measure mutagenicity, their success in ranking substances for further investigation depends upon the correlation between that characteristic and other hazards, especially carcinogenicity. Although many scientists are convinced that the association is strong and the in vitro tests good predictors, others are less sanguine.[8]

In short, concerning the central feature of decisions about hazardous materials in the community--health effects, especially of long-term, low-level exposures--we are woefully ignorant. Continued testing and measurement of new substances and review of the data for old substances will gradually increase our level of knowledge in some areas. Many citizens are inclined to believe that the response "we just don't know" is intended to cover up available information about risks; in fact, it is more likely to be the case that we indeed do not know. Even in cases in which laboratory and other tests have been conducted, however, citizens (and experts) often have trouble in understanding what the evidence means. This problem is considered in the following section.

Assessing and Understanding Health Risks

There are myriad possible delayed adverse health effects of exposure to chemicals; of these, carcinogenicity (ability to cause cancer), teratogenicity (causing birth defects), and mutagenicity (causing changes in the germ cells) are the most commonly mentioned. Three different methods are most often used for determining whether a substance causes one of these effects: animal tests, epidemiologic studies, and in vitro tests. For simplicity's sake, only carcinogenicity testing will be discussed in detail, but testing for the other effects poses analogous problems.

Laboratory Animal Tests

Animal tests are perhaps most frequently encountered. They are conducted in order to answer the question "Is this substance carcinogenic, and if so, at what doses?" Cancers have a natural, or "background," frequency in the population; when they are known, which is not often, these frequencies are usually expressed as rates. Thus, the background rate for bladder cancer is about 15 per 100,000.[9] Although this appears to be a low rate, multiplying 15 by 250,000 (to change the 100,000 into 250 million, the approximate population of the United States) shows that there are about 37,500 cases of bladder cancer annually. The laboratory tests attempt to determine whether the substance causes more, or "excess," cancers in the laboratory animals by comparing the rate of tumor development in controls, which are not exposed to the substance, with animals that are exposed.

Because there are differences between the sexes and among different kinds of animals, a well-designed laboratory test will involve at least two species and both sexes; with controls and two different exposure levels for each of these four groups, which should contain a minimum of 50 animals, the smallest experiment comprises at least 600 animals. A study using rats and mice lasts about two years. For this reason, such studies cost between $400,000 and $1 million.[10]

Another condition of a good laboratory test is that animals be exposed to the test substance in the same way as humans would be. This "exposure characterization," may itself be quite difficult to achieve, inasmuch as exposure depends upon the nature of the substance (solid, liquid, gas, solubility, biodegradation, impurities, etc.), its use and the kinds of problems associated with use, and many other factors.[11] The problems with characterizing exposure accurately may be understood from an example: The lung is composed of over forty different cell types, concentrated in different regions of the lung and exhibiting different responses to different kinds of exposures. Thus, exposure of rats to sulfur dioxide leads to chronic bronchitis, a problem of the upper airways, whereas exposure to nitrogen dioxide leads to emphysema, a problem of the respiratory region.[12] Even an otherwise well-conducted study may not provide precisely the kind of exposure most likely to elicit information about health effects.

One aspect of animal tests that draws public concern is the level of exposure. The relatively small number of animals used means that a cancer that occurs naturally with low frequency may not even occur in the control group. In order to ensure that substances elicit a measurable effect in the exposed group, researchers give the animals a proportionately larger dose. Of a famous study that suggested to the Food and Drug Administration that it should ban saccharin, one congresswoman said, "People are outraged and skeptical. . . . They feel a Canadian study done on rats fed such large doses is ridiculous. . . . No one I know is going to or has ever consumed 800 cans of diet soda a day. Gentlemen of the committee, I have just lost over the past year forty-seven pounds . . . and even in the hot summer campaign, I couldn't drink 800 cans of soda a day."[13] Opponents of the ban frequently made similar arguments, although, in fact, a lower level in the diet (the equivalent of two cans per day, say) could have been fed if several hundred thousand rats had been used. (The result of the protests, it should be noted, is that Congress forbade FDA to ban saccharin, mandating instead a product label that informs interested readers that the substance is an animal carcinogen--RTK for consumer product risks.)

The methods used create other difficulties of interpretation. Because the test animals are fed at high doses, scientists must calculate what the effects would be at lower exposures by a technique called "extrapolation." Figure 6-1 provides a graphic representation of this technique applied to data from a study in which animals were fed DDT; the experimental data are presumed to fit a particular equation or curve and that line is then extended downwards to lower doses. Figure 6-1 shows that the result is quite sensitive to the model chosen; the "safe" dose (causing about 1 excess cancer per 100 million people) ranges from 1 part per 100 billion to 1 part per million. Although most scientists apply a "safety factor" of 10 or 100 to the results of these extrapolations in case humans are more sensitive than rats, there are still uncertainties involved in inferring human health effects from laboratory animal studies. Other uncertainties of interpretation arise

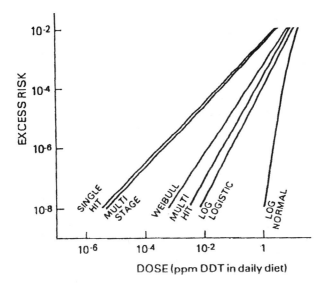

FIGURE 6-1 DDT data extrapolation

Source: Charles C. Brown, "High- to Low-Dose Extrapolation in Animals," in Joseph V. Rodricks and Robert G. Tardiff, eds., Assessment and Management of Chemical Risks (Washington, D.C.: American Chemical Society, 1984), p. 3.

from examinations of the animals' tissues, since reasonable scientists may differ as to whether a particular cellular alteration indicates a tumor.

Because they are based on small numbers of animals exposed at high levels, results of studies are usually provided as ranges or probabilities of excess cancers. More than one decisionmaker has found this to be less than useful:

> *Congressman*: We are talking about statistical probabilities, aren't we?
> *FDA representative*: Yes.
> *C*: What I am getting at, the carcinogens in saccharin that you feel compelled to have banned, is that also . . . only a statistical probability?
> *F*: It is always a statistical probability.

C: That is the point. If I am correct now, if we are basing a decision on these tests, on a statistical probability, that the saccharin produced all of the tumors that you say are bad in the tests, and nothing else could have produced them. Then we are basing that upon another probability, and that is that the mathematical extrapolation from those studies are absolutely correct and we are basing the whole thing on a third probability, and that is that carcinogens may produce cancerous tumors in humans, as a result of all of this.

So in essence, we are coming up with a decision based upon a probability, which is based upon a probability which, in turn, is based upon a probability. I would like to know what mathematical evaluation have you given to this probability to the third power?[14]

The cost of doing laboratory tests constitutes an impediment to creating risk information, and the very nature of those tests allows laypeople to question the accuracy of information when it is created.

Heretofore, these problems have arisen mostly in the regulatory arena, in which experts have contended with one another. Only the occasional congressional or interest group intervention has caused laypeople to take note of the vagaries of the scientific evidence. RTK, however, forces citizens to confront the health effects evidence in order to decide whether the risk posed by a substance in the community is serious enough to merit their concern and political activity. In so doing, they will frequently discover studies like the one for saccharin in which animals were exposed to extraordinary amounts of a substance.

In the case involving saccharin, people objected, in part, because the evidence was supporting a ban they opposed; will they be equally skeptical when the evidence from a laboratory study suggests that there may be a risk from a substance widely used in the community? How will they know whether a study was well or poorly conducted? Will they discern when a discredited extrapolation method or overly conservative assumption is made? Many experts believe that the problem of nonexperts attempting to interpret uncertain data is so serious that the only reasonable response is to discourage forms of RTK that require citizens to understand and act upon evidence of health effects from laboratory studies. Instead, they argue, RTK data should be used primarily by experts within and outside industry to reduce risks. Others take a different tack, arguing that RTK will require extensive efforts at educating citizens to understand both the strengths and the limitations of scientific data.

Epidemiologic Studies

Epidemiologic studies, which rely on human rather than animal data, entail many of the same uncertainties as laboratory studies and engender similar difficulties of interpretation. Because people and their exposures are less controlled than laboratory animals, possible relationships between exposure and health effects found in "epi" studies must be supported by other evidence, such as a laboratory study or an understanding of the physiological basis for the effect, before scientists will accept them. This has proven frustrating for citizens who believe they have detected excess rates of a disease in their communities only to have experts say that the "cluster" could easily have occurred by chance.

One of the most famous cases took place in Woburn, Massachusetts, in the late 1970s, when a resident realized that she was only one of many neighbors whose children had been diagnosed as having leukemia. Around the same time, although for reasons completely unrelated to the parents' concerns, the local drinking water was found to contain high levels of tri- and tetra-choloroethylene, widely used solvents. Convinced that the water was the source of the disease, citizens created a map of leukemia incidence. The state health department, examining its data, also found an excess rate of childhood leukemia in Woburn and conducted a retrospective study comparing life-styles and pregnancy histories of the sick children's families with those of other families.

Officials explained that they didn't really expect to find anything from the study, because trichloroethylene and similar substances do not remain in the body, because the substance had never been related to leukemia in laboratory or other epidemiologic studies, and because there was no way to link the water supply to the children, the pattern of distribution from the six wells constituting Woburn's full water supply being unknown. Although these reasons and the data were strong, citizens felt that "it was hard to have confidence in a study that they themselves don't have confidence in. They went in expecting to find nothing and they found nothing."[15]

A second study was conducted privately, using volunteer interviewers from a local environmental group to survey 8,000 families. The researchers also obtained the city pumping records, overcoming that limitation of the earlier study, and found that the suspect wells served primarily the east (affected) end of town. The new data showed congenital abnormalities and disorders, including childhood leukemia, to be positively associated with exposure to water from the two wells with contaminated water. Critics argued that this study was also wrong, emphasizing methodological problems and lack of supporting evidence from other sources. Using the study and data EPA collected on the presence of excess tri-choloroethylene near the wells, citizens filed suit against local industries known to have stored or used the chemicals. The suit was settled out of court.

The Woburn case clearly illustrates that the results of epidemiologic studies, like laboratory studies, are seldom clear-cut; they are open to interpretation and dispute among experts. For a study of RTK, however, Woburn provides a more important lesson: The gap between citizen and scientist can be closed. By mapping the incidence of leukemia, by collecting and analyzing data for the second study, by pushing agencies to obtain the necessary supporting data, citizens were not just participating in decisions about controlling a risk identified by scientists but were actually participating in the scientific enterprise itself.[16] Citizens could come to appreciate the strengths and the limitations of the data.

Around the nation, citizens are conducting other community health surveys.[17] The data made available under RTK supports the health surveys by indicating which chemicals are present in the community; the health surveys expand and deepen the idea of right to know by allowing citizens to show that those chemicals are creating unwanted health effects. The complexities of analytic methods still limit citizens' abilities to participate in data analysis, however active their participation in data collection. This means that results may still be presented in ways that suit political purposes. A study of mortality and toxics of a type that will be replicated using section 313 data, for example, found both high excess cancer rates and high releases of toxic chemicals to air and water along the Mississippi River. Although the researchers were careful not to state that there is a causal relationship between the emissions and the cancers, few readers would fail to make the inference.[18] Does the fuzziness of the line between interpretation and exploitation of such data suggest the need for limiting RTK, or does it underline the importance of making all data available to everyone?

Understanding Scientific Communications

One effect of RTK will be to expose citizens to a range of scientific and technical concepts and communications. Although in some situations experts use technical language to "snow" lay audiences,[19] in most instances they use it to convey well-defined concepts with minimum ambiguity. Mathematical formulas often serve the same purpose.

Who is responsible for ensuring that citizens understand technical language? Must they take full responsibility themselves, virtually becoming experts in the process, or should experts or even government assist people in understanding the information they obtain under RTK? Two examples illustrate the range of issues.

Suppose, for example, citizens want to compare emissions data with the conditions of a permit, a course that is being urged on them by various interest groups.[20] The following excerpts--only a few sentences out of a forty-page permit--would surely force most citizens to obtain additional information, if not to give up altogether:

> For all constructed soil liners: (1) Laboratory Standard Proctor Density and optimum moisture contents tests performed . . . for a minimum of one representative sample from each 10,000 cubic yards of soil; . . . (3) Atterberg Limits and percent passing No. 200 sieve tests at a minimum rate of one test per 5 field density tests; . . . (5) Hydraulic conductivity measurements expressed in terms of cm/sec for representative undisturbed core samples of the constructed soil liner system. . . . [21]

Of course, citizens may ask the agency that provides the permit to help them understand it; but suppose hundreds of groups request permits and assistance in decoding them. The agency might well find its staff overburdened with the requests and decide to reduce support to citizens. There are costs to that course of action, however; disgruntled citizens might complain to state legislators. Furthermore, the agency would be compromising its supplementary if informal enforcement staff of active citizens. As an alternative, the agency might decide to develop a document that provides laypeople with general guidance in interpreting permits.

Citizens may also seek out other experts or obtain textbooks or other educational materials. The accuracy and relevance of what they learn from such sources is uncertain. Finally, citizens may be referred to the permitted facility itself for assistance; indeed, it could be argued that this is a better outcome for RTK. It brings citizens and industry together, places the costs of educating the public on the industry that is creating the need, and ensures that the affected facility has an opportunity to make its best case to the public.

Another situation in which citizens are often confronted with technical language is during public hearings and meetings, such as the ones EPA is required to hold as part of determining the appropriate treatment for abandoned waste sites. At one public meeting, after a presentation by EPA experts, a neighbor of the site rose and said:

> I can't help but be amused at the little lady, as pretty as she is, tonight made a statement. I don't know what her background is, but I have been a geologist in my past and I understand faulting and salt domes and petroleum reserves. . . . She said that there was no faulting which might affect the migration here. But I would like to know, how does she know that? Now, did you make a structural map of the subsurface from any of the electric logs which are in the South Houston oil field? I got a map from [a local company]. There are faults . . . [and the water will be contaminated].[22]

The "little lady" from EPA, herself a geologist with an advanced degree, replied that EPA had looked at "dozens" of electric logs and made structural maps but had found no evidence of faulting in the top 400 feet; with only 30 inches of soil contaminated and the water table at about 30 feet, other faulting would be irrelevant. The citizen then replied, "Any fault at 600 feet is not just going to peter out suddenly. It is all the way up in the strata unless there has been an erosion or a deformity in a hiatus, then it may not."[23]

This exchange highlights several important aspects of communicating technical information. First, the exchange may represent a legitimate difference of opinion among scientists, which tends to disorient laypeople, who have no means of distinguishing among the positions except by their authors' credentials. Second, under such circumstances, it may be effective to impugn the quality of expertise of scientists with different opinions--"little lady." Finally, the exchange would have been less futile if the citizen had had a chance to see a fuller report on the tests EPA had conducted; at least, he would have known that they had consulted the electric logs. Although simplifying technical information has, with reason, received most attention from experts concerned about right to know, there are some affected citizens who will themselves possess expertise. They will need access to more detailed information.

Technical language and its appurtenances, especially the trappings of a formal presentation including a podium, overhead projector, or flip chart, help to ensure that information flows mostly in one direction--from expert to layperson--and create a sense of resentment. Experts are often afraid to tell lay audiences they don't know something, fearing either a loss of trust or legitimacy if they have already taken a position or a loss of control as the discussion turns to nonscientific issues in the absence of technical information.[24] This fear may be heightened by the "decline of deference" to scientists: The number of people expressing "a great deal of confidence" in the scientific community declined from 58 percent to 42 percent between 1966 and 1982.[25]

Conveying scientific and technical information to nonexperts is an essential feature of at least some forms of RTK. The difficulty of doing so, combined with the resources needed to make technical information clear enough to laypeople to enable them to make informed decisions, has led many experts to conclude that a limited form of RTK is most appropriate. According to this view, citizens would have full access to any data they want--they do have a "right" to know, after all, and some citizens are also experts--but the primary responsibility for actual decisionmaking would and should remain with experts, as it generally has for regulatory decisionmaking in the past.

Material Safety Data Sheets and Scientific Uncertainty

Material Safety Data Sheets, which are one of the most important forms of supplementary information provided by Title III, clearly raise many of the issues entailed in presenting the information from laboratory and epidemiological studies--how to provide a comprehensible summary of available information without ignoring the uncertainties created by the data.

MSDSs were first created for workers to provide them with three kinds of information: instructions for safe handling, emergency response measures, and more general information on the characteristics and health effects of substances. OSHA required that MSDSs be made available widely when it promulgated the Hazard Communication Standard; Congress then referred to MSDSs in Title III. MSDSs constitute the primary means for making available the supplementary information about health effects that citizens would need to make good decisions. Unfortunately, MSDSs do not constitute effective or useful supporting information, in large part because they do not successfully resolve the problem of imparting complex scientific information.

Before discussing this aspect of MSDSs, however, it should be noted that they are unsuitable for RTK purposes for another reason. Devised for workers, they necessarily focus on workplace exposures and workplace practices. Respondents to the Massachusetts survey stated forcefully that they want information about "routes of community exposure, not information about workplaces." The instructions for safe handling and emergency response measures are irrelevant for most citizens. Even the ways in which people are exposed may be different; workers handling the substance may be exposed by touch, whereas citizens would be more likely to inhale the escaped volatilized gas. Yet an MSDS may not mention facts important to such citizens, such as whether smelling a substance on the air is an indication of a concentration that has potential health effects.

Even supposing that citizens want the kinds of information provided by MSDSs, however, they would find the information hard to understand. Brief MSDSs contain difficult abbreviations and cryptic notations; longer ones, running to eight or ten pages, are often confusing, repetitious, and highly technical. Figure 6-2 illustrates part of an MSDS.

MSDSs do not seem to be effective in communicating even to workers:

> They give us a chemical precaution sheet with the hazard level of each chemical. Some say it will affect your liver or kidneys, but it's never explained. It's tossed to people who have maybe just a high school education, and there's a word on there like trichloroethylene. If you've never heard of that word before, you wouldn't even know how to pronounce it, let alone understand it. And the threshold limits are all Greek to people. It's never really taught that this is how to decide when you are being overexposed. They're fulfilling their obligation by giving you the information, but they're not telling you how to understand it.[26]

As this worker suggests, MSDSs provide very detailed information about the sources of the health-effects information and the results of the laboratory studies. It would seem that few workers or citizens would want to know the LD_{50} (lethal dose for 50 percent of the test animals) of a substance, because making use of that information rests on having background knowledge of the LD_{50} of other substances for comparison. Knowing the LD_{50} in rats, mice, and rabbits is probably still more useless for laypeople. Instead, most people would prefer a simple sentence that the substance is poisonous only at high doses but that they should avoid ingesting it. Similarly, few people are interested in reading cryptic descriptions of results of laboratory studies for teratogenicity.

Substance identification
Substance: **Methyl alcohol**   CAS #: 67-56-1
Trade names: methanol, wood alcohol, methyl hydroxide, wood spirit
Chemical family: hydroxyl, aliphatic
Molecular formula: C-H4-O   Molecular weight: 32.05
CERCLA ratings (scale 0-3): health=1, fire=3, reactivity=0, persistence=0
NFPA ratings (scale 0-4): health=1, fire=3, reactivity=0

Physical data
Description: clear, colorless, highly polar liquid with a characteristic alcohol
odor. Boiling point: 148.6F Melting point: -144.0 Specific gravity: 0.7915

Fire and explosion
Dangerous fire hazard when exposed to heat, flame, or oxidizers. Vapors are
heavier than air and may travel to a source of ignition and flash back. Flash
point: 52F Upper explosive limit: 36.5% Lower explosive limit 6.0%
Autoignition temp: 72F

Toxicity
500 mg/24 hours skin-rabbit: moderate irritation; 40mg eye-rabbit: moderate
irritation; 428 mg/kg oral-human LDLo; 143 mg/kg oral-human LDLo; 86.000
mg/kg unreported-man LDLo; 7000 mg/kg oral-monkey LDLo; 1000 ppm
inhalation-monkey LCLo; 7500 mg/kg oral-dog LDLo; mutagenic data (RTEC);
reproductive effects data (RTEC); carcinogen status: none. Methyl alcohol is a
skin and eye irritant, neurotoxin, and a central nervous system depressant.
Persons with chronic respiratory, eye, or skin disease may be at increased risk
from exposure.

Health Effects and First Aid
Narcotic/neurotoxic. 25,000 ppm immediately dangerous to life or health.
    Acute exposure: intoxication may result in a state of inebriation, within 12-
18 hours, headache, anorexia, weakness, fatigue, leg cramps, vertigo and
restlessness occur, followed by nausea, vomiting, dizziness and other signs of
narcosis. Blurred or dimmed vision has occurred, followed by transient or
permanent blindness.
    Chronic exposure: prolonged or repeated exposure may cause symptoms
such as blurred vision, contraction of visual fields.
    First aid--remove from exposure area to fresh air immediately; if
breathing has stopped, perform artificial respiration. Keep person warm and
at rest. Get medical attention immediately.
    Skin contact: may cause dermatitis due to defatting of the skin. It may be
absorbed through the skin to cause systemic effects including narcosis, optic
neuritis, and acidosis.
    First aid--if ingestion is discovered within 2 hours, give syrup of ipecac.
Lavage throughly with 2-4 L of tap water with sodium bicarbonate (20g/l)
added. Get medical attention immediately. (Dreisbach, Handbook of
Poisoning, 11th ed.)

FIGURE 6-2 Part of a Material Safety Data Sheet

Why, then, do MSDSs contain so much data? Because they serve as the official description of the substance as required by the OSHA HCS. Lawyers for companies that must ship MSDSs with their products felt that their employers would be at risk for liability suits if they did not provide all available information. Interpretations of the information would similarly make them vulnerable: Suppose three studies had been conducted, of which two suggested that a substance is a carcinogen and one showed no significant difference between the exposed and unexposed animals. If the company stated that the substance is a suspect carcinogen, readers of the MSDS who had cancer might be induced to sue; conversely, if the company did not mention carcinogenicity on the MSDS, someone who read elsewhere about the first two studies might sue the company for hiding relevant information. The result of these conflicting pressures was to create MSDSs that present a lot of data without evaluating it. The information is thus unusable by workers or, under Title III, citizens. A further result is that MSDSs for the same substance prepared by different companies may contain slightly different information, which is confusing for readers, including emergency response personnel who have received multiple MSDSs through the requirements of Title III section 311.

The New Jersey fact sheets, which the state health department must develop under the state law, attempt to overcome some of these problems; they contain uniform headings, include a list of technical terms, evaluate health effects, and are written in clear, relatively nontechnical English or Spanish. Moreover, they are available for use throughout New Jersey, providing one means of overcoming the differences among MSDSs. Figure 3-1 showed four of the six pages for one fact sheet. The pages not illustrated include a set of definitions of technical terms, considerable information on personal protective equipment, and general questions and answers on health risks. Note that the fact sheets are still long and emphasize (as the law requires) workplace conditions.

Merely putting information into nontechnical or summary form is an important first step but does not necessarily overcome the problem of utility. Consider the label for saccharin: "May cause cancer in laboratory animals." Although the language is not technical and avoids the problem of reporting results of myriad laboratory studies, how is a reader to make a decision based on this statement? The information would be more useful if it were supplemented with the background rate for bladder cancer, the increased cancer rate from saccharin exposure, and the promoters or exacerbating factors, such as smoking. But each additional bit of information is subject to its own uncertainties and qualifications. The same is true for information about chemicals or mixtures that citizens would like to have to make RTK more effective. In Chapter 9, I consider this problem further and offer an alternative approach to presenting information about individual chemicals to citizens.

The Media as Communicators of Technical Information

If experts find it difficult to convey technical information directly to citizens who need it, the difficulty is compounded when the information is filtered through a third party. In today's world, most citizens will obtain much of the technical information relating to RTK from the media. Nearly two-thirds of the U. S. population have acquired information about cancer prevention from the media, while less than one-fifth have obtained it from physicians.[27] It is unlikely that the media will be less influential in an area such as hazardous materials in the community that is of less immediate concern to most people.

Unfortunately, the media are in general not well equipped to publicize the kinds of information we have been considering here: technical information, information that entails uncertainties, information that experts are reluctant to boil down--while citizens and reporters push for a single sentence or word. Few reporters have much, if any, scientific training; in the local media, most staff people have multiple beats or rotating assignments. When an issue with a scientific or technical component arises, these reporters must depend upon press releases,[28] wire service reports, or, if they are lucky, on a local expert with whom they have managed to maintain contact. Despite the growing interest in science-based stories, moreover, the amount of coverage of science in local newspapers is decreasing; more than one-third carried science stories in 1967, and less than one-tenth carried such stories in 1983.[29]

More important, the need to attract an audience forces the media to focus on controversy. Risk issues such as those that RTK may engender concerning a particular substance present in the community often feature controversies about "riskiness." Journalists often present opposing assessments but do not have the time or understanding to present the reasons for these assessments. When they interview a mother who is affected by the disposal site, her assertion that her child's symptoms are caused by leakages from the site is presented right along with those of the experts. If they disagree, the media imply that the views of each are equally valid. The tendency to emphasize controversy is exacerbated by the need to be "fair"; it is more interesting to present two contrasting fringe views than one balanced centrist view. If follow-up stories are presented, complex risk information is often compressed into a standard phrase or buzzword such as "potential cancer-causing chemical."[30]

As a result, journalists are "preoccupied with the existence rather than the substance" of controversies.[31] Editors prefer stories that can be written quickly and understood easily. The predominance of the adversarial mode of legal interaction in the United States also contributes to downplaying substance. In the law, it is assumed that each party will use whichever interpretation of the evidence that suits its own interest.[32] When scientific evidence is subsumed under this theory, the important facts become the existence of the controversy and the nature of its resolution, not why the parties disagree. Identifying a "bad guy" also attracts audiences and allows them to find a satisfying interpretation of the news for themselves. In many risk controversies, this label may be pinned on a facility or company, especially when the company is coming in from outside with a proposed new facility. At other times, it is easier to portray the government as a bungler.

Finally, audiences want to know what the risk means for them. Scientists and regulators often have aggregate risk estimates that cannot form the basis for answers to questions such as "Is it safe for me to eat this?" Unable to tell their audiences what they want to hear, journalists may respond by turning the scientists themselves into the "bad guys," by seeking nonexpert views, or, most often, by allowing the audience to infer its own risk from some dramatic incident, no matter how unrepresentative. When EPA first became concerned about ethylene dibromide (EDB) in ground water, all the major networks showed a film about two workers, who had come into direct contact with liquid EDB, being washed down with a hose and then rushed to the hospital, where they later died.[33] One student of media risk reportage explicitly urges scientists to provide both a risk estimate (1 in 1 million) and a "scariness estimate," in which experts state how they would act under similar circumstances.[34]

Headlines are another source of difficulty. They may contain alarming messages that are not fully merited by the content of the articles. Experiments suggest that readers remember risk estimates no matter how they are presented in newspapers, but find the risks more "scary" if the estimates are associated with vivid or alarming headlines.[35] Unfortunately, journalists seldom control the headlines for their articles.

Many of the first newspaper articles covering the release of emissions data on July 1, 1988 exemplified these problems. Although some reporters simply presented emissions data about particular chemicals and stressed that the information could not yet be interpreted, many others quoted chemical industry representatives interpreting the emissions as generally safe. Some found people to express opposing viewpoints. Very few took the opportunity to tell readers where additional data could be found, to remind them that better information would be available in a few months when EPA had computerized it, or to consult with other experts as to the meaning of the data.[36]

Congress required LEPCs to include a representative of the media in part to overcome some of these difficulties. The media representative could assist the LEPC in getting out information about the planning process, could work with facility representatives to develop sound information to be provided during any emergencies, and might learn by his or her presence at LEPC meetings and interactions with industry representatives and scientists how to convey information about routine emissions. Unfortunately, evidence suggests that few LEPCs have active media representation.[37] At least one newspaper editor has stated that it is a conflict of interest for reporters to be members, because the activities of the LEPC are themselves newsworthy. Thus, the mutual benefits of media membership on LEPCs, and especially any gains in local journalists' abilities to report complex technical information, are not being reaped.

If citizens obtain most of their information about hazardous materials in their communities through the media, as seems likely, their RTK may actually be impeded. They may receive information that is tailored more toward titillation than rational decisionmaking. Without the media, however, citizens may not even know that they have the right to know or that there are facilities in their communities that use RTK. Some means of encouraging media participation on LEPCs is needed.

Conclusion

The absence of scientific evidence on topics ranging from behavior of gases accidentally released into the air to delayed health effects limits RTK: Citizens cannot obtain nonexistent information. Efforts to fill in the gaps have generated new information, but often its meaning is not clear. Neither epidemiologic nor laboratory animal studies provide direct evidence of delayed health effects, for example, so scientists must use extrapolation and inference, giving rise to increased opportunities for conflict. Although professionals might be willing to wait until additional evidence becomes available, regulators and, with the advent of Title III, citizens, to an increasing degree, put pressure on them to interpret the data so that policy decisions may be made immediately.[38] Any conflicts among experts in interpreting evidence then become public instead of remaining within the confines of the scientific community.

These conflicts have several effects. First, they may undermine the legitimacy or authority of science in the eyes of laypeople--How can experts disagree about a straightforward matter such as the teratogenicity of a substance? If experts are willing to testify on both sides of a policy question, it may seem that they are selling their expertise rather than serving "the truth." Second, the conflicts may encourage disregard of the scientific evidence or its exploitation as a political tool. If science cannot answer the question clearly, then other criteria must be used; technical experts have no clear advantage over anyone else in such cases. These problems are exacerbated by the difficulties many experts have in conveying their knowledge to the lay community. Inasmuch as expertise is in part educated intuition, scientists may be unable to articulate the precise factors that tipped the balance toward one conclusion and away from another, further increasing the public's skepticism.

Envisioning the further decline of respect for their disciplines or their expertise, or forseeing a decline in the quality of public decisions if technical evidence is disregarded, many experts are very cautious about increased public participation in policy decisions with a technical component. This caution has led to a view, not confined to experts, of RTK as a limited right. Citizens should, indeed, have access to data; democracy, like science itself, cannot succeed without an open exchange of information and the opportunity for oversight that it provides. But decisions should incorporate available scientific evidence, however uncertain, perhaps through the existing regulatory process or by providing incentives to industry to take voluntary action to reduce risks. As noted, others believe that the uncertainties of scientific evidence are the precise reason that decisionmaking should involve laypeople as well as, or perhaps even more integrally than, experts.

Ironically, both of these views require some mastery of technical information by citizens, either for oversight or for active participation. Thus, an important policy question inherent in RTK becomes that of deciding the balance of responsibility for meeting the demand for technical information that may be understood by nonspecialists. The cost of developing such information can be very high. If the entire burden is placed on interested citizens, then RTK may be the right to become an "amateur expert," devoting time and resources to mastering technical information. Some of the people of Woburn did do this, as do a few citizens in many communities. The burden on these individuals would be reduced if they had strong basic science educations; unfortunately, the quality of science education in the United States appears to be declining.[39] This long-term solution relies heavily on government. In the short term, government or industry could prepare supplementary materials. Many industries are developing one-page descriptions about individual chemicals. Their activities are discussed further in Chapter 9. The precise balance of responsibility among the different actors is just beginning to be debated.

RTK is only the most recent of many public activities to face the quandary posed by incomplete or uncertain scientific information. We are gradually acquiring more understanding of the ways in which the policy process may be designed to take this fundamentally unresolvable problem into account. RTK will create further strains on our existing institutions as citizens demand to be included in scientific discussions and decisions. It is an irony of right to know that we only want and need that right because the risks we hope to control are so difficult to understand.

Notes

1. Citizens have difficulty even distinguishing between emissions and exposure; see EPA, Title III Needs Assessment Project, 1988 General Public Focus Groups, Summary of Findings, (Fall 1988), p. 7.

2. U.S., Congress, Office of Technology Assessment, *Transportation of Hazardous Materials: State and Local Activities*, OTA-SET-301, March, 1986, p. 5.

3. Ronald Koopman, Testimony before U.S. Congress, House, Committee on Government Operations, Government Activities and Transportation Subcommittee, Los Angeles, October 19, 1987, p. 2.

4. Ibid., p. 4. Koopman's testimony was directed toward establishing the importance of continued federal funding of the research, and had no intended implications for right to know.

5. Interview with Guy Crawford, Texaco Chemical Company, Austin, Texas, July 14, 1988.

6. National Research Council, Commission on Life Sciences, *Toxicity Testing: Strategies to Determine Needs and Priorities* (Washington, D.C.:National Academy Press, 1984), pp. 122, 125. (Hereafter, NRC study.)

7. NRC study, p. 118.

8. Bruce N. Ames, "Identifying Environmental Chemicals Causing Mutations and Cancer," Science 204 (1979): 587-593, and Bruce N. Ames, Renae Magaw, and Lois Gold, "Ranking Possible Carcinogenic Hazards," Science 236 (17 April 1987): 271-280. Also see NRC study.

9. U.S., Congress, Senate, Committee on Labor and Human Resources, "Saccharin Study and Labeling Act Amendments of 1985," 99th Cong., 1st sess., April 2, 1985, p. 37 (news release on National Bladder Cancer Study).

10. Office of Technology Assessment, Cancer Risk: Assessing and Reducing the Dangers in Our Society (Boulder, Colo.: Westview Press, 1982), p. 115. (Hereafter, OTA cancer study). There are numerous guidelines for well-conducted laboratory tests, including Office of Science and Technology Policy, Chemical Carcinogens: Review of the Science and Its Associated Principles (Washington, D.C.: OSTP, 1984). Others are listed and compared in Mark Rushefsky, "Assuming the Conclusions: Risk Assessment in the Development of Cancer Policy," Politics and the Life Sciences 4 (August 1985):34-35.

11. For a concise discussion of this step in the bioassay, see K. M. Cunningham, "Exposure Characterization," in W. H. Hallenbeck and K. M. Cunningham, Quantitative Risk Assessment for Environmental and Occupational Health (Chelsea, Mich.: Lewis Publishers, 1986), pp. 9-18.

12. Daniel B. Menzel and Elaine D. Smolko, "Interspecies Extrapolation," in Joseph V. Rodricks and Robert G. Tardiff, eds., Assessment and Management of Chemical Risks, American Chemical Society Symposium 239 (Washington, D.C.: ACS, 1984), p. 27.

13. Statement of Barbara Mikulski in U.S., Congress, House, Committee on Interstate and Foreign Commerce, Subcommittee on Health and the Environment, Hearings, 95th Cong., 1st Sess., March 21 and 22, 1977, p. 6.

14. Ibid., p. 103.

15. Ann Anderson, on "Toxic Trials," a "Nova" program, WGBH-TV, 1986. Entire story recounted from this program.

16. I am indebted for this point to Jerry Zeitz.

17. See Marvin Legator, The Health Detective's Handbook : A Guide to the Investigation of Health Hazards by Nonprofessionals (Baltimore: Johns Hopkins University Press, 1985) for instructions on carrying out a community health survey. A related guide is found in National Campaign Against Toxic Hazards, The Citizens Toxics Protection Manual (Boston: NCAT, n.d.), chap. 13. (Attachment 1 of the manual describes how citizens can do their own environmental testing.)

18. Greenpeace, Mortality and Toxics along the Mississippi River (Washington, D.C.: Greenpeace, September 1988).

19. Peter Sandman, Explaining Environmental Risk: Some Notes on Environmental Risk Communication (pamphlet) (Washington, D.C.: EPA, Office of Toxic Substances, November 1986.)

20. See, among many other documents, Kentucky Resources Council, Waking a Sleeping Giant: A Citizen's Guide to Toxic Chemical Releases Reported Under Section 313 of the Emergency Planning and Community Right-to-Know Act (Frankfort, Ky.: KRC, September 1988), p. 17.

21. Texas Water Commission, Permit No. HW-50143, October 28, 1986, p. 15.

22. Statement by Lynn Brasher, former mayor, city of South Houston, at public meeting regarding Geneva Industry Waste Site Cleanup, South Houston, Texas, Thursday, May 22, 1986. Transcript available at Texas Water Commission, Austin, Texas.

23. Ibid.

24. See statement of Roger Kasperson, reported in J. Clarence Davies, Vincent T. Covello, and Frederick W. Allen, eds., *Risk Communication*, Proceedings of the National Conference on Risk Communication held in Washington, D.C., January 29-31, 1986, p. 45.

25. The phrase and the data from Frank N. Laird, "The Decline of Deference: Political Context of Risk Communication," Paper delivered at the annual meeting of the Association for Public Policy Analysis and Management, November 1987.

26. Dorothy Nelkin and Michael S. Brown, *Workers at Risk* (Chicago: University of Chicago Press, 1984), p. 59.

27. Dorothy Nelkin, *Selling Science: How the Press Covers Science and Technology,* (New York: W. H. Freeman, 1987), p. 77, quoting National Cancer Institute, *National Cancer Prevention Awareness Survey* (Washington, D.C.: Government Printing Office, 1984), pp. 58, 64.

28. Nelkin, *Selling Science*, p. 129.

29. Leo Bogart, "How U.S. Newspaper Content is Changing," *Journal of Communication* 35, no. 2 (1985): 82-90.

30. Janet J. Fitchen, Jenifer S. Heath, and June Fessenden-Raden, "Risk Perception in Community Context: A Case Study," in Branden B. Johnson and Vincent Covello, eds., *The Social and Cultural Construction of Risk* (Amsterdam: D. Reidel, 1987), p. 41. Also see Sandman, *Explaining Environmental Risk.*

31. Nelkin, *Selling Science*, p. 56.

32. I am indebted for this point to an unwitting Rob Coppock, who made it in comments on another paper at the annual meeting of the Society for Risk Analysis, Houston, Texas, November 3, 1987.

33. Harold I. Sharlin, "EDB: A Case Study in Communicating Risk," *Risk Analysis* 6 (1986), p. 62.

34. S. Dunwoody, "Mass Media and the Presentation of Risk," Paper presented at the annual meeting of the Society for Risk Analysis, Houston, Texas, November 3, 1987.

35. Dunwoody, "Mass Media."

36. Based on articles from twenty-six newspapers reprinted in Chemical Manufacturers Association, *Communicating Title III*, vol. 2 (July 1988), and on participation in press conference with representatives of fifteen radio, television, and print reporters, Austin, Texas, July 14, 1988.

37. Anecdotal evidence supplemented by survey of LEPC chairpeople. Also see Campbell Communications, Inc., "Survey of York, Pennsylvania, Emergency Response Committee Members," Final Report, August, 1988 (presented to Georgetown University Institute for Health Policy Analysis). Also see W. David Conn, William L. Owens, and Richard C. Rich, "Interim Report

on LEPC Questionnaire," November 1988, in which the investigators report that few Virginia LEPCs have media members.

38. This point is made especially clearly in John D. Graham, Laura C. Green, and Marc J. Roberts, *In Search of Safety: Chemicals and Cancer Risk* (Cambridge, Mass.: Harvard University Press, 1988), p. 184. I received this book as I was making final changes in the manuscript and could not make use of its insights as fully as I would have liked.

39. A study by the Educational Testing Service found that only 7 percent of the seventeen-year-olds in 1986 were prepared for college-level science courses, and more than half could not hold a job that required technical skills, benefit from on-the-job training, or make informed decisions as citizens. Gregory Byrne, "Science Achievement in Schools Called 'Distressingly Low,'" *Science* 241 (September 30, 1988), p. 1751.

7 / Risk Perception and Risk Communication

Everybody gets so much information all day long that they lose their common sense.

--Gertrude Stein, *Reflections on the Atomic Bomb*

Although Title III emphasizes access to data, there are other elements of RTK that are equally important for those who believe in more than a minimal right. If citizens are to take action based on information, they must understand it; in Chapter 6, I described the impediments to understanding caused by the absence, uncertainty, and technical nature of some of the relevant data. This chapter expands upon the theme of understanding and using information by focusing on risks. Although the idea of risk is implicit in RTK, I have thus far avoided considering it in detail. It is in some ways an elusive concept, and many important points about RTK, information policy, and regulatory policy may be understood without more than a passing reference to risk. Now, however, it is time to come to grips with risk, because the choices envisioned by RTK are fundamentally choices about risks.

In the discussion in Chapter 6 of evidence for long-term health effects I emphasized the extent to which the available data was probabilistic and uncertain. Uncertainty is one of the primary features of risk; indeed, many experts define risk as a combined measure of the probability and magnitude of undesirable effects. Most of us, however, use the word "risk" to indicate a much richer concept that involves balancing benefits against unwanted outcomes and also involves some sense of the fairness of the activities that create the risk. Thus, some of the difficulty that people have in interpreting the policy implications of laboratory and epidemiological studies arises less from the complexity or even uncertainty of the data than from their evaluations of the "riskiness" of the effects being considered. Many people, for example, seem to fear cancer and would, therefore, be alarmed by laboratory studies indicating that a substance is a carcinogen.

Laypeoples' perceptions of risk have often been thought to constitute a barrier to good decisionmaking by causing them to evaluate risks inappropriately--seeking control over minor risks and failing to worry about more serious ones. "Risk communication" (RC) is an effort to provide people with better information about risk, couched in terms they can understand and use. As experts' understandings of the concept of risk widened, they began to realize that risk communication also needed to be expanded. Title III provided another stimulus for rethinking the idea of risk communication, which now encompasses a range of activities that may even include developing new institutions for policymaking.

Risk Perception

Right to know is hardly the first public policy to require public judgments about risks. Decisions about bridges, dams, and airports, for example, entail balancing of risks against potential benefits. Public hearings are now a required component of many policies that will impose risks on citizens. These public hearings--covering not only superfund sites but also proposed new incinerators, waste disposal facilities, chemical plants, or commercial developments--are often characterized by public discontent expressed through screaming, emotional appeals consisting of references to sick babies, or, as in the example given in Chapter 6, impugning the technical competence of outside experts. In these settings, experts have often been confirmed in a belief that the public simply cannot understand risk. In this section, I briefly review the origins and development of that belief and survey some of the evidence that it is incorrect.

Right to know is at least partly about making better decisions. In the view of those who study formal decisionmaking, a "better" decision is one that increases the "expected value"--that is, gives a higher number when the value of each possible outcome is multiplied by its probability. Thus, a result valued at $1,000 is less good than one valued at $500 if the probability of the first is only 20 percent and the probability of the second is 80 percent ($200 as opposed to $400). This view assumes that decisionmaking is rational, in the sense that it is completely thought through, with alternatives listed and weighed against one another. Decisionmaking about health or safety risks is only a special case of this general model; the unwanted health consequences or other risks must be assigned some "value."

It is obvious that on many occasions people do not follow the rational decisionmaking model. One time when it is, in fact, rational not to follow the model is when acquiring the information to conduct a full analysis of a situation is very expensive or time-consuming relative to the expected value of the choice. People may develop heuristics, or rules of thumb, that serve as shortcuts for making such decisions. Although it was long thought that people are reasonably good decisionmakers,[1] beginning in the early 1970s a more pessimistic view developed, which held that commonly used heuristics are systematically incorrect and lead to less-than-desirable or "biased" choices.[2]

Such biases have been widely documented. One of the more famous is the "availability bias," in which probabilities of events are estimated according to the ease with which instances of similar events can be remembered--as in the great white shark scare after public release of the film *Jaws.* Another important bias is "representativeness," in which the probability of a sample is judged by the degree to which it resembles the parent population; still another is "anchoring," in which estimates of probability are derived from some outside source and then adjusted upwards or downwards in light of new information. Finally, presentation or "framing" may create bias; a medical treatment reported as 60 percent successful, for example, is usually preferred to a treatment that has a 40 percent failure rate, although the two are objectively equal.[3]

Note that all these biases affect people's perceptions of probabilities. Because people's values are different, they are expected to display reasonable differences in their evaluations of the outcomes of decisions. But the other part of a decision calculation--probability--seems to be measurable, and based on these experiments, people seem to be poor intuitive measurers. This has especially important implications for risk decisions inasmuch as risk is a measure of both probability and undesired outcome. If people cannot evaluate probabilities, therefore, they cannot evaluate risk. If they cannot evaluate risk, they cannot make good risk decisions.

Proof positive of people's inabilities to evaluate risks may be found, according to many students of formal decisionmaking, in their irrational behaviors concerning them. For example, most people are willing to get into their automobiles, even though each trip creates about a 1 in 4,000 chance of being killed or injured. On the other hand, many Americans have simply refused to support nuclear power, for which there is only a 1 in 10 million chance of dying in an accident.[4] Of course, any accident that did occur might kill thousands of people. But the probability is so low that the risk involved in nuclear power is clearly less than the risk from driving. As a result of these "distorted" individual perceptions of risk, public priorities may also have been distorted. For example, government regulations limit trichloroethylene (TCE) in water to 5 ppm (parts per million), whereas the standard for chloroform, which is twenty times as carcinogenic, is 100 ppm.[5]

The view that people have generally poor abilities to understand and use probabilities came to be widely accepted, even outside the community of psychologists who had conducted the studies on perceptual biases. The findings seemed to confirm the experiences of many professionals in risk-related areas--experiences in which the public would fail to accept logical, probability-based arguments such as the following, offered by representatives of a company hoping to install a waste incinerator: "We have calculated the additional cancer risks from the incinerator using worst case assumptions; namely, that the incinerator does not operate at maximum efficiency and that someone is constantly in the plume from the incinerator. And that unlikely risk is lower than the risk you face from using hair coloring regularly."[6] Similar situations regularly arise at public meetings such as the one described in Chapter 6 concerning the best alternative for reducing the risk from hazardous waste at a superfund site. Even nonprofessionals have adopted the view that citizens have difficulty understanding risk information; of the thirty-four Texas LEPC chairpeople who answered a survey question on this topic, twenty-one stated that they did not think citizens could understand or make use of RTK data.

Studies documenting perceptual biases have only served to deepen the concerns of those who question the public's ability to participate in policy decisions concerning risks. On fundamental level, these studies call the whole notion of RTK into question, because they suggest that even with information people will make poor decisions. Supporters of RTK believe that this conclusion is incorrect for at least two reasons.

First, they suggest that the studies that documented perceptual biases, conducted in the laboratory, are not necessarily generalizable to the real world. In these studies, questions were posed to experimental subjects that offered them choice between only two, often similar, answers. In the real world, people seldom face such finely tuned choices, and usually more than one alternative is available.[7] Moreover, the experiments often showed the expected result precisely because the subjects were not provided with full information.[8] Finally, they argue that the experiments only document, but do not explain, perceptual distortions; just as epidemiologic studies require supporting evidence to make causal inferences, so do laboratory psychological experiments. It is thus inappropriate to derive policy implications--

that people are poor risk estimators and need to be educated or informed--from the studies.[9]

Second, supporters of RTK point out that the studies embody a very limited conception of "risk." For ordinary people, risk is not simply composed of probability and outcome. In fact, risk is a much richer, multifaceted concept that includes perhaps twenty other characteristics. One analyst has called these the "outrage" factors. These characteristics include the following: voluntary or involuntary; familiar or unfamiliar; with immediate effects or with delayed effects; natural or artificial; controlled by the individual or controlled by someone else; with visible benefits or without visible benefits. In this list, risks displaying the first characteristic of each pair are rated as less "risky" and more tolerable than risks displaying the second characteristic.[10] Other features, such as "dread," may inhere in some activities--nuclear power is often mentioned in this regard--and make calculations of probabilities simply irrelevant.[11] Thus, citizens who rejected the incinerator argument mentioned above believed that the comparison was invalid, since hair coloring is voluntary, has clearly defined benefits, and affects only one individual in contrast to the involuntary and communitywide risks from the incinerator.

This richer concept of risk has several important implications for RTK. First, it suggests that laypeople have an important role to play in risk decisionmaking, if only because they evaluate risks in ways that are likely to differ systematically from risk evaluation by regulators, industry representatives, and other experts who have typically defined "riskiness" for policy choices. Second, it suggests that explaining risk to people comprises much more than merely describing probabilities and outcomes; this topic is considered in the section of this chapter on risk communication. Finally, it raises fundamental questions about the determinants of risk perception and how risk decisions should be made to take into account the differences in people's evaluations of risk.

Determinants of Risk Perception

The more different characteristics risk has, the more likely individuals' risk assessments are to differ. How controllable, voluntary, natural, or fair risk seems to be depends upon variety of personal experiences and upon the cultural context within which the perceiver operates.[12] Americans in the 1980s, for example, generally have perception of greater risk to their health than they did in the 1960s. Although much of their concern arises from increased awareness of risks associated with life-style choices such as smoking, drinking, eating high cholesterol foods, and using seat belts, some concern also derives from increased awareness of environmental risks. Both of these concerns derive in turn from the decline of infectious disease as a cause of death and the concomitant rise of heart disease and, especially, cancer. The media, already discussed in the context of conveying difficult technical information, played an important role in apprising citizens of new discoveries about hazardous substances and activities.

Even within the same society, however, individuals may respond differently based on other determinants of risk perception. Advised of these health risks, many individuals, especially among the middle class, have undertaken "personal reconstruction," metaphorically taking back control over rapidly changing economic and social environment by seizing control of their lives and health.[13] Other Americans have rejected the healthful life-style changes, saying in effect, "You only go around once. Enjoy it." These are often people who are themselves controlled by outside forces, expressing either rebellion or hopelessness in their unwillingness to adopt personal health-protection measures.

Individuals' stakes in policy decisions that arise after risk is identified also affect their perceptions of its seriousness. At Love Canal, retired citizens whose houses often represented an important part of their estates were less likely to perceive the risk from seeping wastes as serious than were younger residents with children.[14] In another instance, workers with higher seniority (and, therefore, previous experience with jobs that did not entail chemical exposures) "resisted viewing chemicals as hazardous and were concerned more about routine safety problems."[15]

In sum, people's perceptions about the less measurable characteristics of risk will affect their assessment of its riskiness. But their perceptions that risk is controllable, voluntary, or reasonable are affected in turn by their attitudes, economic situations, and cultural milieus. Individuals with "secure or accepting coping styles" are more likely to believe that sudden accidents can be controlled than those with "vigilant or defensive" styles of coping.[16] Secure coping styles, in turn, are fostered by previous successes in coping, higher education, greater wealth, and other standard correlates of success in our culture.

The hypothesis that risk perception is in large measure cultural phenomenon suggests that evaluations of riskiness, along with other understandings of the world, are formed by interactions with peers. Indeed, one of the easiest ways to gain information, including risk information, is to talk to friends. Friends not only provide information, they also comment on it; these evaluations assist in easy acquisition.

Moreover, friends are likely to offer information that reinforces existing perceptions--and, not coincidentally, reinforces the friendship as well.

It is perhaps not too strong to suggest that interactions among members of the community create a "community risk perception" that both affects and is affected by the risk intuitions of each individual.[17] Evidence for community risk perceptions comes from cases like Woburn, in which health effect or residue measurement creates concern about an existing facility, and especially from cases in which new, potentially hazardous facilities are proposed. These studies suggest that community perceptions are also subject to the same formative factors that affect individual risk perceptions. For example, risks that arise from familiar or well-understood phenomena are generally more acceptable than risks that arise from unfamiliar ones. Attempts to site nuclear power plants, nuclear or hazardous materials disposal facilities, and, more recently, waste incinerators have provided ample evidence of this effect. People are often more concerned about the disposal facilities, for example, than by the trucks carrying the hazardous materials to or from the sites. Presumably, trucks are well understood and disposal technologies are not, even though in many areas transport presents higher "objective" risk than disposal.[18]

As the NIMBY (not-in-my-backyard) syndrome has become more widespread, it has taken on an additional feature. Communities are now frequently heard to argue that they are willing to take the risks arising from disposal of their "own" wastes but do not want to be the repository for wastes from other areas. Citizens speaking at the public meeting on a superfund site (discussed in Chapter 6) explicitly stated their fears that once the proposed incinerator had been used to clean up the local site, it would be used to reduce wastes from other sites.[19]

I call this the "proximity" factor. It appears to incorporate a risk/benefit calculus: "We derive the benefits from the manufacture and/or use of these products; therefore, we will, however reluctantly, accept the risks of disposal. But we don't want additional risks from other people's wastes, which do not have associated benefits for us--or at least benefits large enough to merit taking these risks." It also incorporates a bit of xenophobia that surfaces as a community phenomenon even when individual citizens would not articulate such views. Finally, and perhaps most important, this bias incorporates view of fairness that seems to be uniquely American. It is not "fair" that "we" should have to bear the risks from disposing of "their" waste, even though the overall social risk level would be lower for one waste-disposal facility than for many.

In a study of several otherwise similar communities, researchers found very different reactions to the news that the drinking water was contaminated. Although there were differences among citizens within these communities, there were also important differences among the communities as a whole. One factor that affected community reactions was the circumstances surrounding discovery of the contaminant; if residents first suspected the problem themselves and had to work to call it to the attention of public officals, they exhibited stronger concern than when the problem was discovered in the process of routine testing. The willingness of public officials to provide desired information also affected public perceptions of the risk, as did the nature of the presumed polluter, strength of local identity, and other specific local events.[20]

At the beginning of this chapter, we considered people's risk perceptions as a possible barrier to effective decisionmaking. The old argument held that people are poor at understanding or using information about probabilities, which makes them inherently poor at understanding risk. In this view, all the data provided by RTK are more likely to result in worse, not better, public decisions because people will misapprehend what the data are telling them about risk. This argument, however, has been shown to be only partly valid, because probability is only one of many important characteristics that people consider in evaluating risk. Moreover, cultural, economic, and other differences make people weigh these other factors, including controlability and fairness, in different ways.

Increased understanding of the determinants of people's risk evaluations may have two very different outcomes for RTK, however. On the one hand, it may suggest need for greater access to information and broader participation in policymaking, in order to obtain more representative sample of the range of risk perceptions. On the other hand, it may confirm the belief that lay risk evaluations are based on factors--individual and cultural--that are or should be irrelevant to policymaking. Better understanding of these factors could then be used to convey information in ways designed to elicit the desired response from lay participants in the policy process. Conveying information, often called "risk communication," is the topic of the following section.

Risk Communication

The term "risk communication" has a bad name among many advocates of increased public participation in risk decisionmaking. To understand why, we have only to examine a brief history of risk analysis, since RC consisted until recently of merely conveying the results of risk analysis. At first, engineers and other experts quantified risks; the results were often of the form, "This risk of this is 1 in 1 million." Risk analysis was then expanded to include calculations of "acceptable risk," in which experts attempted to justify certain risky decisions by such methods as comparing the new risk with existing widely accepted risks. Driving automobiles was favorite example.[21] An extension of acceptable-risk calculations was risk-benefit analysis, in which not only other risks but also benefits were quantified. Unfortunately, such comparisons often entailed putting values on human life, usually by estimating income or accumulated wealth, and--in many ways even more difficult--on the value of prevented losses.

One reason for each of these expansions of risk analysis was public unwillingness in many cases to accept risks that the experts thought were small enough to be acceptable. "If they can't or won't understand our risk analysis, surely comparison with another common risk will persuade them. No? Well, let's show them what the benefits are. They won't accept that analysis either? What fools!" Still hopeful that "if only they had the information we had, they'd see it our way," risk analysts came to realize that they had to put across their information in ways that were responsive to the needs of the audience.[22] Thus, RC came to be associated with one-way flow of information from experts (and policymakers) to citizens--more an attempt to justify preferred policies than to implement policy of information provision.

The passage of Title III, and especially the prospect of releasing the emissions data under section 313, occasioned a groundswell of interest in RC by affected industries. Industry representatives were especially concerned about the effect that data about large-scale emissions would have without complementary information about exposure or actual health effects. The new insights about determinants of risk perception were used to try to improve the effectiveness of RC.

Risk comparison, for example, was a standard tool of RC, but, as noted, it was not very successful. The realization that risk is a multidimensional concept, however, suggested a better approach to risk comparison. Because risk has so many different characteristics, it is virtually impossibile to find a comparison that is completely analogous. Thus, the citizens rejected the hair coloring vs. incinerator comparison because the two differed in such important dimensions as voluntariness and understandability. Comparing the risk to itself--for example, at different times, with existing standards, or with the risk level that would result from using alternative production methods[23]-- avoids this problem. Following these suggestions, a facility manager might tell the neighbors that emissions are below the standards set by EPA. A slightly less effective strategy is to compare risks of doing something with risks from not doing it or to compare alternative solutions to the same problem. Risk-benefit comparisons and comparisons with other specific causes of the same risk are poor, because they begin to invoke some of the "outrage" factors; the kinds of risk comparisons mentioned, such as waste disposal compared to driving, are to be avoided altogether precisely because they ignore completely the importance of risk characteristics other than probability.

Although use of these formulations is likely to elevate considerably community residents' grasp of the level of risk posed by chemicals in their environment, one might also argue that a more important result is to update and strengthen traditional RC--that is, to enhance the ability of those providing the information to anticipate and control the reactions of the recipients. Such critic might note, "The word 'communication' comes from the Latin: communicare=to share. It does not mean 'sending messages,' for messages cannot possibly be 'sent' in the sense that we speak of sending goods or commodities. Communication is always a social activity, an act of sharing."[24] Until RC includes an exchange of views, according to this argument, it should not be called "communication." Many adherents of this approach believe, moreover, that the term "risk communication" is so tainted by its earlier history that it would be a disservice to any real communication to use it. To my knowledge, no acceptable alternatives have yet been proposed, so I will simply call it "the new RC."

The New (?) Risk Communication

As noted, the essential element of the new RC is mutual exchange of information, in contrast to the old RC in which experts convey risk information to a passive audience, usually in the hope of persuading people to accept risk assessment or related policy decision. In the new RC, experts might continue to provide risk comparisions, explain the scientific basis of existing standards, estimate costs of mitigation alternatives, or describe why contamination of the water supply is unlikely, but in response, laypeople would explain what levels of risk seem acceptable, when the uncertainties of the data appear to them to call for political decision, and what they would like government or industry to do to reduce risk. Experts and affected parties would reply, and conversation would ensue, not only between industry and citizens but also between citizens and government officials.[25] There are several conditions for achieving the transformation from the old to the new RC, including mutual trust and the creation of mechanisms or institutions through which the parties can communicate. These two conditions are very difficult to meet.

Although better risk comparisons and better training in statistics may improve citizens' understanding of particular risks, these can never overcome all the problems we have discussed: lack of information, scientific uncertainty, the need for supplementary information, and, above all, the need to interpret whatever information is available so that individuals can comprehend the nature of the risk for themselves or their families. Thus, citizens must continue to depend on experts for information and especially for an interpretation of its implications for them. This dependence, in turn, requires that citizens trust the experts.

Psychologists and politicians have long known that the influence of a message depends upon the credibility of its source.[26] Unfortunately, the United States is experiencing a "decline of deference."[27] The number of people expressing "a great deal of confidence" in institutions generally declined between 1966 and 1982: For the medical community, it declined from more than 70 percent to below 50 percent; for the scientific community, from 58 percent to 42 percent; for the executive branch, from 41 percent to 25 percent; and for the press, from 55 percent to 20 percent.[28] Voter turnout, perhaps an indicator of respect for political institutions, has declined to about half the population even in years of presidential elections. Citizens appear less, not more, inclined to trust risk communicators; in set of workshops about Title III for citizens living in industrialized areas, the only sources consistently cited as credible were environmental groups, but they were believed to have the disadvantage of lack of access to good information.[29]

Trust, like Rome, is not built in day. Parties must work together over long period to allow time for evaluating whether promises have been kept or whether the other party has lived up to the spirit as well as the letter of an agreement.[30] Initial agreements must concern well-defined matters that are not critical to either party, in case expectations are not met. Once these interactions are successful, the parties may work out agreements about more complex and critical matters.

Aside from any mutual distrust or contempt that may exist, one of the primary barriers to building up trust is the absence of organized ways in which to begin interacting. Our society has developed some mechanisms through which citizens and government may interact, including the public meeting, lobbying of legislators, and citizen membership on policy advisory boards. We have virtually no institutions through which citizens may meet in an orderly and systematic way with representatives of the private sector; indeed, we operate almost entirely on the assumption that government must serve as an intermediary in such interactions, in part because industry is so powerful in comparison with individual citizens or even citizens' groups. How to build such institutions is a central question raised by Title III. Can LEPCs be adapted to this purpose?

Cynics may note that the new RC would raise serious concerns even if the barriers to interacting created by lack of trust and lack of institutions were overcome. They point to potential abuses that arise from the unavoidable need for laypeople to rely on experts for at least some of their information. Even if community residents and a particular industry had agreed on the need to reduce emissions, for example, citizens would be forced to rely upon the facility to provide cost estimates for different levels of emissions reduction as well as an accurate picture of the company's ability to pay these costs. RTK could be extended to cover additional financial information beyond that provided under the rules of the Securities Exchange Commission (SEC), but there will always be areas beyond the purview of amateurs. Thus, trust built up during the early phases of the new RC could be used to mislead citizens on issues of real importance. There are, of course, no rebuttals to this argument; democracy is built upon trust, and attitudes such as this may erode the foundations of our nation. Good institutions do provide, however, for checks and balances and procedural safeguards that may help overcome these concerns.

The idea of the new RC is inextricably linked to RTK. The need for it became very apparent as the various parties contemplated the effect of Title III on their activities. Increased sophistication in our understanding of risk and risk perception provided support for those who realized that the old RC was inadequate. Those, however, who accept the need for the new RC are implicitly advocating a much expanded form of RTK--a form in which citizens are active participants in decisions about hazardous materials in their communities rather than passive recipients of chemical inventory data and risk evaluations prepared by experts.

Risk and RTK

Citizens' perceptions of the risks they learn about from RTK information will determine what kinds of community decisions they seek. If the risks seem reasonable--understandable, balanced by relevant benefits, not too great--then citizens will not press for great changes in the present system. If the risks seem unreasonable--unfamiliar, unfair, involuntary--then citizens will seek change. Experience with attempts to site new facilities and the NIMBY syndrome have made many public officials and industry representatives expect that citizens will "overreact" to RTK information. Their pessimism is increased when they consider the outrage factors of risks, since both kinds of data that Title III makes available--data about daily low-level emissions of hazardous chemicals and data about large accidental spills--appear to many citizens to describe risks that are involuntary, unfair, unfamiliar, uncontrollable, and benefiting industry rather than the whole community. In short, risks of hazardous chemicals used by industry exhibit all the characteristics that increase people's perceptions of riskiness.

Reactions to this dilemma have focused on three different conceptions of RTK. First, those who advocate the limited form of RTK have concentrated their efforts on developing more effective methods of conveying assessments of riskiness to citizens in hopes of eliciting the "right" responses. (It is important to remember in this context that although industry has focused especially on the likelihood that people will perceive low risks as unacceptable, laypeople may also fail to take note of serious risks.)

A related reaction has been what might be termed the "preemptive strike." If laypeople are unable to appreciate the subtleties of the technical information and overrate risks, then experts may alleviate their fears by reducing those risks from the outset. This approach has been widely adopted in the chemical industry. Among the activities that chemical companies undertook near the July 1, 1988, deadline for reporting emissions under section 313 were these: establishing advisory committees made up of community members and employees; establishing on-site information centers with computers and MSDSs; aggregating emissions data, measuring concentrations of major substances, and holding public meetings to discuss the findings; holding plant tours; and, most important, pledging to reduce emissions by large factors in the coming years.[31] Any decrease in community distrust achieved by reducing risk also opens the door to more effective negotations for other desired changes.

Finally, as we have seen, the third response has been the development of a new idea of RC. It is the most radical of the responses, because the new RC is a waste of resources unless it is intended for citizens to act as equal partners in risk decisionmaking. Chemical companies may as well simply reduce risk and then tell people about it if they are not planning to work with citizens to achieve a balanced response to emissions and chemical storage. The rhetoric of the new RC may, however, be more widespread than belief in its implications for citizen participation.

These three different ideas about RTK and risk reflect a continuing dilemma about risk information. This dilemma, common to all essentially political situations, is to obtain reasonable balance between individuals' different (but not inherently wrong) risk perceptions and experts' assessments of the risk compared to other risks whose mitigation will absorb social resources. How much can, how much should, risk communication or risk information change citizens' risk perceptions? What social resources should be expended on providing such information if people's minds are already made up? Thus, we come to the final major issue of RTK--determining the proper balance of government and private action to implement the right and make it effective. This issue is the subject of Chapter 8.

Notes

1. See C.R. Peterson and L. R. Beach, "Man as an Intuitive Statistician," *Psychological Bulletin* 68 (1967):29-46. I am indebted to Lola Lopes for pointing out that the literature on perceptual biases marked a real turning point.

2 See R. Nisbett and L. Ross, *Human Inference: Shortcomings of Social Judgment* (Englewood Cliffs, N.J.: Prentice-Hall, 1980), and, especially, the pivotal research of Tversky and Kahneman collected in Daniel Kahneman, Paul Slovic, and Amos Tversky, eds., *Judgment Under Uncertainty: Heuristics and Biases* (Cambridge: Cambridge University Press, 1982). This early work is summarized in "Judgment Under Uncertainty: Heuristics and Biases," *Science* 185 (1974):1,124-1,131. Of thousands of shorter articles that present the information, two of my favorites are Amos Tversky and Daniel Kahneman, "The Framing of Decisions and the Rationality of Choice," *Science* 211 (1981): 453-458, and Paul Slovic, "Judgment, Choice, and Societal Risk Taking," in Kenneth R. Hammond, ed., *Judgment and Decision in Public Policy Formation* (Washington, D.C.: American Association for the Advancement of Science, 1978), pp. 98-111.

3. Tversky and Kahneman, "The Framing of Decisions and the Rationality of Choice," *Science* 211 (1981):453-458.

4. Auto risks: R. Wilson and E. Crouch, *Risk-Benefit Analysis* (Cambridge, Mass.: Ballinger, 1982), p. 176. Nuclear power: B.D. Dinman, "The Reality and Acceptance of Risk," *Journal of the American Medical Association* 244 (1980):1126-1128.

5. Richard Wilson, "Communicating Perspective Without Minimizing Hazard," Paper delivered at the annal meeting of the Society for Risk Analysis, Houston, Texas, November 3, 1987.

6. Interaction described at the Texas Risk Communication Project Workshop, The Woodlands, Texas, October 16, 1987.

7. Lola L. Lopes, "The Rhetoric of Irrationality," Paper presented at the colloquium in Mass Comunication, Madison, Wisconsin, November 19, 1987.

8. W.W. Lowrance, *Of Acceptable Risk : Science and the Determination of Safety* (Los Altos, Calif.: William Kaufmann, 1976), chaps. 2 and 9. The data on fallible probability perceptions may be overinterpreted or at least overpublicized as well; nearly half the articles on decisionmaking published in psychological journals between 1972 and 1981 reported good performance rather than bad. Unfortunately, the articles reporting bad performance by the experimental subjects were cited about twenty-eight times, whereas those reporting good performance were cited about five times. J. J. Christensen-Szalanski and L.R. Beach, "The Citation Bias: Fad and Fashion in the Judgment and Decision Literature," *American Psychologist* 39 (1982): 75-78.

9. Natalie A. Kishchuk, "Causes and Correlates of Risk Perception: A Comment," *Risk Abstracts*, 4: no. 1 (January 1987):1-4. Another problem with the laboratory studies (not discussed by Kishchuk) is that they require careful calculation to obtain a correct answer, whereas many decisions are best made by "satisficing," or settling for the first acceptable choice rather than by exhaustively enumerating and evaluating all choices. When the data upon which the choice is to be based are not very good, a situation that arises frequently in RTK, satisficing and use of other resource-conserving heuristics represent a sensible deployment of resources.

10. Peter Sandman, ""Risk Communication in the Chemical Industry: Explaining Hazard or Coping with Outrage," Talk for Exxon Chemical Americas, Houston, Texas, September 29, 1988. Sandman coined the term "outrage" for these features, but they were already thoroughly documented in the work of Fischhoff, Slovic, and Lichtenstein. For a review, see Paul Slovic, "Perception of Risk," *Science* 236 (April 17, 1987). The notion that voluntary risks are more acceptable was first made public by Chauncey Starr, "Social Benefit vs. Technological Risk," *Science* 165 (1969): 1232-1238.

11. On dread, also see Slovic, "Perception of Risk."

12. On cultural context, see Mary Douglas and Aaron Wildavsky, *Risk and Culture* (Berkeley: University of California Press, 1982), as well as other works by Douglas. Also Steve Rayner and Robin Cantor, "How Fair Is Safe Enough?" *Risk Analysis* 7 (1987): 3-9.

13. The quoted phrase and many of the ideas of the previous paragraph are from Robert Crawford, "Cultural Influences on Prevention," in Neil D. Weinstein, ed. *Taking Care: Understanding and Encouraging Self-Protective Behavior* (Cambridge: Cambridge University Press, 1987), pp. 95-115.

14. Martha R. Fowlkes and Patricia Y. Miller, "Chemicals and Community at Love Canal," in Branden B. Johnson and Vincent Covello, eds., *The Social and Cultural Construction of Risk*, (Amsterdam: D. Reidel, 1987), pp. 55-78.

15. Michael S. Brown, ""Disputed Knowledge: Worker Access to Hazard Information," in Dorothy Nelkin, ed., *The Language of Risk: Conflicting Perspectives on Occupational Health* (Beverly Hills: Sage Publications, 1985), p. 80.

16. George Cvetkovich, Charles Vlek, and Timothy C. Earle, "Designing Public Hazard Communication Programs About Large-Scale Technologies," in Vlek and Cvetkovich, eds., *Social Decision Methods for Large-Scale Technologies* (Amsterdam: North Holland, 1988).

17. Janet M. Fitchen, Jenifer S. Heath, and June Fessenden-Raden, "Risk Perception in Community Context: A Case Study," in Johnson and Covello, *The Social and Cultural Construction of Risk*, pp. 31-54.

18. Texas Risk Communication Project Workshop, October, 1987.

19. For another example, see Fitchen, Heath, and Fessenden-Raden, "Community Context." Brandon Johnson, "Public Concerns and the Public Role in siting Nuclear and Chemical Waste Facilities," *Environmental Management* 11:571-586 reviews much of the literature.

20. June Fessenden-Raden, Janet M. Fitchen, and Jenifer S. Heath, "Providing Risk Information in Communities: Factors Influencing What Is Heard and Accepted," *Science, Technology, and Human Values* 12 (1987): 94-101.

21. Harry Otway, "Experts, Risk Communication, and Democracy," *Risk Analysis* 7 (1987):126.

22. This is embodied in the title "Risk Communication: A Marketing Approach," Paper prepared for an NSF/EPA workshop. Timothy C. Earle and George T. Cvetkovich, 1984.

23 Vincent T. Covello, Peter M. Sandman, and Paul Slovic, *Risk Communication, Risk Statistics, and Risk Comparisons: A Manual for Plant Managers*) (Washington, D.C.: Chemical Manufacturers Association, 1988).

24. Colin Cherry, quoted in Harlan Cleveland, *The Knowledge Executive* (New York: E.P. Dutton, 1985.), p. 74.

25. Texas Risk Communication Project, *Final Report on Seminar/Workshop* (Houston, Texas: TRCP, February 1988). Based on workshops built around chemical risk "scenarios," the working group of industry and community people evolved the following guidelines for action: (1) Risk communication is not a one-way process. All parties must participate and be granted opportunity to speak; each must listen and respect the others' positions. (2) Risk communication depends upon trust among the parties; this is only established over a long period of time. (3) Credibility is also acquired by being honest, saying "I don't know" when appropriate, and having the person who needs to communicate be directly involved rather than acting through intermediaries. (4) Spokespeople need communication skills and training and must have authority; use a team or even third-party experts as backup to the authoritative speaker. (5) Vary the communication process to fit audience and situation.; public hearings and news conferences with their "us-versus-them" arrangement may not be as effective as roundtables, one-to-one, small groups, and even telephone hot-lines. (6) Listen to the questions asked. Taking notes shows concern. For guidelines for government officials, see B. Hance, C. Chess, and P. Sandman, *Improving Dialog with Communities: A Short Guide for Government Risk Communication* (Trenton, N.J.: New Jersey Department of Environmental Protection, 1988).

26. W. J. McGuire, "Theoretical Foundations of Campaign," in R. E. Rice and W. J. Paisley, eds., *Public Communication Campaigns* (Beverly Hills, Calif.: Sage Publications, 1981), discusses this effect for political issues.

27. Frank N. Laird, "The Decline of Deference: Political Context of Risk Communication," Paper delivered at the annual meeting of the Association for Public Policy Analysis and Management, November 1987. All the data in this paragraph are cited by Laird.

28. Data reported by Laird from a variety of sources.

29. Campbell Communications, Inc., "EPA Title III Needs Assessment Project: 1988 General Public Focus Groups, Summary of Findings," (Summer 1988), p. 11.

30. On the need for trust in relationships spanning more than one interaction, see Robert Axelrod, *The Evolution of Cooperation* (New York: Basic Books, 1984). See also Howard Raiffa, *The Art and Science of Negotiation* (Cambridge, Mass.: Belknap Press of Harvard University Press, 1982, (paper edition), pp. 12, 200, 344ff.

31. See, in general, *Communicating Title III: A Newsletter on Outreach Activities* 1, no.1 (June 1988) (a publication of the Chemical Manufacturers Association). Information also based on interviews with facility managers or environmental managers at plants in Delaware, Pennsylvania, Texas, Kentucky, and Missouri. On reducing emissions, see Bill Dawson, "Release of Toxic Chemicals Disclosed by Area Plants," *Houston Chronicle*, July 17, 1988, section 3, p. 6; also Robert Steyer, "Monsanto Volunteers to Cut Toxic Emssions at All Plants," *St. Louis Post-Dispatch*, July 1, 1988; and Charles L. Elkins, "Toxic Chemicals, the Right Response," *New York Times*, November 13, 1988, p. F4 (national edition).

8 / The Political Economy of RTK

Many of the issues concerning RTK raised in Chapters 4 through 7 could be resolved if more resources were available. If only we had enough money, time, or staff, we could computerize all the data, design user-friendly software with maps and interpretations, conduct additional animal studies to learn more about health effects, measure concentrations of thousands of chemicals in the air and water, educate citizens about probabilities, test and use innovative formats for presenting information that would enhance understanding, overcome agency rivalries by giving them all additional resources, and create new mechanisms for public participation. Not only do we not have that much money; even if we did it is not clear that hazardous-materials information or RTK is the matter on which we would like to spend it. Housing, jobs, economic development, the arts, defense, and many other areas are also deserving of support. Thus, a very important decision for RTK concerns how many resources should be devoted to it.

Other issues cannot be resolved by devoting additional resources to RTK. Instead, their resolution turns on deciding who should provide the resources to be expended and who has responsibility for various activities. Answers to these questions depend in large part on underlying attitudes about the proper roles of government and the private sector in the United States as well as about the nature of citizenship and democracy.

In the 1980s, it has become fashionable to denigrate government and reduce its role relative to the private sector. A variety of analytic techniques, such as cost-benefit analysis, have been used to justify decisions to divest government of various responsibilities. But RTK calls these assumptions into question, or at least forces a serious reconsideration of the proper role of government, in part because RTK is an information policy, and information is, from an economic standpoint, an unusual commodity.

In this chapter, I consider issues at the intersection of politics and economics. The economics of information provision as a regulatory policy could fill a volume all its own. This chapter provides only a review of certain of the important ideas as they affect right to know. I begin with a discussion of individuals' use of information, picking up some of the themes from Chapters 4 and 7. I then turn to a discussion of social costs and benefits of information provision under RTK, focusing especially on the amount and kind of information government, as opposed to the private sector or citizens, should provide.

Government and Information

Government has gotten into the "information business" for three reasons: because information is difficult to evaluate before it is "consumed"; because information is a regulatory strategy that seems to maximize individual freedom; and because information is, at least in part, a "public good," or one from which it is difficult to exclude people, even those who do not pay. The most frequently cited example of a public good is perhaps national defense, as we cannot produce national defense for some citizens while excluding others. Although we can sometimes exclude people from using information--through patent protection, for example, or by making it available only through a database operated by a private company--in general once information is available to some people, it is available to all. (This formulation ignores any difficulties raised by the fact that something that is meaningful information to some people is meaningless, and therefore not information, to others. The discussion here would not be advanced by making this distinction.)

One characteristic of public goods is that there is seldom as much available as people would like, in large part because they are so easy to get without paying that there is no market incentive to produce them. For this reason, many public goods, again including national defense, are produced publicly and paid for by everyone, willing or not, because citizens are coerced by the power of the government to pay through their taxes. Without a real market operating, however, it is difficult to determine what the demand for a public good is, and too much or too little may well be produced.

Although information is not a perfect example of a public good, it does partake of the characteristic that not enough is likely to be produced without government action. As noted in Chapter 6, the costs of laboratory tests for delayed health effects are very high, and no individual or neighborhood group would be likely to be either willing or able to defray them. Government requires such tests to be conducted as a condition of obtaining a license to market the product, however;

the costs of the tests are included in the price of a product and, for costs incurred by government in enforcing and assessing the tests, in taxes.

The difficulty of assessing the value of information is another reason for governments to act to ensure its availability. Information is not free even if it is created and provided by government, as under RTK; people must expend resources in acquiring it (finding out where the LEPC keeps it, for example) and understanding it (such as learning to interpret the results of epidemiologic studies). But people cannot fully evaluate what the information will be worth until after they have made the commitment to acquire it.[1] This difficulty applies especially to information that is novel or unlikely to be used frequently, because people will not have developed the same kinds of heuristics for evaluating the likely benefits that they have for more usual sources of information. For example, viewers often choose a particular television channel for the news, because experience suggests that they prefer its format or content to that provided on other channels; similarly, they listen to or disregard the views of the local movie or restaurant reviewer (or of certain friends) based on past experience with the congruence between those views and their own. With unfamiliar kinds of information, such as risk information, people cannot decide whether to acquire the information. Government can make this assessment for citizens and make important information readily available.

The third reason for government to provide information is that, as noted in Chapter 1, many citizens prefer information provision to other possible strategies for regulating risks. Direct regulations, such as design standards, impose costs on all parties: on the regulated community for compliance, on government for setting the standards and enforcing them, and on consumers. The costs to consumers are of two kinds: first, direct increases in product price and, second, a reduction in the range of choices of products available. If all producers must conform to certain standards, the products are more likely to be similar. Individual choice may be increased by providing information about product risks and allowing consumers to chose the combinations of risk and price that best suit them.

Although information provision has become the policy of choice for reducing risks from consumer products in the United States--and through Title III, has been extended to risks in the environment as well--the suitability of an information-provision policy for reducing risks depends upon several factors. If we can not only describe the nature of the risk but also prescribe an action the reader can take to reduce or avoid the risk, information provision will be successful. It is also especially appropriate when only a small part of the populace is affected--as with allergies. When a risk is universal, standards may well be more appropriate, because there are often significant costs for individuals to acquire, understand, or use information.

Thus, information provision through such means as product labels, while maximizing individual freedom, may also impose higher costs on those less able to afford them. People who cannot read, for example, will not benefit from written information; evidence suggests written information is also less appealing to the elderly. In one large study, individuals whose homes were found to have radon, a naturally occurring radioactive source, in their basements were provided with different kinds of information and offered the opportunity for different follow-up services. Participants in the study who were over sixty-five years old were found to have much lower interest in the information and less willingness to pay for additional services.[2] Perhaps their disinterest arises from a shorter time horizon, perhaps from increased difficulty in processing risk information, or perhaps it is similar to the relative disinterest retired homeowners at Love Canal expressed in risk information that could threaten the economic stake they had in their homes.[3]

Individual variations in risk perception and ability to acquire and process information call into question the assumptions underlying the preference for information provision as a risk control policy. Perhaps government should ensure a minimum level of safety for all, including those who cannot or will not make use of the available risk information. Perhaps government should go farther in providing more information through public education programs or additional label requirements. In short, selecting an information policy does not eliminate the need for the same kinds of balancing decisions about the nature and extent of government activity that are made when direct regulations are being formulated.

Title III raised many of the standard questions about apportioning the costs of regulation. For example, in order to minimize the costs of compliance, Congress specified that industry should not have to generate new data in order to comply with section 313 reporting requirements, specifically mentioning measurements of emissions. EPA, therefore, bore the costs of developing some methods for estimating emissions using readily available information. As noted in Chapter 6, the estimation methods were not very accurate, and many companies preferred the known costs of direct measurement to the possible costs of a public outcry that might be engendered by reports of very large emissions.

Similarly, the other bits of data that EPA added to the section 313 reporting form were not "new," although by requesting them the agency did force many facilities to seek out and compile data that would otherwise not have been readily available. For example, smaller facilities may not know their Dun and Bradstreet numbers or even the SIC codes of their businesses; virtually every facility was expected to have to consult with the U.S. Geological Survey to learn its latitude and longitude, incurring a one-time cost of about $22.50 per facility.[4]

The decision to impose the collection costs on facilities rather than on users highlights an important consideration for all information policies: the extent to which it is appropriate for individual reporting entities to bear the costs of pulling together existing data. Two different considerations support the answer implicit in EPA's actions that the facilities should bear the cost in the case of Title III. First, a large part of the supplementary data on the reporting form "exist" in only a limited sense. Although facilities were already required to report the identities of off-site facilities to which they shipped their hazardous wastes, for example, the disposition of any particular chemical could have been inferred only in a few cases and then with considerable effort.[5] Although such information may be able to be teased out from existing aggregate data, it is generally more efficient for individual facilities, which keep track of the information as part of normal operations, to report it directly.

Second, not imposing the collection cost on the facilities imposes it instead on the users. Each user, moreover, would incur the same collection costs over and over. Thus, a regulator in Seattle and a public interest group representative in Atlanta would each have to spend forty-five minutes calling the U.S. Geological Survey to obtain location information for the same facility. Furthermore, the likelihood of error increases with the number of times the data must be retrieved and correlated.

In short, to the extent that the information sought is already in the possession of the facilities, the social cost of aggregating it is reduced by including it in the report form rather than requiring hundreds of users repeatedly to seek out such data individually. Although it always requires a cost-benefit analysis to justify imposing costs on the regulated community, this is the kind of decision that has repeatedly been made by EPA and other regulatory agencies as they implemented environmental and health policies. As shown in the next section, right to know increased the complexity of the values to be balanced.

Government Responsibility for Information Content

At the time Title III was first being implemented, there was considerable pressure on federal agencies not to undertake any tasks that could be performed as well or better by the private sector. The OMB had promulgated guidelines for acquiring computer hardware and software that explicitly required agencies to use private vendors if possible.[6] The justification for this approach was that if information has value to its users, they should be willing to pay for it. If they are willing to pay for it, a private company can probably provide it at a lower cost or with more amenities for the same price than the government can.

Citizens, on the other hand, are placing increasing demands on government to make the information it provides easier to use and better. EPA has been criticized for the unfriendly or inaccessible form of much of its data.[7] EPA's computerized Tolerance Assessment System, which allows users to predict pesticide residues in individual food products and to estimate exposures for populations, such as children, with different food consumption patterns, would be of great use to the growing number of citizens concerned about pesticide residues, but it has "never been packaged for public use."[8] Other agencies have also been asked to make their data easier to use or to analyze them more fully for citizen use.[9]

The TRI Database

EPA faced this choice between public and private provision of information for the Toxic Release Inventory data that it was to collect under section 313 and make available in electronic form to the public. In fact, EPA identified four options for locating the publicly accessible TRI database: (1) maintaining the TRI database on its own or a contractor's computer and operating a clearinghouse for public access to the data; (2) making the TRI database available to the public through commercial bibliographic retrieval services with the National Technical Information Service acting as broker for agreements; (3) making the TRI database available through the National Library of Medicine in return for a loading fee paid by EPA; and (4) making the database available through a nonprofit organization, such as Purdue University, which distributes NPIRS, the National Pesticides Information Retrieval System of the U.S. Department of Agriculture.[10] As OMB's directive ordered, the agency expected to prefer the second option,[11] but in fact it adopted the third. The change appears to have been motivated by two considerations: special user needs and uncertainty about the number of users.

As noted in Chapter 6, late in 1987 several public interest groups became concerned that the TRI database, perhaps the most valuable result of Title III, would be given to a private firm to maintain and distribute, resulting in high user fees and concomitant loss of real public access. At the same time, they began to consider the kinds of features that a public access database would need to make it useful to people not familiar with database technology.

Among the features they identified were the following:

- The database must be user-friendly;
- the database must be located in an institution with a "service orientation";[12]
- the database must provide access to other related databases;
- the system must support downloading data to microcomputers; and
- access charges must be low.[13]

When the four options were ranked as to their abilities to provide fifteen features, most of which were these kinds of user amenities, both the EPA clearinghouse and the nonprofit organization received low marks. The EPA clearinghouse was found to be especially deficient in user support, accessibility of complementary files, and, perhaps surprisingly, crosslink to EPA databases, whereas the non-profit ranked generally low on all features except accessibility of the system for the public.[14] EPA had obtained considerable information from two private vendors, whose proposals, along with the interagency agreement with the National Library of Medicine, rated notably higher, especially on the more user-friendly services.

The choice between the remaining two options rested heavily upon the number of users, because commercial viability depends in large part upon the payments received from users. One of the commercial vendors contacted during the investigation period, for example, proposed a contract that would require EPA to pay data storage fees if less than a certain number of users decided to access the system.[15] Under such a contract, the public cost of privately developed or delivered systems declines as the number of potential paying users increases. In the case of the TRI, for which Congress has mandated "reasonable" fees associated with the actual costs of developing the database, an increased number of users is essential for a vendor to recapture the costs of developing and disseminating the database.

Estimating the number of likely users is always difficult. In the case of the TRI, the difficulty of the task was compounded by the lack of experience with the wide range of possible users, who include not only the usual government agencies, consulting firms, environmental attorneys, information research specialists, chemists, and medical personnel but also new groups, such as land developers, local citizens, public interest and environmental groups, the media, and others. EPA's first estimate was based on the experience of NLM with "chemistry-related" databases; later, it estimated users as a function of the number of reports filed.[16] Neither estimate makes much sense. Surely a more plausible assumption would have been that the number of inquiries would be proportional to the number of facilities rather than reports. In any event, the estimates were extremely uncertain.

The uncertainty was compounded by questions about the actions of public-interest users, who were thought to be especially sensitive to price and database features.[17] In addition, Title III requires EPA to provide access to the same data by "other means," on the assumption that not all users will have appropriate computer equipment. Indeed, Congress noted that the agency should plan to respond to "reasonable" requests for printouts as well as analyses and summaries of the data.[18] Would people who obtain information by these "other means" be less likely to use the database, thereby lowering the number of electronic users, or would access to hard copies instead stimulate wider interest in obtaining more detailed information through use of the database?[19]

The great uncertainty in estimating the number of users caused EPA to question the stability of any relationship with a private vendor.[20] Without a guaranteed market, an EPA contractor report argued, a private vendor might find itself losing money and anxious to stop providing access to the TRI. Moreover, the wide variation in the kinds of contracts, services, and hardware that private vendors could offer to EPA would entail an extended evaluation of the complex tradeoffs among the features. Because a final decision among the options for the database was still pending in April 1988, and the reports were scheduled to be submitted no later than July 1, there was no time for such a thorough review. An agreement with the National Library of Medicine appeared to offer almost equal user amenities at a much lower risk, so EPA opted for the NLM.[21]

In short, for the private sector to fulfill its promise, several conditions must be met, including the following: Potential users must know that the data are available and understand clearly the data's relevance to their concerns; they must have some way of estimating the value of the information; and there must be a clear pool of potential users large enough to pay back the information speculator, to whom the private entity can direct its marketing efforts. In the case of the TRI database, however, several conditions suggested the need for the government to retain control over the data, including extreme uncertainties about the number and nature of potential users and difficulty in estimating costs and benefits of information collection and use. These factors might not have been decisive without the statutory mandate to provide the information. Thus, RTK did expand the government role in a significant way, at least until the effects of the policy became clearer.

Supplementary Database Features

Even after the decision had been made to house the TRI at NLM, EPA still had to resolve other issues of citizen access, especially the degree of user-friendliness of the NLM database and the cost of access. As noted, potential users had argued to EPA that the public database should allow even minimally trained citizens to receive direct answers to their questions. They emphasized especially the need for answers to questions about particular geographical areas. Individuals may want to know how close they live to certain kinds of emissions. Maps, which are logically associated with geographic information, were, therefore, a common demand.[22] Such user amenities obviously increase the cost of the database; inclusion of mapping capabilities, links to other databases, and menu-driven screens could, by one estimate, more than double the costs of a basic system.[23]

In addition to defining the sphere of interest in geographical terms, users often wish to obtain data focusing on a chemical, a facility or company, an industrial sector, or a health hazard. To answer the question "List all the facilities emitting chemical x," for example, the system must be able to help users with synonyms for chemical names and with other identifiers. The system must have computational capacity to answer a related question, "What are all the facilities emitting chemical x in amounts greater than y per year?" Users are also likely to want to know whether a particular facility or industry has been reducing its emissions over time and whether total emissions in a particular area are increasing or decreasing. People also want to ask about all the chemicals that present a particular health hazard that are being released in a certain area.[24]

Even data sorted in the desired ways might be difficult to understand. Computers could provide additional support, such as graphic presentation, summary, and analysis, that would make the information more useful for the average citizen.[25] Answering questions that require supplementary data that are available in other databases compounds the problem by requiring the user to know both how to access another database and then how to use it.

Each feature designed to aid the public user thus elicits the need for additional features. Even the availability of menu-driven screens will not obviate the need for training programs, on-line help, and manuals.[26] How many of these amenities should be provided and at what cost? EPA's general approach to the TRI database was to ensure that user aids would be available, but not all in the first year. For example, the agency argued that it was not necessary to support time-series analysis (comparing data from more than one year) in the first year or two of the database. Without funding for Title III, EPA had to limit the amenities it provided.

The decision about the extent of user aids was not examined in detail because resources were so limited. When Title III is more adequately funded, however, EPA will have to consider the appropriate level of user-friendly services to provide. How should it do that?

One answer parallels answers to similar questions for all kinds of government services or regulation: EPA should provide those services whose social benefits exceed their costs and for which people could not afford to pay individually. The problem with this guideline, as we have seen in the decisions concerning the TRI database, is that it is very difficult to judge that point with any exactitude. Some more extreme cases are reasonably clear: No single person should have to pay to have Title III data put onto the computer, just as no single person should have to pay for a laboratory study of a proposed food additive. On the other hand, government should not pay to conduct an analysis of the data that allows a citizen to file a successful personal injury case against a neighborhood polluter. User-friendly software falls somewhere between these two cases; if, as suggested in the discussion of computerization of sections 311 and 312, it costs local governments less to develop such software than to pay for staff to answer citizens' questions, government should pay for the software development.

But why should a single local government pay for such software, when all the local governments need it? Surely some additional benefit would be obtained if a more central unit of government paid for the development of the software and then provided it to the localities at cost. Would the resulting product be insensitive to different local needs? Are the benefits to be gained by making it responsive to any individual differences large enough to offset losses from having many government agencies create or cause to be created similar but not identical software?

Another important consideration in this calculation is that RTK data differs from some other kinds of data in that it is generally of more use to the community as a whole than to any single citizen. Whereas product labels contain instructions for safe use that the individual may choose to follow or risk ignoring, RTK data only has effect if groups of citizens decide that it has pointed out an unacceptable risk and agree to take action together to limit that risk. The reader might reasonably draw either of two contradictory conclusions from this statement: first, that the collective nature of the enterprise devalues RTK information for any single person, so that government must do a lot of manipulating and analyzing just to make it likely that citizens will avail themselves of the right to know; conversely, that it is not worthwhile for the government to add all that value to the information, because any collective actions citizens take will ultimately be taken through the agency of the government anyway.

In short, economic or regulatory analysis alone cannot provide the answers to these questions. The TRI database remains in government hands in part because the data needed to complete a useful regulatory analysis were simply not available. An ideology or philosophy of government must also play a role in deciding just how much the government should do for citizens in providing, computerizing, and analyzing the data that Title III has made available. The TRI database also remains in government hands in part because some citizens believed that government would be avoiding its responsibilities, even denying them the right to know, by privatizing Title III data.

Conclusion

Information is not free. EPA estimated that the cost to industry of providing the section 313 emissions data would be $591 million, or about $12,900 per facility in the first year and about $9,000 per facility in subsequent years, and the cost of fulfilling the section 311 and 312 reporting requirements would be $708 million over ten years, of which $162 million would be incurred in the first year.[27] Industry believes that these estimates, especially the one for emissions data, are low; EPA assumed it would take about 400 hours to make the estimates, but it is taking three or four times that amount.[28] After the data are submitted, moreover, EPA must computerize them; the agency also bore the costs of designing the database.

Once the data are public, individuals incur costs in acquiring them, even if they are "free." For RTK data, these costs will include going to the relevant agency to look at the forms or learning how to manipulate the TRI public database to receive answers to questions. There are also costs entailed in making the data into useful information; supplementary information about individual chemicals and general risk assessment will be needed in order to make sense of the data provided by each facility. There are costs entailed in understanding the information. People have to perform mental manipulation of the data--not only adding together pounds of chemicals reported or ranking substances on the basis of their risks, but evaluating what the ranks mean: Is this risky enough for me to worry further about it? If it is, what actions shall I take? In short, cognitive capabilities are limited just as money is limited, so information processing is not free even if the information itself appears to be.

Earlier information-provision policies did not usually take these problems into account, assuming that the government's responsibility ended when it had ensured that information became available. Citizens could reduce risk or not as they chose; meanwhile, government obtained the benefit of being able to say that regulation was occurring without incurring the costs of creating or enforcing standards. Title III forced EPA to confront the problems more directly because it seemed to be more than a risk reduction policy--it called for citizens to *know*.

Each of the four kinds of RTK implies a different level of government effort (and individual effort) concerning information about hazardous materials in the community. The basic and the risk reduction forms of RTK are merely extensions of earlier information policies--make the data public and see what people do with it. The risk reduction form assumes that industry might prefer to change its habits rather than making certain potentially inflammatory information public. The other two forms of RTK impose a greater burden on government and also on citizens. The better-decisionmaking form requires meaningful information to be disseminated to the public; EPA must either analyze data or build easy-to-use software that allows citizens to analyze the TRI data for themselves. "Change the balance of power" is the form of RTK reflected in the requests for EPA to make such sophisticated software available immediately and, more important, in the pressure on EPA to keep the TRI database inside the agency. In both cases, citizens incur a responsibility to acquire and act upon the data with enough understanding that their demands are reasonable.

If present policy can be inferred from EPA's actions concerning the TRI database, it would seem to fall in the middle of the continuum, between risk reduction and better decisionmaking; the agency has kept the data within the government but is moving deliberately on the access software.

In the long run, this choice may be only a temporary one. If Congress decides to extend public access to other data acquired by EPA or other regulatory agencies in the course of their duties, it may turn out to be cheaper and more effective to establish an agencywide or even governmentwide clearinghouse, in which a few government employees are given the expensive training needed to acquire and manipulate a wide variety of data, rather than designing friendly software and training thousands or millions of citizens to use the data less effectively. Most likely, a combination of both approaches will be needed to meet the differing abilities and interests of our heterogeneous population. The balance that is ultimately achieved will depend on the demands of citizens for RTK data; in the short run, however, government must focus on reducing the costs of the data so that citizens can and will make use of them. Like so many rights, RTK must be nourished before it takes root and grows on its own.

Notes

1. This point is made eloquently in Michael O'Hare, Lawrence Bacow, and Debra Sanderson, *Facility Siting and Public Opposition* (New York: Van Nostrand Reinhold, 1983), pp. 103-104, and is made fully in Michael O'Hare, "Information Management and Public Choice," in John Crecine, ed., *Research in Public Policy Analysis and Management*, vol. 1 (Greenwich, Conn.: JAI Press, 1981), pp. 223-256.

2. V. Kerry Smith, William H. Desvousges, Ann Fisher, and F. Reed Johnson, *Communicating Radon Risk Effectively: A Mid-Course Evaluation* (Washington, D.C.: EPA, July 1987).

3. This study is discussed in Chapter 6. Martha R. Fowlkes and Patricia Y. Miller, "Chemicals and Community at Love Canal," in Branden B. Johnson and Vincent T. Covello, eds., *The Social and Cultural Construction of Risk*, (Amsterdam: D. Reidel, 1987), pp. 55-78.

4. This is my calculation based on the RIA's estimate that technical personnel work at $29.92 per hour and assuming that it will take approximately 45 minutes to contact the U.S. Geological Survey. Other documents, including the RIA (see note 16) and the ICF report (see note 10), have slightly different estimates.

5. See the Final Rule for Submission of Section 313 Reports, 53 Fed. Reg. 4516 (February 16, 1988). (Hereafter, Final 313 Rule.)

6. OMB Circular A-130, 50 Fed. Reg. 52748 (December 24, 1985).

7. Hampshire Research Associates, Inc., *User Friendliness of OTS: Information Resources and Systems*, March 28, 1986. (OTS is the Office of Toxic Substances of EPA.)

8. Warren Muir, "Some Thoughts About Toxic Substances and Hazardous Waste Data Policy Issues," prepared for the Bauman Family Foundation Right-to-Know Meeting, October 8-9, 1987, p. 23.

9. See, for example, the discussion of the Securities Exchange Commission in Henry Perritt, "Electronic Acquisition and Release of Federal Agency Information," Report prepared for the Administrative Conference of the United States, Washington, D.C., October 1, 1988.

10. ICF, Inc., "Draft Economic Analysis for Section 313 Rulemaking," prepared for U.S., EPA, Office of Toxic Substances, Regulatory Impacts Branch, December 10, 1986, pp. 4-9 (part of a package entitled "Section 313 Reporting Rule Package Collection of Draft Documents," January 1987). (Hereafter, ICF report.) Also see CRC Systems, Inc., "Public Report for Options to Make the Toxic Release Inventory (TRI) Data Base Accessible to the Public," March 4, 1988, which evaluates these options in more detail. (Hereafter "Public Report.")

11. ICF report, p. 51.

12. Hampshire Research Associates, Inc., "Packaging and Disseminating SARA Section 313 Toxic Release Inventory Data," Alexandria, Va., November, 1987, p. 18. Gary D. Bass, executive director, OMB Watch, "Testimony Before a Public Meeting of the Environmental Protection Agency on the Toxic Release Inventory Database," Washington, D.C., March 30, 1988, passim. (Hereafter, Bass testimony). Also see "EPA Public Meeting on Database Access" (summary report of public meeting, Washington, D.C., April 30, 1987, typewritten), in which potential users argue for ease of use.

13. In addition to the sources listed in note 12, see also Draft Memorandum from Jerry Berman to the Toxic Release Inventory Working Group, March 30, 1988 (hereafter Berman memo) and EPA "White Paper," a report from several regional EPA adminstrators on Title III policy, February 1988. The "Public Report" identifies some of these features as "Tier B" or "Tier C" amenities that would enhance the utility of the database but are not requirements. The Bass testimony and Berman memo in particular disagree with this contention.

14. "Public Report," pp. 3-14, 3-15.

15. Described in "Public Report, "pp. 3-9, 3-10.

16. Preliminary estimate: developed by multiplying the total estimated user population (about 250,000) by the ratio of users of existing chemistry-related databases to all database users (about .8 percent). The number of users would therefore be about 2,000; if access costs $100 per hour, experience suggests that the database will be used about 88,000 times a year. "Public Report," pp. 2-2 through 2-4. Later estimate: reached by assuming that the annual number of public inquiries would equal 20 percent of the total number of reports filed, yielding an estimate of 64,000. See ICF, Inc., "Regulatory Impact Analysis in Support of Final Rulemaking Under Section 313 of Title III

of SARA," February 1988, pp. 5-17. (Often called the RIA.) The basis for selecting 20 percent is not documented.

17. See "Public Report," pp. 2-2, 2-6. A representative of the Local Government Commission estimated that only 20 to 30 percent of local governments in California have appropriate equipment. Hampshire report, p. 9.

18. U.S., Congress, House, *Superfund Amendments and Reauthorization Act of 1986: Conference Report*, 99th Cong., 2d sess., Report 99-962, p. 299.

19. On reducing the number of users, see "Public Report," p. 1-2. The idea about stimulating additional interest from interview with Gary Bass, executive director, OMB Watch, Washington, D.C., May 11, 1988.

20. "Public Report," pp. 4-3, 4-4.

21. "Public Report," p. 4-4. Also see Hampshire Research Associates, "Packaging Title III Data," p. 20. In a letter written on April 26, 1988, to Charles Elkins, director, Office of Toxic Substances, Environmental Protection Agency, Gary Bass of OMB Watch, writing as a member of the Working Group on Community Right to Know, stated, "Because we were informed . . . that an Interagency Agreement with NLM would be arranged by April 19, and because of the need for moving quickly . . . we concentrated on the NLM option. This is not to say that NLM is the first choice of the Working Group. We believe there are fundamental long-term policy questions that still have not been adequately addressed. For example, does placement of the TRI database at NLM set a precedent for other mandates from Congress to make information publicly accessible? . . . How will placement at NLM complicate the ability to link TRI information with other pertinent data housed within EPA's own databases?"

22. Hampshire report, p. 9; Bass testimony, p. 2. These sources as well as interviews conducted with a wide range of potential users inform the following two paragraphs.

23. "Public Report," p. 3-7. Several commentators have questioned both the cost estimates and the separability of some of the system characteristics. See Bass testimony and Berman memo: also telephone interview with Ben Goldman, Public Data, Inc., May 13, 1988.

24. On these questions, see Hampshire report, Bass testimony, and Berman testimony.

25. Goldman interview.

26. See, for example, the results of early interactions reported in Working Group on Community Right to Know, "Initial Outline: Toxic Release Inventory Database Interagency Agreement," April 25, 1988, p. 11. (Report prepared by Denise Vesuvio, Bruce Geisert, and Jerry Berman.)

27. For section 313 costs, see the Final 313 Rule, 53 Fed. Reg. 4521 (February 16, 1988). For the others, see 52 Fed. Reg. 38362 (October 15, 1988). Costs to government for sections 311 and 312 were estimated at about $43 million in the first year.

28. Elizabeth Grillo Olson, "When a Chemical Company Is Forced to Tell All," *New York Times*, July 3, 1988, business section, p. 8 (national edition), reports that Nepara, Inc. has spent 1,400 hours on the estimates. Texaco, Inc.,

in Austin, Texas, was able to monitor about 6 elements a day of the total of 700 in their small research facility: interview with Guy Crawford, Texaco, Inc., July 18, 1988. The increases in estimation time are a result of the inapplicability of EPA's estimation techniques; facilities therefore undertook direct measurement.

PART 3
Remedies: Making RTK Work

Where is the wisdom we have lost in knowledge? Where is the knowledge we have lost in information?

--T. S. Eliot, *Choruses from the Rock*

9 / Improving Right to Know

It is easier to criticize than to propose remedies for problems. In the previous chapters, I have described implementation of Title III, the statute that embodies right to know for most Americans today, and have uncovered some barriers to RTK and some problems that afflict it. The purpose of this chapter is to begin to describe an RTK program that would overcome many of these difficulties. Although the remedies are phrased specifically for Title III, they would apply to most information-provision or RTK programs. The chapter is divided into two major sections: statutory and programmatic recommendations and a discussion of the nature and format of the information that is provided.

Some of the problems discussed in Chapters 4 through 8 are not amenable to immediate solution. These issues are intertwined with the whole fabric of life in the United States: the proper role of government, the tort liability crisis, the decline of deference to experts and social institutions, economic growth and environmental protection, democracy and citizen participation. In Chapter 10, I consider these larger issues, focusing on the importance of the right to know in the context of U.S. democracy. In this chapter, I suggest more immediate ways of making right to know more effective.

A Better Statute Better Implemented

One important criticism implicit throughout the earlier discussion is that the authors of Title III did not think carefully about the kinds of information that would be needed to fulfill the four different purposes of the law: emergency planning, emergency response, right to know, and emissions inventory. (I am not alone in making this criticism. Shortly after Title III was passed, one senator said that the law's complexity showed that the conferees had lost sight of what they were trying to achieve.[1]) Thus, the statute requires that the same information be reported more than once but does not require that some other information be reported at all. For example, Title III apparently assumes that the data submitted under the right-to-know sections will also be useful for emergency planning and response; we know this because these data are to be provided to fire departments as well as to LEPCs. In fact, the data to be reported under sections 311 and 312 are more obviously tailored to the needs of emergency planners than to the needs of citizens hoping to acquire useful information about chemicals in their communities. I have discussed the other kinds of information citizens might want in Chapters 5, 6, and 7. Several of the following suggestions are directed to this concern--not by asking Congress to rewrite the statute to indicate the ties between particular data and their purposes but by trying to ensure that appropriate information is readily available to those who want or need it. Table 9-1 summarizes the recommendations and indicates which of the four purposes of Title III would be advanced by implementing each of them.

Not all of the recommendations are appropriate to all the different conceptions of RTK. Those who believe that RTK is simply ensuring the availability of data would not think it necessary or appropriate for Congress or EPA to expend resources ensuring that supplementary information is readily available. The more extended definitions of RTK would, however, be improved by adoption of policies designed to improve delivery of data. Thus, the recommendations are arranged in a hierarchy: The earliest ones should improve all forms of RTK, whereas ones later in the list have a more restricted application. The subheadings describe the RTK goals that the recommendations are most likely to further.

Recommendations to Improve Provision of Data

Availability of accurate and consistent data is essential to all forms of RTK. The recommendations in this section are intended to improve the availability, quality, and accuracy of data. The reports and reporting formats, designation of covered facilities and chemicals, and other data to be reported can all be rationalized to ensure that citizens and emergency responders have the data they need without imposing confusing and duplicate reporting requirements.

For example, requiring separate reports for sections 302, 311, and 312 imposes unnecessary costs on reporting facilities, on agencies receiving reports, and on citizens attempting to acquire and understand the data. If each facility could submit only one form, even citizens in localities without computers would be able to obtain information easily about a particular facility and to compare data provided by facilities more readily. LEPCs and SERCs would have many fewer pieces of paper to manage and store; data entry would be easier when computers

TABLE 9-1 Recommendations and Title III Goals

	Goals[a]			
	1	2	3	4
1. Rationalize the reporting requirements.	√		√	
2. Untie Title III from the OSHA HCS.	√		√	
3. Designate a single hazardous chemical list.	√	√	√	√
4. Simplify the threshold quantities.	√	√	√	√
5. Extend Title III to all government facilities.	√	√	√	√
6. Create a demonstration program for direct emissions measurements.				√
7. Provide for more orderly updates in reports.	√		√	√
8. Provide for limited preemption.	√		√	
9. Ensure that MSDSs include the 5 hazard categories.	√		√	
10. EPA should monitor effects of trade secrets.	√		√	√
11. EPA should develop a database of databases.			√	√
12. EPA should continue to sponsor relevant research.			√	√
13. SERCs should help LEPCs with the fewest resources.	√	√		
14. Refine methodology for hazardous materials transportation plan.	√			
15. Provide for funding of Title III.	√	√	√	√
16. States should adopt Title III legislation.	√	√	√	
17. EPA should assist computerization of SERCs/LEPCs.	√	√	√	
18. EPA should develop basic information about chemicals.			√	
19. SERCs/LEPCs should emphasize public outreach.			√	
20. LEPCs should regard emergency planning as ongoing.	√			
21. Support LEPCs as a focus for government/business/citizen interaction.	√		√	

[a] Goals: 1=emergency planning; 2=emergency notification; 3=right to know; 4=emissions inventory.

are installed; and reporting facilities would be more likely to report fully and accurately. With computers, the data on the single form are easily routed to different databases designed for the particular needs of different users.

Tier 1 reports are disliked both by many reporting facilities, because double-counting of substances that fit into more than one of the five hazard categories misrepresents the true amount of hazardous substances they store, and by users, especially emergency responders for whom they provide no real idea of what kind of substances to expect. Social resources are squandered when 3,000 LEPCs and 50 states have to pass laws or write rules saying they don't want Tier 1 reports. Presumably, the purpose of Tier 1 was to provide some protection for facilities beyond that offered by the trade secret provisions, allowing them not to list chemicals by name. Trade-secret protection should be adequate to this purpose. Therefore, RTK would be improved if Congress would

1. *Rationalize the reporting requirements--specifically, create one single reporting form that applies to sections 302, 311, and 312; eliminate the section 312 Tier 1 form; and prohibit facilities from providing bales of MSDSs to LEPCs in lieu of lists. Instead, allow LEPCs and SERCs to determine how they want to obtain the kinds of information provided on MSDSs, asking facilities for specific ones as needed.*

The definitions of covered and exempted facilities also limit the quality and consistency of the data available under Title III. For example, Congress tied section 311 and 312 reports to the OSHA Hazard Communication Standard. When Title III was passed, the OSHA HCS applied only to manufacturing facilities; under court order, OSHA then extended the standard to all private facilities. Sections 311 and 312 of Title III would have applied to tens of thousands of stores and facilities starting in May 1988 if the OSHA HCS had not become mired in judicial jockeying. The LEPCs and SERCs thus won a reprieve from inundation by paper until November 1988, and facility representatives won more time to become familiar with the requirements of both the OSHA HCS and Title III. Congress presumably did not expect the HCS to be expanded quite so radically and, therefore, never considered whether it is appropriate or useful for Title III to apply to so many facilities. If Congress would decide which kinds of facilities should be covered and state so in an amended statute, community right to know and emergency planning would not be caught up in the fate of employee right to know.

2. Sever the ties between Title III and the OSHA Hazard Communication Standard. Designate the kinds of facilities that need to report using criteria relevant to the purpose of the law.

Title III specifies two separate chemical lists and gives a more general definition of hazard for chemicals to be reported under sections 311 and 312. Congress presumably hoped to tailor lists to particular regulatory purposes. In this case, any benefits of keeping the chemical lists small are at least partly outweighed by the costs to regulated facilities of keeping track of which chemical is covered by which section of Title III (and other related laws with similar but not identical lists). Industry representatives with whom I have spoken indicate that they would rather have one somewhat longer list than several partly overlapping shorter lists. Citizens and regulatory agencies would benefit from the higher compliance rate that simpler reporting requirements engender. EPA has taken one step toward this goal by making the CERCLA (superfund) and Title III section 304 spill-reporting requirements and lists of covered substances the same.[2] Congress should

3. Designate a single hazardous chemical list appropriate for sections 302, 304, and 313; clarify that all chemicals on the list are covered by section 312; and consolidate other chemical lists insofar as possible.

Another factor that complicates compliance and thereby compromises data quality is the differences in the reportable quantities required by sections 302, 311/312, and 313. Again, industry representatives indicate that lower but consistent thresholds are preferable to higher ones that vary among the sections and among substances. Inasmuch as EPA has stated that threshold amounts are not to be taken alone as indicators of risk,[3] the diverse quantities impede both compliance and RTK. At this writing, EPA was reportedly going to propose to keep the reporting quantities at 10,000 pounds, which is inconsistent with many state laws. Congress should alter the provisions of the statute to allow EPA to

4. Simplify the threshold planning quantities and reportable quantities.

Another impediment to acquiring all the data citizens need is that Title III does not cover public facilities. Some states have included such facilities in their laws, but federal facilities are never included. But government facilities include city water-treatment plants that store and use great quantities of chlorine, a dangerous airborne toxic, and federal army bases that store and use a range of substances from explosives to poisons. Congress should

5. Extend Title III to all government facilities.

The quality of data provided under section 313 is likely to be worse than the quality of data provided under the other parts of Title III because of difficulties with the techniques for estimating and even measuring emissions. Although Congress hoped to protect the regulated community from the high costs of direct measurement of emissions, the result of this requirement in the law is data that cannot readily be compared across facilities. EPA's present guidelines for estimating emissions drew heavily on a study of emissions from large petrochemical plants whose processes and equipment differ strongly from those at many other kinds of facilities. As it acquires additional data, EPA will be able to refine its estimation methods. To make this work, however, EPA will need to conduct some field tests to check on the quality of the data submitted. Incentives or a demonstration program to make direct measurements in a variety of industries and sizes of facilities would allow EPA to develop better estimation techniques in concert with industry while keeping industry costs reasonable. Congress and EPA should

6. Provide incentives or a demonstration program for direct measurements of emissions for two years under section 313, so that EPA in concert with industry can develop more accurate emissions models.

Failure to update chemical inventory information may also affect the quality of data. Section 302 provides that any facility experiencing significant changes in the reportable on-site substances must notify the LEPC, SERC, and fire department within sixty days. Because data from the chemical inventories submitted under sections 311 and 312 are also to be used by emergency planners and responders, and because those sections cover additional substances not covered by section 302, facilities should be required to report major changes in their inventories as well. Representatives of emergency responders, especially firefighters, and affected industries should be brought together to develop a reasonable approach to updating information relevant to emergency response more frequently than once a year.

One related action was taken by the Travis County, Texas, LEPC, which added a question to its section 311/312 reporting form asking whether a substance will be on site in the year following the reporting year. It took this action when one of the facility representatives on the LEPC mentioned that in response to Title III, his company had decided not to use a particular substance any more. This decision would not have been apparent to the LEPC until more than eighteen months after it was taken (decision made in July 1988 and report for 1988 filed in March 1989; report for 1989, the first full year without substance, filed in March 1990) without the additional question. Congress and EPA should

7. Provide for more orderly updates in reports.

Another source of complexity in the reporting requirements may be conflicting state laws. Agencies do not willingly give up power or programs. To the extent that conflicting state or local laws impede RTK by creating additional reporting forms, requiring the same data in different formats, or otherwise making information more difficult to understand and use, the laws at the lower levels of government should be preempted. Lower reporting quantities alone would not constitute grounds for preemption.

One important area for preemption is reporting dates. All facilities should file all required information on the same date, not some on one date and some on another. The March deadline should provide ample opportunity for facilities to gather information about the previous year.

8. Provide for limited preemption of conflicting state and local laws, especially provisions concerning reporting dates and duplicative reporting requirements. Lower reporting quantities alone should not be grounds for preemption.

A final source of confusion in data is MSDSs. Congress specified the use of Material Safety Data Sheets in Title III, probably because they were the primary source of health-effects information available at the time. Under the OSHA Hazard Communication Act, which prescribes the use of MSDSs, suppliers are free to choose their own descriptions of hazards using more than twenty hazard categories described by OSHA. This means that the recipients of MSDSs are left to determine into which of the five EPA hazard categories the substance fits. If suppliers were required to provide this information right on the MSDS, different facilities would not provide different hazard descriptions for the same chemical, impeding RTK.

9. *If MSDSs are retained as the primary method of disseminating health-effects information, ensure that they report the five EPA hazard categories.*

Finally, trade secrets may impede access to data. In Chapter 5, it was reported that EPA had to collapse ten hazard categories into four in order to preserve the trade secrecy of the chemical identities of certain substances. Thus, citizens are prevented from making as detailed risk assessments as they otherwise could. Recognizing that both trade secrecy and RTK are important values, EPA should continue to explore these circumstances so that the actual balance between the two may be more clearly understood and more informed choices made. At the same time, EPA should keep track of the number of trade secret requests that are submitted; if there are very few, the level and need for trade secrets should be reevaluated as RTK is extended into more areas of governmental activity.

10. *EPA should continue to monitor the extent to which citizens will not be able to assess risks in their communities because of trade secret declarations.*

Recommendations to Improve Risk Reduction

Four recommendations concern ways to improve government agencies' capacities to use Title III data and other powers under Title III to reduce risks from hazardous materials in the community.

One impediment to regulation is the difficulty of tying together information received under the different programs. EPA has more than seventy "information products" concerning hazardous chemicals.[4] A database of databases, which would describe the particular items of data in each as well as the chemicals included, could assist people in finding the information they want. EPA's "Roadmaps" computer program is a good start on this task. Ultimately, a "gateway" computer program should be available that asks users what information they seek and helps them find it among many different databases.

11. *EPA should continue to develop a database of databases about hazardous materials.*

There are many other areas in which missing data complicates the task of risk analysis and management. Many of them are detailed in Chapter 7. Although many of these questions will never be fully answered, EPA and other agencies should not reduce their efforts to acquire better information about health effects, emissions, and environmental fate.

12. EPA should continue to develop better models for estimating releases from facilities, conduct research on the environmental fate of such emissions, and work with other federal, state, local, and private agencies to acquire health data as a basis for future epidemiological research about the delayed effects of chemical exposures at low levels.

One important form of risk reduction comes from formulation and implementation of the emergency response plans. However, the ad hoc implementation of Title III that has occurred thus far has resulted in a two-tier system: LEPCs that were formed in areas where local governments were providing similar services, especially emergency response, have generally managed to collect data and formulate plans, whereas LEPCs in areas without similar infrastructure are performing their functions poorly or not at all. SERCs need to ensure that the latter group receive assistance of various kinds. In Texas, one form of assistance many need is on-site training courses; because the state is so large, traveling to the usual training centers entails missing several days of work and a concomitant loss of pay for volunteer emergency responders. Nighttime and weekend courses offered in remote areas could help overcome this problem. These more disadvantaged LEPCs should also be the first to be tied to any computer networks that are established; SERCs that do not establish networks should seek ways to get computers and coded data out to the LEPCs. If EPA developed some planning software, that could also assist the second tier of LEPCs.

13. SERCs should develop means of providing technical assistance to LEPCs with the fewest resources.

Another area in which LEPCs are experiencing difficulty is in transforming chemical inventory data into information that would be useful in preparing for emergencies involving transport of hazardous materials. EPA could commission some studies to develop methods for achieving this goal and then ensure that the best results are made available directly to the LEPCs, perhaps through intelligent computer software.

14. EPA should work with LEPCs to develop a method for using chemical inventories to develop a hazardous materials transportation plan.

Improving Citizens' Participation in Decisionmaking

Citizens can only be full participants in decisions about hazardous materials in their communities if they can interpret the data provided under Title III and decide what it means for themselves, their families, and their communities. Not only does this form of RTK create a greater role for government in refining information, but it also seems to require a larger governmental role in breaking down institutional barriers to acquiring data and participating in their use, including barriers raised by relationships among the different levels of government. The recommendations in this section are relevant for those who believe that these are proper governmental activities.

Perhaps the most serious barrier to a strong form of RTK is lack of funds. Although access to data and risk reduction would both benefit from additional resources, lack of money becomes the critical factor in limiting implementation of a more participatory form of RTK.

The RTK program is now at the point where lack of funding is having two undesirable effects. First, it has created two classes of citizens--those whose areas have emergency plans or who have access to RTK data and those whose areas do not have effective plans or who cannot get the data. The former usually live in jurisdictions that had existing programs whose staff and equipment could be deployed for RTK, whereas the latter do not. Second, social resources are being inefficiently deployed as many different local and state agencies attempt to discover for themselves how to accomplish the same tasks. With resources, EPA could develop guidelines, software, or technical assistance that would minimize such duplication of effort.

A sound RTK program would incorporate the elements that are included in the following recommendations, ranging from information products suitable to the needs of different audiences to enforcement staff. Training grants for emergency response and emergency planning, which were deleted from the 1990 federal budget, should also be restored. If Congress imposed a fee of $1 per worker for the RTK program (to fund both worker and community RTK), EPA and OSHA would each have more than $80 million. If these funds were used initially to help SERCs and LEPCs, they would have the greatest impact on citizens. Another source of income could be the fines that EPA imposes for noncompliance. Congress should allow monies from fines to be returned to the agency for use in further implementation, rather than going to the Treasury Department, as they now do.

EPA would not have sufficient funds to help every LEPC or SERC. Two different approaches could be taken to distributing the money initially. One would be based on need, as measured by a combination of population and number of reporting facilities. An alternative method would focus on areas without other resources. Although EPA would presumably like to reward states (and states reward localities) that have taken the initiative in obtaining funding, such an approach would increase the differences that are already apparent among the have and the have-not areas. Any granting agency should adopt an "each one teach one" approach so that areas without technical expertise can learn from better-endowed areas.

15. Congress should provide for funding of Title III.

One of the important institutional barriers to RTK arose because Title III established state and local bodies not accounted for by state law. State statutes adopting many of the provisions of Title III may help overcome these barriers. State statutes are most useful when they include the following provisions: allow state and local officials to enforce the provisions of Title III/the state law; provide for collection of penalties; fund the program through fees or appropriations; provide liability protection for SERC and LEPC members; clarify responsibilities of SERCs and LEPCs; and remove technical incompatibilities between existing state law and the federal law.

16. States should adopt legislation implementing Title III.

Computerization is essential to the broader form of RTK because it allows citizens to obtain an overview of the community as a whole--a comparative framework within which to assess risks. Computerization also aids emergency responders, can reduce costs for both the regulated industry and regulatory agencies, and may provide special benefits for small business under certain circumstances.

One important lack is in software that allows the public to acquire information easily. Many database packages are hard to use and some require that each potential way of sorting the data has been thought through in advance. Governmental intervention in this area is especially important, since there is no "market" in any conventional sense for such software. The kinds of amenities that the public-interest groups asked EPA to provide for the public TRI database should also be available at the local level for the chemical inventories. EPA and SERCs should ensure that LEPCs receive the section 313 emissions data to supplement the chemical inventories.

17. EPA should assist SERCs and LEPCs in computerizing. If it cannot or does not want to provide hardware, it should provide software or guidelines for software for data acquisition and dissemination, "smart forms," and relevant expert systems.

Health-effects information is central to the broader form of RTK. For a variety of reasons, most information about hazardous chemicals concerns workplace exposures, safe handling, and emergency response. In the surveys of citizens in New Jersey and Massachusetts, however, citizens asked for information about "routes of community exposure." Actual formats for providing such information are discussed in more detail in the following portion of this chapter. Here it is important to note that an important impediment to providing citizens with brief health-effects information is the concern that they will misinterpret it and the providers will incur liability thereby. If a multidisciplinary committee (leavened with the realism of some citizen consumers of information) sponsored by a range of organizations developed a brief description for each of the chemicals on the section 313 list and later expanded to the section 302 list and others, however, we would have a single standard description that everyone could use. We know that workers and citizens find unsettling the fact that different MSDSs for the same substance contain different information; the program described here would help overcome this problem as well.

18. EPA should establish a committee including representatives of the public, academia, and industry and covering a wide range of disciplines to develop a noncopyrighted set of basic information about chemicals that is useful for citizens.

Another barrier to citizens' participating in decisions is lack of knowledge of their new right. In the survey of more than 600 citizens in Texas conducted in February 1988, 80 percent stated that they had not previously heard about a federal law passed in 1986 that allows citizens to gain access to information on hazardous materials stored and used in their communities. The survey of thirty-six LEPC chairpeople conducted a month later revealed that only half the LEPCs had met, and less than half of those had discussed RTK or public access to data. The survey of citizens who had actually filed requests in Massachusetts and New Jersey also indicated that people have heard much more about worker RTK than about community RTK; New Jersey is working on a model citizen outreach program for LEPCs.[5] Outreach programs do not need to be conducted in perpetuity; after a few years, citizens will be used to exercising RTK and will tell others about it. RTK and emergency response should certainly be mentioned in schools during discussions of environmental policy and consumer services.

19. SERCs and LEPCs should give added attention to public outreach and public access to data.

Citizens' abilities and desires to participate will increase as they hear more about RTK and develop interest and even expertise. In many cases, the short deadline and citizens' lack of knowledge about the law combined to prevent them from participating in work on local emergency plans. Citizens should still have the opportunity for meaningful participation, however, because other factors tended to prevent LEPCs from developing high-quality plans: the relatively short time between submission of chemical inventory data in March 1988 and the deadline for submitting the emergency plan in October 1988, the general lack of computers at the local level, and the lack of information about Title III among potential reporting facilities. LEPCs that sought additional data from facilities were even more likely not to have the data available during the planning period.

In short, LEPCs should not consider that they have finished their tasks by submitting a plan in October 1988. Planning is of necessity an ongoing task; one effect of Title III is that facilities will reassess the quantities and nature of the substances they store and use. These changes must be reflected in future plans. At the same time, the ongoing planning process will allow for additional citizen participation. EPA has reflected these points in a late fall 1988 publication called *It's Not Over in October*.

20. LEPCs should regard emergency planning as an ongoing activity.

Finally, an important institutional barrier to participation is the lack of any formal mechanisms in most localities through which citizens may meet and work with the private sector. In many communities, mechanisms for ensuring citizen input even to government are minimal. Participatory RTK seems to call for creating and supporting such institutions; perhaps the LEPCs can serve in such a capacity. Although some citizens will be able to develop institutions for themselves, government assistance in ensuring that citizens can participate on an equal basis may be necessary at least for a while.

21. EPA, SERCs, and local leaders should support LEPCs as a focus for citizen-government-industry interactions.

Better Information Formats

My recommendations, to a greater or lesser degree, cover three of the five issues elaborated in Chapters 4 through 8: institutional constraints, quality and quantity of data, and resource constraints. The remaining issues are also central to RTK: the technical difficulty and the form of information relevant to decisions about risks. In this section, I consider these problems, suggesting an approach to providing information that should be applicable to a wide range of programs.

In short, I suggest that agencies implementing RTK use public resources to make available a "first level" of information that is brief and simple; people who want more information, including affected citizens, LEPC planners, and regulators, would be directed to it, while people who did not want more information would not be provided with it. This approach is based on three important considerations: First, different people have different predilections for information in general; second, different people want the information for different purposes; and, third, as suggested in Chapter 8, society should provide information that is unlikely to be provided otherwise.

One well-known analysis of information policies suggests that people have inherently different interests in information: Some are "fact respecters," who prefer to base their opinions on substantive information; some are "expertise takers" who adopt opinions of policy proposals from others who have relevant expertise; others are more responsive to other cues, including leadership, peers, or personality.[6] These attitudes are tied to other aspects of personality but may also differ according to the issue. Some people who are not generally information gatherers may be very interested in the facts about an issue that is especially germane. People like some of the Woburn residents discussed in Chapter 6 become experts on technical subjects when the issue is very important.

Quite apart from the predilections of information consumers, information may serve many different purposes. For example, researchers studying the presentation of information to people whose homes have high levels of radon, a naturally ocurring radioactive substance, identified four different goals for a risk communication program: transferring information about radon to individuals; helping them form a perception of their risks from radon; reducing demand for additional information; and motivating high-risk households to take actions to reduce their exposures.[7] We have seen that Title III also has a variety of purposes, each of which makes use of the reported data in a somewhat different way. Emergency responders want to have immediate access to the names of chemicals stored in particular locations and to information about appropriate response measures. At least under the participatory form of RTK, citizens presumably want more information--first for ranking substances or facilities according to risk and then for making more precise decisions about the particular substances in question.

Information would be easier to understand if it were clearly related to these purposes. Some of the difficulty laypeople have in comprehending technical information and using it for making decisions lies in their difficulty in deciding which particular items are most relevant to the decision at hand. Is the LD_{50} of a substance germane to a decision to ask for additional air monitoring? Is it important to know the exact location of a substance within a facility in order to determine which citizens are at risk from a spill? The approach implicit in Title III is to lay out a large amount of information, allowing the users to choose what is best for their purposes--an approach that is more likely to exacerbate than to alleviate problems arising from citizens' difficulties in understanding technical information.

Material Safety Data Sheets constitute an excellent example. They are the primary source of health-effects information mandated by Title III. They are usually several pages long and include a lot of detailed information that may put citizens off. Figure 6-2 included a few excerpts from an MSDS. Note the extent to which it uses technical terms, such as anorexia, narcosis, LDLO, and ACGIH TLV. Because MSDSs are legal documents under the OSHA Hazard Communication Standard, moreover, they contain a lot of information about the results of laboratory experiments, such as the LD_{50} for inhalation in dogs, and not very much evaluative information that would allow the user to understand what those experiments mean or how that LD_{50} compares to the LD_{50} for other substances. MSDSs also emphasize safe handling and emergency response.

Part of the problem arises from the fact that Congress took a tool intended for one purpose--helping employees use substances safely in the workplace and identify possible overexposures--and deployed it for the very different purpose of giving information to members of the community about hazardous substances. Thus, MSDSs contain a lot of information about things citizens don't generally care about, such as safe handling, and too little about others that they do care about, especially likely routes and levels of community exposure. In the New Jersey/Massachusetts survey, the Massachusetts residents, in particular, complained about the difficulty of reading MSDSs to extract the information they wanted. A couple of respondents were especially upset by the availability of different MSDSs for the same substance that differ from one another in form and even content; many fail to include information on chronic health effects. Again, this is a result of the status of the MSDS under OSHA; because the law requires each shipper to determine whether the product is hazardous, the accompanying MSDS reflects the shipper's individual assessment of the hazard.

Instead of MSDSs, New Jersey residents may receive fact sheets prepared by the New Jersey Department of Health. These documents are also long (six pages) but include much less technical language and evaluate health risks. (They are also available in Spanish.) Four pages from a fact sheet are shown in Figure 3-1. In spring 1988, EPA decided to make the New Jersey fact sheets available to SERCs for distribution along with the section 313 emissions inventory information in an effort to overcome some of the problems associated with MSDSs. The fact sheets still emphasize workplace exposures and emergency response, however, in compliance with the state law, and some users have complained about their length and technical nature as well.[8]

Many chemical companies, recognizing that the very complexity and unintelligibility of MSDSs might stimulate fear rather than contribute to a reasoned debate, developed their own fact sheets. An example of a typical one is found in Figure 9-1. Although easier to understand than either the MSDS or the New Jersey fact sheet, this presentation still avoids the important questions citizens have about exposures in the community rather than the workplace. This is not surprising, as little information is available in this area. Companies are often unwilling to incur potential liabilities by describing diseases that are not *known* to occur at low levels of exposure. Moreover, it is at precisely this point that any difficulties people experience in understanding probabilities come into play: Workplace exposure data, itself probabilistic, must be extrapolated to lower exposure levels and a probability determined for the unwanted effect; individuals must then interpret how that probability applies to themselves.

Right to know does not allow us the luxury of throwing up our hands in despair or hoping that citizens will be sensible enough to believe the interpretations provided by experts. Instead, it forces us to think though the kinds of information people need for particular decisions and to devise ways of presenting it that are responsive to those needs. Focusing only on "citizens," who, of course, comprise audiences with widely varying backgrounds and interests, and recognizing both the different demands for information by different people and the different purposes to which information may be put, we can still identify two related principles of information provision that will assist in understanding and using RTK data:

Product: Benzene

What is it?

Benzene is a colorless liquid used to make certain plastics, latexes for carpets and paint, Sytrofoam, and in the production of gasoline.

Where is it produced?

It is manufactured by ___ plants in ___ and ___.

How is it stored?

It is stored in steel tanks and underground salt domes.

What are exposure limits?

The federal government's workplace Permissible Exposure Limit (PEL) is 1 part per million for an eight-hour day.

What are possible effects of excessive exposure to humans?

Benzene is classified as a suspected carcinogen by certain government agencies. It can irritate the eyes and cause burns to the skin. If excessive amounts are inhaled, effects to the central nervous system and blood-forming organs may result. The inhalation of extremely large amounts of benzene in confined spaces may cause death.

How are workers protected from excessive exposure?

Employees wear protective equipment including goggles, rubber gloves, and boots. Respirators are available. The area is kept well ventilated and an air-monitoring system is used to ensure the workplace is kept below proper exposure levels.

What medical attention is needed for excessive exposure?

If the liquid comes into contact with the skin or eyes, irrigate immediately with flowing water. If inhalation occurs, remove to fresh air. If breathing is difficult, administer oxygen or apply mouth-to-mouth resuscitation. If swallowed, do not induce vomiting. Consult a physician.

How is product kept from entering the environment?

Benzene is kept tightly contained during production. Dikes and paved surfaces in storage and processing areas are used to prevent contamination to the ground and water. The substance is best disposed by incineration.

For more information, contact Jane Jones (333) 333-3333.

FIGURE 9-1 Sample industry chemical fact sheet

1. Allow users to have some control over the nature of the information they receive and the rate at which they receive it. The importance of this is illustrated through analogy with a visit to the doctor's office. If the doctor diagnoses a dread disease, he or she may immediately begin to list the treatment options, perhaps even asking the patient to choose one right then. On the way home, however, the patient thinks of dozens of additional questions that would bear on a decision. The patient could not mentally process the treatment alternatives because he or she was still coming to grips with the diagnosis. Similarly, citizens cannot absorb all the information about a new facility, a waste disposal site, or the chemicals at an existing facility in one dose. They have follow-up questions, different abilities to understand information, and different desires for additional data. Thus, public meetings, the traditional forum for risk communication, are seldom completely successful at transferring information.

2. Provide information that is branched and/or layered. Both are techniques for allowing individuals to exercise control over the information received. Branching recognizes that information is often hierarchically arranged, whereas layering emphasizes increased depth of understanding of a particular idea. Figure 9-2 illustrates both these approaches. Computers facilitate presenting information in this format by allowing citizens to delve deeper or move to other information contained in connected databases.

For citizens, most RTK purposes will be well served by a relatively simple first level of information that provides an introduction to the subject and includes pointers both to more detailed information and to branches. Figure 9-3 illustrates a format for introductory information about a particular chemical. (This is the simplified fact sheet mentioned in recommendation 18 earlier in this chapter.) It could serve as a handout at a public meeting, providing citizens with a reminder of what they learned and a reference for additional sources of information, or it could be the first information they acquire about a chemical as they peruse the LEPC database.

The choice of a particular chemical as an initial entry into RTK information is deliberate. (One advantage of computers is that properly programmed they can allow entry on any of the branches, whereas when information is given on paper we have to choose one branch.) Some experts, taking note of the scientific uncertainties surrounding health effects, especially of long-term, low-level exposures outside the workplace, believe that the best approach is to teach people about risk assessment in general. The Food and Drug Administration, for example, has a program to teach the public about the drug approval process as a way to get them to understand that

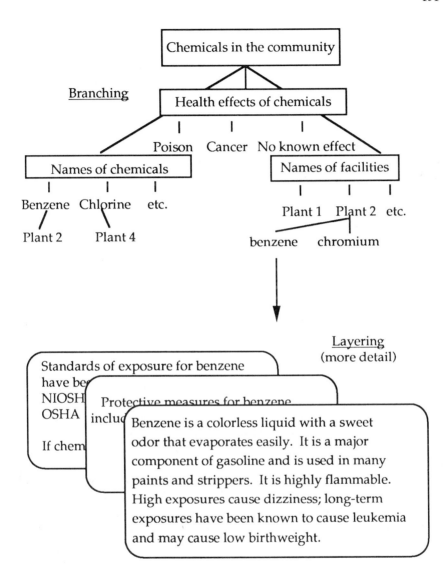

FIGURE 9-2 Branching and layering of information

there are inevitably risks in prescription drugs, but these are offset by the benefits and, moreover, that there are risks in not taking the drug properly. EPA is also working on public understanding of risk assessment as part of its Title III activities. However, I believe that people pay little attention to that kind of general information unless there is a reason to do so. Instead, they want specific information concerning particular chemicals to which they know they are being exposed, or perhaps about the chemicals known to cause symptoms they are experiencing. Once they begin to learn about the particular chemical or chemicals that interest them, some people will want to dig deeper to learn how we know about the health effects and will thus seek more general information about risk assessment.

The information sheet shown in Figure 9-3 embodies several findings from the surveys and other sources. It provides simple factual information about the chemical and its uses--a partial response to the often-asked question, "Why are they using that substance here?" It specifically answers a basic question that experts forget people may need answered: whether a substance is solid, liquid, or gas at usual temperature and pressure. It also describes sources of exposure other than emissions or spills from commercial facilities and available means of avoiding those exposures. This information serves two purposes: First, it puts the facility emissions into perspective; and, second, it helps to alleviate the frustration and concern aroused when people learn about a risk but are not told how to mitigate it.

The health-effects information is more controversial. The presentation rests on two assumptions: (1) Even when some desirable information does not exist, people should have ready access to whatever is known; and (2) even disagreeing experts can achieve consensus at some high-enough level of abstraction, creating information that is usable by nonexperts for "satisficing" decisions. The certainty with which we know about the health effects is embodied in the phrases "known to cause" and "may possibly cause"; levels of exposure are not described as "workplace" or "animal study" but as multiples of community levels. Thus, the source of the data, along with any complications or uncertainties entailed therein, is treated as less important than its substance. Although experts will be horrified by the serious qualifications and temporizings obscured in this presentation, it is important to remember that people are using it to make only very general decisions--decisions about whether to acquire more information, for example, or whether to stop worrying about emissions of this substance.

The information sheet also draws on the lessons learned by risk communicators about comparison. Two factual comparisons are

BENZENE

CAS# 71-43-2   DOT # 1114

What is it?
- A colorless liquid at ordinary temperature and pressure.
- Evaporates easily, has a sweet odor, and is highly flammable.

What are its major uses?
- A component of many consumer products, including gasoline.
- A common industrial chemical used in the manufacture of plastics, textiles, rubber, adhesives, solvents, and other products.

How can I be exposed?
- **Breathing** is the most likely route of exposure.
  Note: Benzene may get into the air from industrial emissions, gas stations, auto emissions, cigarette smoke, some paints and paint strippers, some glues, some household cleaners.
- May also be absorbed through **skin** from contact with liquids containing it.
- **Eating or drinking** are usually less important routes of exposure but are possible if water or food is contaminated.

What can it do to me?
Note: Harmful health effects increase as length of time exposed and/or concentration of exposure increase.
- Brief exposures at high levels--drowsiness, dizziness, and headaches (only during the time of actual exposure).
- Long-term exposures at typical community levels--no known reliable data.
- Long-term effects at exposures 100 to 1,000 times greater--known to cause leukemia (cancer) and aplastic anemia; may possibly cause miscarriages, lowered birth-weight, and reduced resistence to infections.

FIGURE 9-3 Chemical fact sheet

How much is in our air and water?
- Concentrations of benzene in the air in the United States range from 3 parts per billion (ppb) in rural areas to 30 ppb in heavily exposed urban areas.
- Concentrations in water range from less than 1 ppb to 50 or more in polluted wells.
- Your LEPC or local health department may have more specific local information.

Are there standards or exposure limits?
- For workplace exposures, Threshold Limit Value and OSHA Permissible Exposure Limit are both 1 part per million (ppm) (8 hours, air).
- For air in the environment, there are some state and local guidelines. Ask your LEPC or see the attached sheet, Benzene in Our Community. Texas Screening Value: 0.001 ppm.
- For drinking water, the EPA maximum contaminant level is 0.005 milligrams per liter.

Can I reduce exposure to benzene? Yes, some, by doing as follows:
- Work with local facilities to reduce benzene emissions.
- Stand so you don't smell gasoline when filling your car. Encourage gas stations to install the devices that allow you to start filling the pump and then walk away.
- Use paints, glues, and cleaning products with the windows open to provide fresh air.
- Use protective equipment. Always use impermeable gloves to avoid getting skin wet. Use a cartridge respirator if you are a frequent user of paints, glues, etc.
- If skin contact occurs, wash thoroughly.
- Choose paints and glues without benzene if possible.
- Read product labels and follow instructions for safe use.

Sources of additional information
- Sax, N. Irving. *Dangerous Properties of Industrial Materials.* Van Nostrand Reinhold.
- U.S. Public Health Service, Agency for Toxic Substances and Disease Registry, *Toxicological Profile for Benzene.*

FIGURE 9-3 Chemical fact sheet *continued*

provided: a comparison of levels of exposure to the substance typically occasioned by different activities; and a comparison between any known concentrations and the concentrations allowed by any government exposure standards. Risk is not mentioned at all.[9]

In sum, the proposed information format is not intended to serve as the basis for complex choices about appropriate levels or kinds of chemicals in the community. It is intended to provide enough information to allow a concerned citizen to decide whether to obtain additional information by providing some implicit comparisons with other sources or levels of exposure. It bypasses explicit discussions of risk and so reduces the ill effects of any cognitive biases on the part of the readers; on the other hand, it avoids providing any overall assessments--especially that the substance is safe--which are likely to be both incorrect and irritating to the reader. It provides the kinds of information citizens say they want, especially information about routes of community exposure, to the extent that this information is available. By listing familiar products manufactured with the chemicals, and by describing its everyday properties, moreover, the format (and the one shown in Figure 9-2) has the effect of making the chemical seem more familiar and, perhaps, reducing its apparent riskiness. (Some substances will appear to be more risky when this information is provided. Since the purpose is to promote more accurate assessments, such an outcome is to be expected and even desired.)

If this information is introductory, other data should be available. One branch of particular importance is information specific to the locality, including a listing of the facilities that store or emit the chemical and whatever is known about local concentrations and special local conditions such as a contaminated aquifer. A sample of such information is provided in Figure 9-4. An example of the kind of deeper level of information that citizens might seek is provided in Figure 9-5, which provides data about comparative exposures. Any studies that are used as evidence should include an evaluative annotation--significance, for laboratory studies; "power," which indicates the chance of detecting an effect of a given size, for epidemiological studies.[10] An indication of how many studies have been conducted would also assist people in evaluating the significance of the health effect.[11] The rich variety of existing sources of information, including handbooks, journals, and especially databases, would, of course, be available for those who wish to probe more deeply. In general, it does not seem socially efficient to duplicate these sources, although development of a good source of sources would be helpful.

BENZENE IN OUR COMMUNITY

CAS# 71-43-2

DOT# 1114

Why is benzene in our community and in what amounts?
The following table lists facilities in our area that use benzene, how much they store, the amounts emitted annually into air and water, and the products they manufacture using benzene.

Amount Stored	Annual Air Emissions	Annual Water Emissions	Products Manufactured
Facility 1	60,000 lb	0	Glues
Facility 2	50,000 lb	0	Petroleum products
Facility 3	500 lb	0	Paint
Facility 4	7,000 lb	0	Semiconductors

How much is in our air and water?
Recent measurements at the corner of Broad and Main showed an average concentration of benzene of 8 parts per billion daytime, 5 parts per billion 9PM to 6AM.

How does benzene get into the environment in our community?
• From the facilities listed in the table above.
• From vehicles.
• From gasoline stations.
• From consumer products such as glue and paint.
• From cigarette smoke.
• Leakage from underground storage tanks at 42nd and Broad. These tanks are now being closed and steps taken to reduce leakage.

What should I do during an acute release of benzene?
• If a very strong odor is detected, shut off sources of ignition (car, gas valve, stove).
• Stay indoors, turn off the air conditioner, close doors and windows.
• Get information from radio, CAER hotline, [describe local alarm system].
• If directed, evacuate (going cross-wind if possible); proceed to shelter as directed.

For additional information about benzene, consult the following:
• At the Univ. of Ourtown: Prof. Jack B. Zene, toxicologist. 477-4567
• Contact people at community facilities producing benzene--

Facility 1	Mary Walker, Facility Manager	465-5555
Facility 2	John Jones, Public Relations Specialist	465-2222
Facility 3	Richard Hanna, Health Specialist	464-0000
Facility 4	Jorge Juarez, Site Manager	475-8888

• Poison Control Center   464-2000
• Ourtown LEPC Bill Bailey, Chairman   465-0421 days 465-3214 evenings

FIGURE 9-4 Supplementary local information fact sheet

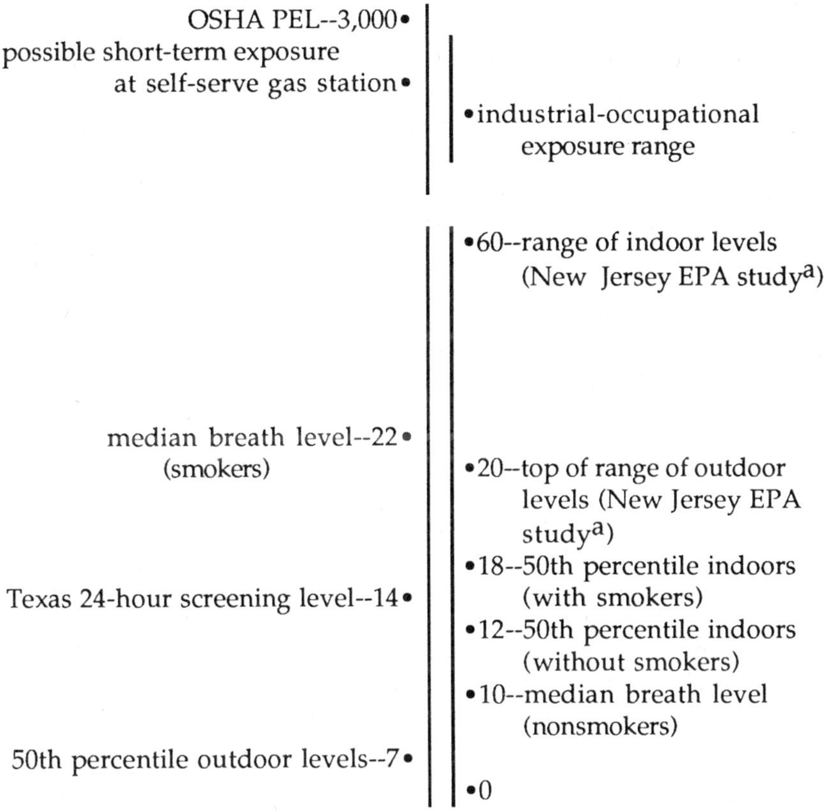

OSHA PEL--3,000•
possible short-term exposure
at self-serve gas station•

•industrial-occupational
exposure range

•60--range of indoor levels
(New Jersey EPA study[a])

median breath level--22•
(smokers)

•20--top of range of outdoor
levels (New Jersey EPA
study[a])
•18--50th percentile indoors
(with smokers)

Texas 24-hour screening level--14•

•12--50th percentile indoors
(without smokers)
•10--median breath level
(nonsmokers)

50th percentile outdoor levels--7•

•0

FIGURE 9-5 Comparative exposures graph

[a]Concentrations measured as 12-hour averages.

Notes: "Range" means 10-90th percentile. Standards and levels of exposure to benzene (by breathing) in micrograms per cubic meter (3,000 micrograms per cubic meter is equal to about 1 part per million in air)

Source: L. A. Wallace, *The Total Exposure Assessment Methodology (TEAM) Study: Summary and Analysis*, vol. 1, EPA, Office of Research and Development, EPA/600/6/87/002a, June 1987.

In the radon study mentioned previously, information was judged effective if, among other criteria, users did not request additional information. The fact sheet, a brief form of information, was least successful at this compared with several longer brochures.[12] I have implicitly argued against this criterion of effectiveness in the case of right to know about hazardous materials in the environment, stating rather that the purpose of the first level of information is to help people make good choices about their need for more information. Thus, some people should demand more information, while others should find themselves satisfied and feel free to turn to perhaps more pressing concerns such as job, family, and budget. In the case of radon, the researchers were concerned with increasing awareness of the risks, which people tend to downplay. The RTK program requires a somewhat different and more flexible approach suitable to the wide range of communities, individuals, and substances it covers.

A Utopian Scenario

Ms. X is the owner of a dry-cleaning establishment that has adopted a new process in which chemicals, machines, and training for employees are provided as a package. She does not own a computer. One afternoon she drives downtown with a chemical list and the MSDSs provided by the supplier. She tells the librarian in the public library that she wants to file Title III reports. The clerk gives her two computer disks, asks if she has ever done this before, and, upon receiving an affirmative answer, leaves her alone. Ms. X sits down at the computer, inserts the disk, and sees a display that provides her with several choices of activities. She indicates that she wants to file chemical inventory reports, and the computer asks if she has ever filed before from this office. When she says yes, the computer asks for the employer ID number, retrieves facility identification information, and asks her to confirm that it is still correct. The computer then shows the inventory she reported last year and asks whether there are changes to be made. When she indicates that there will be a lot of changes, it asks a series of questions to assist her in entering the chemicals' names and identification numbers. Once, when she types in a number, the computer asks her to check it, because this is not the number of a chemical usually associated with dry cleaners. She discovers that she has indeed made a typographical error, which she corrects by highlighting the wrong number and changing it. At the end of the session, the computer prints out a hard copy of the report for her, copies the report to the second disk for government use, and reminds her to give both disks back to the clerk. At the end of the week, the library mails the disks with the facility reports to the LEPC, which uses them to update its own files and those of the emergency management department.

A few days later, Mr. Y, a citizen, enters the library, and asks the librarian for help with a Title III information request. The librarian asks what the problem is. Mr. Y notes that a nearby dry-cleaning establishment has recently begun to emit strange smells. The librarian shows him to the computer and hands him a disk. The disk starts up the computer and displays a series of questions that the user might wish to ask. Mr. Y indicates interest in a particular facility; the computer asks for its name or address. Mr. Y gives the address and is asked whether it is a dry-cleaning establishment he is interested in. When he says yes, it displays full identification information and asks whether he wishes to see a chemical inventory. He says yes, and a list of some thirty chemicals is displayed. The computer tells him that he may highlight the name of a chemical to learn more about it; he chooses the one that is shown as being stored in the largest quantities. The information tells him it is an odorless liquid. The computer also includes a menu of characteristics; he decides that it would be faster to indicate that it is smell about which he is concerned. He chooses "smell" from the menu, and the computer displays a list of six chemicals that are in the dry cleaner's inventory that have characteristic odors. He learns more about each of them and finds two that might be causing the problem. The description of one chemical indicates that it is newly in use by dry cleaners. Mr. Y prints out the list of two and their descriptions, returns the disks to the librarian, and leaves.

He goes to visit his public health department with the reports in hand. A staff person calls up the information on the database to confirm that Mr. Y has provided her with the best two chemical choices, then checks with several other databases for supplementary information on the known health effects and industrial uses of the chemicals to narrow the selection to one chemical. The public health staff person then asks for all the establishments in the locality that are using the substance, and obtains the names of some forty dry cleaners and the total amount that is being stored. She also finds the name and telephone number of the suppliers of these chemicals. She checks an agency database for citizen complaints and finds that complaints about smells from dry cleaners have increased noticeably in the last six months. She tells Mr. Y. that an investigation appears to be merited and takes the necessary steps to begin it.

Mr. Y also tells his LEPC that he has concerns about this chemical. The LEPC has completed a qualitative risk assessment comparing community risks from many chemicals, the method and results of which are included in a computer program available on both the public library and LEPC computers. The data from the suspect substance are entered into the risk-assessment format, and the computer provides a comparison; although the substance presents a relatively low health risk, it has the potential to affect a very large number of local residents and, therefore, achieves a rating that places it high enough on the list to merit attention. Eventually, the LEPC and the health department together conduct a study of the concentrations of the chemical in the air at several distances from eight dry-cleaning establishments, working with neighborhood volunteers who ensure that the collection devices are working properly. The LEPC convenes a meeting of citizens and cleaners and their suppliers; the latter explain the benefits of the new method in reducing costs as well as reducing risks by substituting new (although smellier) chemicals. Citizens strongly favor efforts to reduce emissions, and, using a grant from the state RTK program, hire an expert to determine the costs of emissions reduction. The expert comes up with a surprising method, which the cleaners happily adopt because it reduces the amount of the most expensive chemical they must purchase. The LEPC relays both the results of the study and the methods for reducing emissions to the state health department via modem. The state in turn passes it on to EPA and OSHA, who check the information against similar data coming from other states. Mr. Y, meanwhile, returns to the library and calls up the name of the chemical, rather than the facility, on the Title III computer. There he finds that the chemical is the subject of a proposed federal rule based on the new technology.

Conclusion

Just as information must be tailored to the needs of each individual, federal support should to be tailored to the needs of the states, and state support to the needs of localities. No support at all is not an appropriate option; Congress imposed a large burden on the regulated community to report and on governments to manage the reports and plan and it raised the expectations of citizens concerning the availability and utility of information about hazardous substances in the environment. Title III and right to know should be funded at the federal level.

When that happens, the other recommendations presented here could combine to make a strong program; they would make the information-collection and dissemination portions of the program more efficient, increase localities' abilities to undertake emergency planning and response, help government work with industry to reduce the likelihood that emergencies will arise, and give citizens new understanding of the nature of the risks they face from hazardous materials in their neighborhoods and environments.

The recommendations do not address several more fundamental issues, however, especially the real nature of the right to know and what information citizens need to be full participants in public decisionmaking. These questions are the subject of Chapter 10.

Notes

1. Senator Dave Durenberger in an interview with the Bureau of National Affairs, reported in *Superfund II: A New Mandate* (vol. 17, February 13, 1987, part 2 of BNA Environment Reporter), p. 128. Durenberger is also quoted as saying that the law was so "awful we are going to have to come back in a couple of years and redo it. The paperwork flow and burden will be just overwhelming."

2. *Community and Worker Right-to-Know News* 2, no. 16 (May 22, 1988).

3. See, for example, 51 Fed. Reg. 41570ff. (November 17, 1986), especially pp. 41575 and 41580.

4. Hampshire Research Associates, *User Friendliness of OTS: Information Resources and Systems*, Washington, D.C., March 1986.

5. Telephone interview with Barbara Sergeant, New Jersey Department of Environmental Protection, August 9, 1988.

6. Michael O'Hare, Lawrence Bacow, and Debra Sanderson, *Facility Siting and Public Opposition* (New York: Van Nostrand Reinhold Co., 1983), especially pp. 104-106.

7. V. Kerry Smith, William H. Desvousges, Ann Fisher, and F. Reed Johnson, *Communicating Radon Risk Effectively: A Mid-Course Evaluation* (Washington, D.C.: EPA, July 1987), pp. 1-9. (Hereafter, Radon study.)

8. EPA, Title III Needs Assessment Project, 1988 General Public Focus Groups, "Summary of Findings," (Fall 1988), pp. 21, 30. Some readers took more than twenty minutes to read a fact sheet distributed at a meeting. People nevertheless wanted to take copies home. The information format I propose is intended precisely to be taken home for further reference, not to serve as a complete source of data.

9. Members of the working group that helped devise this format believed that it should include a "risk statement" to let readers know that the adverse symptoms would be evident in the absence of any exposures (the "base rate" in the population) and that the likelihood of exhibiting the

symptoms depends on a variety of factors in addition to exposure, including life-style. Comments from experts and citizens suggested that this statement was more confusing than helpful, and it is omitted here. Such risk-assessment information is available along one or more of the "branches" or sources of additional information.

10. David Ozonoff and Leslie I. Boden, "Truth and Consequences: Health Agency Responses to Environmental Health Problems," *Science, Technology and Human Values* 12 (1987):70-77. Also see Marvin Legator, *The Health Detective's Handbook: A Guide to the Investigation of Environmental Health Hazards by Nonprofessionals* (Baltimore: Johns Hopkins University Press, 1985).

11. See National Wildlife Federation, "Critique of EPA's Hazardous Substance Fact Sheet," and sample fact sheet, Washington, D.C., February 9, 1989.

12. Radon study, pp. 5-14, 6-10.

10 / Empowering Citizens

Free people are of necessity, informed; uninformed people can never be free.

--Senator Edward Long

In Chapter 1, I postulated four different kinds of right to know. The exploration of RTK in practice in the subsequent chapters has confirmed that there are different approaches to RTK but has also suggested that they are not entirely distinct, blurring into each other on the edges. Thus, a more appropriate image would be that of a continuum of rights to know, with the four points marking transitions. I called those forms of RTK basic, risk reduction, participatory, and changing the balance of power. Each implies a somewhat different role for government and for citizens, so the continuum on which they are arrayed might run from less to more social change. (Figure 10-1 illustrates this continuum with some additional forms of RTK added.)

Congress appeared to have more than one of these notions of RTK in mind when it passed Title III; although some of the chemical inventory reporting requirements seem to embody the basic information access form, provisions for citizen suits and a computerized emissions inventory suggest a stronger vision of RTK. The law is, of course, further complicated by its embodying not only several visions of RTK but four distinct programmatic purposes--emergency planning, emergency notification, chemical inventory reporting, and emissions reporting. The emergency planning provisions appear to be most supportive of the risk-reduction goal of RTK.

We would expect different actors to endorse different versions of RTK as well. Intuition might suggest that industry, for example, would be most supportive of the basic form, because, as we have seen, mere access to the basic data would not necessarily inform citizens well enough to enable them to know whether present storage and emissions practices are adequate. Yet, concern that the raw data would be more frightening than a well-balanced interpretation has caused many people in industry to look to other forms of RTK, especially the risk reduction form. Several companies have announced voluntary

Type of RTK	Social change	Recipient of information
	(Less social change)	(Individual as target of RTK)
Just knowing	No notable change	Individual
"Informed consent"	No change	Individual
Reduce risk	Minor change	Individual, regulator
Maintain balance of power	Minor change	Individual, experts
Decisionmaking	Some change	Community
Informed consent	Possible major change	Community
Change balance of power	Major change	Community
	(Increased social change)	(Collectivity as recipient of information)

FIGURE 10-1 Diverse kinds of right to know

programs to reduce emissions by significant amounts over the next several years.[1] Conversely, one might have expected government agencies to endorse the risk reduction form; in many states and localities, however, lack of resources has constrained agencies to support the basic form of RTK more strongly. Interviews with LEPC members and chairpeople suggest that beliefs as well as lack of resources have contributed to this attitude in at least some localities.[2]

Some of EPA's activities, in contrast, are shading over into the participatory-decisionmaking form of RTK. Pushed by interest groups and pulled by the ease of manipulating and interpreting data with computers, the agency has found that the public database of emissions is rapidly becoming a tool for disseminating information rather than mere data. Many of the interest groups that have been lobbying EPA about the database, as well as others at the state and local level, have been conducting other activities directed at changing the balance of power. It is probably too soon at this writing to judge their effectiveness.

The discussion in Chapters 4 through 8 touched on many other issues in which differing visions or versions of RTK have been implicitly or explicitly endorsed by various parties. The issues raised in each chapter, moreover, were pertinent to every form of RTK. For example, each form provides citizens with data or information in ways that will elicit different perceptions of risk; similarly, each form could benefit from computerization. So far, however, we have not considered one important issue that is especially pertinent to the forms of RTK that hope to enable citizens to become effective decisionmakers-- citizen participation. This chapter rectifies that omission only in part; in common with so many of the other issues discussed here, participation is a subject worthy of a book of its own.

Drawing on the discussion of citizen participation and extending it slightly, in the second section of this chapter, I consider some subtle variations on the four kinds of RTK that have so far informed this study. In the final section, I return to the theme of information policies in a more general way, drawing lessons both from and for right to know.

Participating in the Policy Process

Participation is a central doctrine of democracy. Not only did the authors of the Constitution assume that citizens would vote and join in community discussions of issues, but each crisis since then that has resulted in expanded government authority has also resulted in demands for increased citizen participation.[3] The growth in federal regulatory powers that began with the Interstate Commerce Act of 1887 was accompanied by the participatory demands of the populist movement, including direct election of senators; progressivism and the New Deal brought expansions of government power and expansions in citizen power. Since World War II, government power has extended into vast new areas, each overseen by a great bureaucracy and each faced with demands for citizen participation in administrative decisionmaking.[4]

The nature of participation has changed as government power has changed. Initiative, referendum, and recall, reforms sought by the Progressives early in this century, gave way to neighborhood planning councils and the ombudsman. The "cafeteria" of participation techniques that were developed for social and distributive policies during the 1960s and early 1970s turned out to be less useful for environmental and other policies with a critical technological or scientific component.[5] Three methods of participation are especially popular for these latter policies: public hearings, providing citizens with their own experts, and citizen members of advisory panels.

Of these, the public hearing or meeting is surely the most common; several laws, including superfund, require such meetings before a final decision may be made. Among the disadvantages of this form of citizen participation, many of which were implicit in the excerpts provided in Chapter 6, are these: Hearings are often held late in the process so that attendees cannot really affect the decision; large numbers of attendees prevent each from having a say; technical experts and representatives of authoritative groups stand in front on a podium, while the audience sits below and receives information; and meetings are often held to meet the formal requirements of the law rather than to help decisionmakers hear other opinions. SARA also includes a provision that makes funds available to citizens so that they can hire their own experts; citizen groups can thus be equal participants in procedures that require considerable technical or legal expertise.[6] The Science for Citizens program formerly in the National Science Foundation had a similar purpose; experts were to be available for a wide variety of policy decisions, not just for a particular program such as superfund.[7]

It is important to note that both these participation techniques-- public hearings and allowing citizens to hire experts--are part and parcel of the standard methods of administrative decisionmaking, reinforcing rather than expanding or changing existing methods of public choice. In one model, public decisions are made by administrators who listen to and balance demands of contending interest groups. At best, public hearings provide an opportunity to hear from some of these groups; at worst, they provide an opportunity for the administrators to offer public justifications of decisions. Experts can make the citizens' case in terms that administrators are used to. In the 1980s, the method of making decisions by balancing interests has been supplanted in part by benefit maximization, in which the administrator defines policy options, compares their costs and benefits, and selects the one with the greatest social utility.[8] Although participation is less important in this mode of decisionmaking, public hearings may still serve as tools for imparting decisions to citizens and for allowing feelings to be vented. Citizens' experts take on added importance, however, because they are in the best position to exploit opportunities provided by the law to respond to administrative cost-benefit analyses, again employing the administrators' own terminologies.

Robert Reich criticizes both interest-group mediation and net benefit analysis as methods of making governmental decisions, arguing that neither bolsters public confidence in the accountability or responsiveness of administrators (and the governments they represent). If government is experiencing a "decline of deference," in which citizens are reluctant to accept its decisions, then decisions should be made in a way that increases rather than dampens citizens' interest in and respect for government. Equally important is the fact that both approaches take public preferences as given--to be revealed through group interaction.[9] By assuming that citizens' preferences are fixed, they both give further support to the adversarial mode of policymaking, a mode that is also implicit in the two participation techniques. The variety of legal remedies available in environmental laws (including Title III, whose primary enforcement provisions are suits by citizens against industry or government and by government against industry) reinforces the adversarial mode.

The paradox of participation is that to be successful, given the politics of the 1980s, citizens' groups must employ adversarial methods, yet an adversarial process overall is wasteful of resources and often works to the advantage of those who already have the resources. It is in the adversarial context that experts might be especially tempted to use their superior knowledge to downplay information that would otherwise be expected to spur citizens to action--the old form of risk communication.

A third technique of participation that fits the needs of technological policymaking is that of employing citizen experts. It differs from the others because citizens themselves are placed on the deliberative bodies and given the resources to become near-experts. The Food and Drug Administration has citizen members of the technical groups that evaluate new medical devices; many states have placed citizen members on professional licensing boards. Some states have also established procedures for ensuring that citizens are members of the boards that review permit applications for hazardous waste disposal sites.[10] Although it brings the citizen much closer to the locus of decisionmaking, there are still problems with this method: (1) The citizen must expend a lot of time and effort to become expert enough to affect other members' opinions; (2) by becoming an expert, the citizen may lose his or her "citizen perspective"; and (3) the citizen is still only one member of a large body and may not be able to have much effect on the decision. Citizen experts must make a special effort to go back to their constituencies to explain what is going on; their tasks become full-time jobs. "Regulatory negotiation," a participation technique with a growing group of supporters, gives the citizen a stronger role, because the decisionmaking body must achieve consensus, but does not necessarily overcome the other disadvantages.[11]

New techniques for participation are needed. The need has been understood for some time, but the advent of RTK makes it more urgent, because one barrier to participation--lack of relevant information--has been at least partially eliminated. One method that might enable citizens to use the knowledge they have obtained under RTK to mold decisions in their communities is the citizen review panel.[12] Citizens convene like a jury to hear testimony, question experts, deliberate the issues, and reach a conclusion over a period of several days. Success of this method depends on ensuring that panelists obtain a balanced view of the issues. LEPCs could be adapted to become citizen review panels or perhaps to serve as the means for recruiting such panels and ensuring that appropriate testimony and experts are available to the panels. LEPCs could also serve as local level regulatory negotiation mechanisms focusing first on hazardous materials and then, perhaps, expanding their purview to other environmental issues.

Citizen review panels and related participatory methods rapidly absorb social resources. All parties must devote considerable time and effort to providing and acquiring information, discussing its meaning, evolving policy options, and selecting among them. If the costs are high, however, the benefits are also high. We know that people learn better if they think the resulting knowledge will benefit them--the barriers to understanding technical information are a lot lower if people believe that their mastery of it will result in decisions that reflect their interests. Moreover, building support for institutions through participation is ultimately less costly than the social chaos that results from an unhindered decline in respect for these institutions. The method that had the most positive effect on community attitudes toward a proposal to site a hazardous waste disposal facility in Massachusetts was not financial incentives but one that allowed local citizens and public officials to conduct regular safety inspections.[13] Under RTK, citizens have already asked to participate in factory tours and conduct parallel worst-case spill analyses; in the future, they could learn to check on pollution monitoring devices, accompany inspectors on safety tours of facilities, and participate in other related activities.

I am suggesting that developing and refining new methods of participation, although costly, is an essential component of RTK. In Chapter 1, I presented data that showed a vast reservoir of concern about environmental pollution and hazardous chemicals, combined with a general lack of knowledge about the subjects and, furthermore, a lack of knowledge about Title III itself. In the survey of 600 Texas residents, 85 percent did not know about "the new federal law giving citizens the right to know about hazardous materials in the community." Moreover, 14 percent said they did not know whether there were hazardous materials in their own communities, and 47 percent thought there were none. When Title III information starts to be publicized by the press or by public interest groups, people who are generally concerned but did not know about problems in their own areas are going to be surprised and unhappy. Their discontent could be exploited to create social unrest. With strong institutions already in place for participating in decisions about environmental concerns, however, discontent may be mobilized in more productive ways. Therefore, even those who believe that RTK should consist only of the basic provision of access to data should consider the need for government or other agents to establish more effective methods of citizen participation--especially methods such as the citizen panel that combine education and outreach with actual decisionmaking.

Another Right to Know

In the previous section, I presented a strong case for citizen participation as a necessary component of RTK. There are also strong arguments against participation in decisionmaking, some of which I explored in the chapters on risk perception and on scientific uncertainty. The essence of those criticisms is that citizens cannot participate effectively in decisionmaking because they will always be forced to rely on experts by virtue of the complexity and technical nature of the information. Some citizens, of course, may well be or become expert enough to make a difference; as we have seen, the citizen-expert form of participation also has some drawbacks.

A very different kind of criticism of participation focuses not on citizens' capabilities but on their apathy and selfishness. Not a few observers believe that the United States is experiencing a decline of the ideal of the common good. Naked self-interest, it is argued, determines individuals' positions on public issues; the result is that all issues are decided by power plays among contending interest groups.[14] In this context, individuals participate only when they have a particular stake in the outcome, and they are uninclined to accept modifications in their positions unless forced to do so. The argument goes on to suggest that policies involving such public goods as the environment are especially troublesome because no single individual benefits enough to offset the costs of ensuring that the socially beneficial course is taken. Finally, critics note that general public

The notion that people are unwilling to take public action is partly confirmed by some research concerning Title III. Six small groups of seven to eleven people living in communities with significantly polluting industries were convened to discuss hazardous materials as part of a "needs assessment" for risk-communication strategies arising from the availability of Title III information. The report of the meetings states that participants "were concerned about personal risk, not community risk, and there was no indication that these participants would feel compelled to act if a pollutant affects the broader 'community' as opposed to them individually."[15] This attitude is often combined with one that assumes that pollution control is the job of "the government." Thus, apathy is also expressed in the view that someone else should be taking care of the problem.

Not all data confirms this attitude, of course. In the Kanawha Valley of West Virginia, for example, where many chemical plants are concentrated in a relatively small area, a survey found that citizens want to obtain additional information and to work with public officials and plant managers to reduce emissions.[16]

In the survey of Texas residents in February 1988, people were asked specifically about the kinds of activities they would undertake if they heard about a new facility proposed for their community that manufactures a carcinogenic substance. We suggested four kinds of activities: talking to friends and family, talking to public officials, joining a group, and organizing a group. Not surprisingly, the numbers of people who said they would be willing to undertake each of these declined as the activity became more onerous: 64 percent, 49 percent, 39 percent, and 23 percent, respectively. However, the fact that nearly one-fourth of respondents said they would organize a group seems indicative of a high level of interest, even though we know it is easier to say you would do it than actually to do so. Willingness to participate in these political activities was positively correlated with level of concern about the facility locating in the community.[17] But the Texas data are distinguished from the other two studies in a very important way that may undermine their validity: In the Texas survey, questions concerned a proposed facility, whereas the other two studies involved existing facilities. Citizens seem to have a higher sense of both concern (NIMBY) and effectiveness in opposing new facilities than in seeking changes in existing facilities.

Earlier we saw that any lack of interest in participating that citizens do evince need not be attributed entirely to selfishness. Participants in the small-group study also expressed "considerable frustration and low expectations about the ability of personal efforts to 'make a difference' in the face of 'big government' and 'big industry.'"[18]

frustration and low expectations about the ability of personal efforts to 'make a difference' in the face of 'big government' and 'big industry.'"[18] Procedural impediments--getting the runaround from agencies when trying to locate data, for example--also raise the costs of participation. We have already considered the costs associated with becoming expert enough to make a difference.

Participation has been a difficult idea to put into practice for the more than two hundred years of U.S. democracy. On the one hand, there is no democracy without participation; on the other, it is impossible to expect or ensure that everyone participates in all decisions. It would not only be wasteful of social resources but would fly in the face of what we know of human nature to expect each citizen to learn about every issue and take an active stance on it. Our compromise has been to allow interest groups to represent the various points of view; critics of interest-group liberalism question their representativeness and the procedures by which decisions are reached, but they do not question the fundamental need to rely on groups as representatives or agents of individuals.

These considerations led me to seek a form of RTK that does not rule out participation in decisionmaking but does not rely so heavily on it that apathy or selfishness would call the entire right into question. I call this kind of RTK "informed consent," after the concept developed in the medical literature. Like RTK, informed consent is an idea that seems to be difficult to put fully into practice. Most of us are familiar with the "consent" wrested from us fifteen minutes before an operation as we sign a form that contains a clause allowing the doctor to do anything medically prudent without further consultation with the anesthetized patient. Such consent could characterize RTK as well-- under this definition, people are informed about the presence of hazardous substances in their communities and are thereby assumed to have consented unless they take further action. Thus informed consent could be considered a way to rationalize the status quo. In short, this kind of informed consent is similar to the basic form of RTK in that the government's duty has been fulfilled by making the information available; indeed, it is stronger because the government's action has acquired moral force through citizens' "informed consent."

A more ideal sort of informed consent is quite different in form and implications, both in the medical realm and for RTK. Drawing on both moral and legal theory, Ruth Faden and Thomas Beauchamp have argued that "autonomy" is a central feature of informed consent. In the case of medical procedures, autonomy is achieved when the patient understands the benefits and risks of the procedure and freely and intentionally chooses a course of action.[19] For collective choices such as those required for decisions concerning hazardous materials in the community, individuals may act at two levels. First, they must decide whether this issue is of sufficient concern to induce them to participate; and second, they must then make substantive choices about acceptable levels of emissions or other potential risks. "Autonomy" is achieved not when individuals are disconnected from the import of the social choice but when each of these separate decisions is or may be made by an individual on the basis of accurate, readily available information that is understandable. The format proposed in Chapter 9 for presenting health-effects information is intended to fulfill part of this need.

By specifying two stages to true informed consent, I have attempted to account for the unreasonableness of expecting each person to participate in decisions about hazardous materials while still ensuring that those who want to participate more fully may do so. Note that this formulation does not remove the responsibility from government to ensure that mechanisms for participation are available. On the contrary, a citizen making the first choice--Does the issue merit the expenditure of effort to participate?--weighs the salience of the issue against the costs of participating and the likelihood of achieving change. Just as only a collective institution such as government can provide the information needed to make the decision, there is some public responsibility to even out the costs of participating as well.

Figure 10-1 shows two continua on which the six kinds of RTK are arrayed--the original four and two kinds of informed consent--according to the amount of social change entailed and according to the agent or recipient of RTK. The genuine type of informed consent appears just before participatory decisionmaking on the social change continuum, because it postulates participation in ways somewhat more similar to those we now have.

Genuine informed-consent RTK assumes that citizens have an absolute right to obtain relevant information if they want it, without implying that they must do so. The right to know consists partly in knowing that you could exercise oversight, even if you don't choose to, for whatever reason, but especially because others are keeping tabs while you take an active interest in some other problem. This approach was well summarized by a university official during the 1970s, when students had demanded to participate in governing the university and then failed to take advantage of their new right. He said, "It turned out they didn't really want to participate in managing (the institution). They wanted to watch it being managed through an open door."[20] If the door is really open and there are no protests, it is fair to say that citizens have given their informed consent.

Government, Citizens, and Information

Adding informed consent to the list of types of RTK helps answer another question that has troubled the preceding chapters: What is the proper balance between government and the private sector in providing information under RTK? I imagine a line that comprises all the kinds of data, information, and other support that would be needed in order to allow citizens to make sensible, informed decisions about hazardous materials in their communities, or whatever other risk is the subject of policy, and I imagine government and citizens walking toward each other from opposite ends of the line. The question is how far each ought to go in order to meet the other.

Remember that earlier information policies were, in part, dictated by the desire for minimal government regulation; that is, providing information about risks was a substitute for direct regulation to minimize the risks, and, at the same time, it provided citizens with maximum choice among risks. Advocates of these policies implicitly argued that it was not reasonable to foist the higher costs of safer products on people who did not wish to pay. They often conveniently ignored the fact that people without resources were thus forced to "choose" higher risk. Not only safer products but even the information itself is often too expensive for many people lacking education or having difficulty gaining access to the background information needed to understand risk data. Thus, within the limits allowed by the courts, an information policy may become an excuse for placing both burdens-- of information collection and interpretation and of risk-bearing--on the citizen: "We provided the information; it's not our fault if they didn't pay attention."

In November 1986, California voters adopted a toxics information program, embodied in Proposition 65. The law prohibits knowing or intentional exposure of people to carcinogens or reproductive toxins without giving "clear and reasonable warning" to them.[21] Inasmuch as the regulations allow warnings to be conveyed by signs or labels, most employers have posted generic signs reading "WARNING: Products known to the State of California to cause (cancer) are present in this facility." These signs do not indicate which substances people should avoid or how to reduce exposure; moreover, the sheer number of such signs, in gas stations, grocery stores, and offices was so great as to cause "information overload." As a result, "operators and patrons . . . appeared indifferent . . . about newly posted warnings."[22] Many observers believe that these signs are intended to shield those who post them from liability, shifting the burden to the consumer despite the notices' obvious deficiencies as sources of risk information. (Others, more charitable, argue that the effect of posting signs will be to encourage businesses to reduce their use of regulated substances rather than admitting to the presence of hazardous substances, just as industry decided to reduce emissions because of the disclosure requirements of section 313 of Title III.)

The data-only, or basic, form of RTK is a continuation of these earlier kinds of information policies. Under the old policies, individuals were given risk or, more often, safety information and then allowed to decide what actions to take. Under Title III, citizens are given direct access to at least some of the data underlying the health or safety advice--data about emissions and chemical inventories, which may in turn and with effort lead to access to the laboratory and epidemiologic studies of the health effects of exposure. Under the old information policies, government played a large role in assessing the quality and meaning of the data; under Title III, citizens seem to have that responsibility.

If, however, government were to continue assessing the data, turning them into information, then RTK would serve to extend rather than contract citizens' rights, because citizens could have access, not only to the analyzed information they have received from government almost throughout the twentieth century, but also, if they so choose, to the actual underlying data. This is the essence of true informed consent: Government provides both (1) analyzed data to allow citizens to make a quick determination about the seriousness of the underlying problem and their own interest in acquiring additional information and (2) raw data for those who want to exercise direct oversight. (With computers, the added cost of providing another kind of data is very low.) This enlargement of citizens' rights, I have suggested, places still greater burdens on government. The most important of its new tasks is ensuring that the right to know does not stop with data or information--ensuring that citizens can act upon the information they receive by creating or supporting institutions that allow for participation and for citizens to work directly with the private sector.

Our examination of the implementation of Title III suggests that government has not yet assumed all these responsibilities. EPA is still groping for an answer to how far it should go in providing data analysis or even user-friendly software. State and local governments are generally trying just to keep up with the immediate demands of the law for emergency plans and data management. Returning to the image of the line or continuum of activities, there is presently a gap between the point at which government responsibility stops and the one at which citizens' abilities take over. This gap, as I have tried to suggest in earlier chapters, is more the result of resource constraints and inadvertent decisionmaking than it is a conscious choice by anyone about the proper role of government in RTK.

A third actor--industry--has stepped in to fill some of the gap, however. Not only have individual facilities established citizen advisory councils and other means of working or at least communicating with their neighbors, but groups of facilities have banded together to conduct other activities supportive of RTK. For example, a large group of facilities in the Houston area conducts a continual air-monitoring project, completely independent of any government agency, at a cost of more than $1 million a year. In another area, a group of facilities has banded together to establish a telephone answering service; in case of an accident, even one not reportable under Title III's criteria, details about the accident and the chemical involved will be available on tape, while at other times general information on chemicals and the local sponsoring facilities will be available.[23] Many other groups are providing these and other services elsewhere.

Should private industry be filling the gap? On the one hand, these are services that would not be available unless provided privately, and both are activities that enhance the quality of RTK. They are provided at no direct cost to taxpayers, although presumably the costs are included in the price of the products; there is certainly a case to be made that the producers and consumers of products creating risks to health should bear the cost of informing people about the risks.

On the other hand, there are two very different but important arguments against this approach to meeting the needs of RTK. First, not all affected businesses participate. For the regional air-monitoring project, the only disadvantage would be to the participating companies, who must bear more than a fair share of the cost. However, for the telephone project, this limited participation would mean that the information available to citizens is incomplete. Some outside agency may be needed to ensure that all relevant facilities participate so that full data are available. Second, if industry conducts the projects, industry may control the nature and quality of the information that is provided. One point of RTK seemed to be to ensure that citizens are able to assess the data for themselves if they know how. If industry should decide to cease its activities, furthermore, citizens would be left without services crucial to the exercise of RTK.

In short, relying upon the private sector to ensure the right to know--or any other right, such as the right to housing or food--is abdicating responsibilities that are appropriate and necessary to government. We have government to undertake those tasks that cannot be entrusted to others; throughout U.S. history, protection of individual rights has been the most important of the government functions that cannot be delegated. Although we should welcome the innovative efforts of the private sector to fill citizens' information needs, we should also be leery of allowing policy to be made by default. Private responsibility may lead to private control, returning us to the same earlier point at which citizens realized they needed the right to know. The right to know is, in part, the right not to have to rely on other people's assessments of what we can understand or what risks we should have to assume.

What then should be the responsibilities of the several actors? Citizens should, first and foremost, exercise the right to know, either individually or through organized groups. A right only exists by being exercised.[24] Citizens should use the data they obtain responsibly, inform other citizens about what they have learned, and work with industry to achieve greater safety. They should press government to ensure that the data they receive are accurate and timely and that supplementary information sources are readily available.

Industry must, of course, provide the data that are the foundation of the whole RTK program, ensuring to the best of their abilities that the data are accurate. They must work with government and citizens in a cooperative way to try to meet goals for risk reduction. They should also be open-minded about the opportunities for economic gain inherent in RTK. Hazardous waste, for example, is waste first and hazardous second. No one aware of national and global resource constraints could reasonably argue that waste is a good thing. Using information required under Title III, citizens will press industry to reduce their waste--to conserve resources. In the past, however, businesses have sometimes argued that the cost of conservation is too high. This emphasis in the private sector on maximizing short-term gains has purportedly reduced the U.S. investment in basic and applied industrial research and put us at the mercy of world competitors. By responding to demands for waste reduction based on RTK data, companies can realize both short-term public relations benefits and the long-term cost reduction of waste-minimization programs, simultaneously improving corporate balance sheets and the state of the environment.

Similarly, citizens who have persuaded facilities to reduce the amounts of certain hazardous chemicals they routinely store have helped to reduce inventory and storage costs as well as to diminish the costs of accidents. If accidents are less likely to occur, governments and private industry need to support less emergency response capability--a very expensive resource because it is so technical, but one that remains largely unused. Resources now devoted to emergency response may be diverted to more productive uses. In short, industry should at least consider that working with citizens and government officials to reduce risks may reduce costs of operating as well.

Finally, the role of government is to ensure that the other parties can exercise their rights and fulfill their responsibilities. This means collecting and disseminating data and providing data analysis and easily understood computer software. It means designing and, if necessary, redesigning public policies so that the means are appropriate to the end--not merely a burdensome new reporting requirement. Most of all, it means supporting and, if necessary, creating new means by which all the affected parties may come together in a nonadversarial way to achieve reasonable risk reduction. By "opening the door" on the operations of both private industry and government, RTK can foster more trust in social institutions, which in turn reduces the resources that must be spent on a variety of adversarial proceedings.

If citizens have the right to know--and its very name suggests a right that is closely related to the notion of democracy embodied in Senator Long's statement, quoted at the beginning of this chapter--then government should guarantee that right. With institutions in place that allow and encourage citizens to work with both government and private industry, right to know would be transformed from a right merely to oversee and check government policies into a right to participate in formulating those policies. Thus would knowledge truly become power.

Notes

1. See note 31 in Chapter 7 for a list of some of these industries.

2. See note 2 in Chapter 4 for this.

3. Theodore Lowi, *The End of Liberalism: Ideology, Public Policy, and the Crisis of Public Authority* (New York: W. W. Norton, 1969), especially pp. 93-96.

4. This paragraph and the latter half of the one following were strongly influenced by Daniel J. Fiorino, "Citizen Participation in Risk Policy Making: Perspectives, Issues, and Prospects," Paper presented at the Symposium on Decision-Making and Environmental Risks: Economic and Political Issues, University of Wisconsin at Madison, April 14, 1988.

5. The quoted term from Judy B. Rosener, "A Cafeteria of Techniques and Critiques," *Public Management* 57:12 (December 1975), reprinted in Stuart Langton, ed., *Citizen Participation in America: Essays on the State of the Art* (Lexington, Mass.: Lexington Books, 1978), pp. 108-122.

6. See EPA, *The Citizens' Guidance Manual for the Technical Assistance Grant Program*, OSWER Directive 9230.1-03, April 1988.

7. For the argument for the program, see Joel Primack and Frank von Hippel, *Advice and Dissent: Scientists in the Political Arena* (New York: Basic Books, 1974). For one assessment of the Science for Citizens program, which was established by Congress and then discontinued by the same body, see Susan G. Hadden, "Technical Information for Citizen Participation," *Journal of Applied Behavioral Science* 17, no. 4 (1981), pp. 537-549.

8. The two models are well described in Robert Reich, "Public Administration and Public Deliberation: An Interpretive Essay," *Yale Law Journal* 94 (1985):1617-1641.

9. Reich, "Public Administration," especially pp. 1619-1625.

10. On professional licensing boards, see Deborah Barger and Susan G. Hadden, "Placing Citizen Members on Professional Licensing Boards," *Journal of Consumer Affairs* 18 (1984): 160-170.

11. Of the growing body of literature on "reg neg," see Daniel J. Fiorino, "Regulatory Negotiation as a Policy Process," *Public Administration Review* 48 (July/August 1988): 764-772; Philip J. Harter, "Negotiating Regulations: A Cure for the Malaise?" *Georgetown Law Journal* 71 (1983): 1-118; and Henry H. Perritt, Jr., "Negotiated Rulemaking in Practice," *Journal of Policy Analysis and Management* 5, no. 3 (Spring 1986):482-495.

12. Ned Crosby, Janet M. Kelly, and Paul Schaefer, "Citizens Panels: A New Approach to Citizen Participation," *Public Administration Review* 46(2) (1986):170-178.

13. Kent E. Portney, "The Potential of the Theory of Compensation for Mitigating Public Opposition to Hazardous Waste Facility Siting: Some Evidence from Five Massachusetts Communities," *Policy Studies Journal* 1 4 (1985): 81-89.

14. Robert N. Bellah, Richard Madsen, William M. Sullivan, Ann Swidler, and Steven M. Tipton, *Habits of the Heart: Individualism and Commitment in America* (San Francisco: Harper and Row, 1985), makes this argument.

15. EPA, Title III Needs Assessment Project, 1988 General Public Focus Groups, "Summary of Findings," (Fall 1988), p. 9. (Hereafter, Focus Groups Report.)

16. Lewis Crampton, statement in J. Clarence Davies, Vincent T. Covello, and Frederick W. Allen, eds., *Risk Communication*, Proceedings of the National Conference on Risk Communication, Washington, D.C., January 29-31, 1986, p. 105.

17. The percent of those wiling to undertake an activity who were less than "highly concerned" about hazardous materials dropped from 15 percent for "talk to friends" to 7 percent for "organize a group."

18. Focus Groups Report, pp. 12, 18.

19. Ruth R. Faden and Tom L. Beauchamp, *A History and Theory of Informed Consent* (New York: Oxford University Press, 1986), especially chap. 7. An application of these notions to environmental pollution that is similar to mine is found in Mary Gibson, "Consent and Autonomy, " in Mary Gibson, ed., *To Breath Freely: Risk, Consent, and Air* (Totowa, N. J.: Rowman and Allenheld, 1985), pp. 141-168.

20. Quoted in Harlan Cleveland, *The Knowledge Executive* (New York: E. P. Dutton, 1985), p. 62.

21. California Health and Safety Code section 25249.6.

22. "New Toxics Signs Draw a Ho-Hum," *Sacramento Bee*, February 27, 1988, p. B1, quoted in Matthew L. Kuryla, "California's Proposition 65 and the Chemical Hazard Warning: Risk Management Under the New Code of Popular Outrage," April 1988, p. 50.

23. Statement of Walt Buchholz, Exxon Chemical, about the Houston Regional Monitoring Project, and Jack Coe, Rohm and Haas, about the regional telephone line, at American Chemical Society Southwest Regional Meeting, Corpus Christie, Texas, November 30, 1988.

24. Richard Flathman, *The Practice of Rights* (Cambridge: Cambridge University Press, 1976).

Appendix: The Surveys

Throughout this book, I have referred to the results of four surveys concerning different aspects of community right to know: a mail and telephone survey of citizens who had submitted right-to-know requests under the state RTK laws of New Jersey and Massachusetts; a telephone survey of 600 Texans that included twelve questions on hazardous materials in the community; and a two-part survey of local activities to implement Title III: a field survey of local public officials in eleven Texas counties, and a follow-up telephone survey of forty chairpeople of the Local Emergency Planning Committees. This appendix provides a brief description of the method of the surveys and a few selected results that do not appear in the main body of the book.

The New Jersey/Massachusetts Survey

I conducted the New Jersey/Massachusetts survey with the cooperation of the New Jersey Departments of Environmental Protection and Health and the Massachusetts Department of Environmental Quality Engineering. The New Jersey DEP funded the mailing of the survey in that state; other costs were supported by the Stephen F. Spurr Faculty Research Fellowship. The intent was to mail a survey questionnaire to every citizen who had filed a community right to know request in each of the two states. Differences in the states' programs required slight differences in procedure and in the questionnaire itself.

In New Jersey, names of citizens who file RTK requests are confidential. To maintain confidentiality, therefore, DEP mailed the questionnaire to respondents, including on each return envelope an identifying number. Because the agency was conducting the mailing, it composed a cover letter explaining the purpose of the survey; it also made some suggestions concerning the content of the survey. Questionnaires were returned directly to me.

In New Jersey, the DEP is the primary implementing agency for the community RTK program, although citizens may also contact DOH. In the period from the first implementation of the state law in 1984 until September 1987, DEP had retained records about 63 requests for information; in addition, DOH supplied DEP with a list of 118 people from whom it had received a variety of kinds of requests concerning right to know. One DEP and 11 DOH questionnaires were returned as undeliverable; of the remaining 62 and 107 questionnaires, 28 and 43, respectively, were returned. (A second mailing was made to nonrespondents one month after the initial mailing.) The overall response rate was 42 percent; for DEP and DOH, respectively, the response rates were 45 and 40 percent, which is respectable.

Massachusetts's right-to-know law was passed in November 1983. It provides employees and community residents with access to information about hazardous substances in the workplace and community. As in New Jersey, employers must train employees about safe handling of hazardous substances and make available Material Safety Data Sheets that describe the known health effects and other details about each substance. The Massachusetts Department of Health must determine which chemicals are placed on the Massachusetts Substance List and with dissemination of toxicological information about these regulated chemicals. The Health Department receives about 20 calls per week requesting information on hazardous chemicals.[1]

Massachusetts's community RTK provisions, which went into effect in April 1985, differ significantly from those in New Jersey, however. In order to obtain information about substances in local workplaces, citizens must petition the designated municipal coordinator to have access to MSDSs. If the petition is complete, the coordinator notifies the employer, who provides a response. In addition, the coordinator may decide to undertake an investigation, which adds ten days to the statutory fifteen days he has for responding to the petitioner. His report must also be sent to the Massachusetts Department of Environmental Quality Engineering (DEQE), the agency responsible for implementing right to know. DEQE, in turn, reviews the petition, response, and report and may decide to undertake its own investigation to determine whether there is a threat to public health, whether an MSDS should be released, or whether some other action is necessary. The decision is transmitted to petitioner, employer, and municipal coordinator.

Another important feature of the Massachusetts law is that citizens who obtain information under community RTK may not pass that information along to anyone else. Physicians treating patients who are ill as a result of an exposure and municipal officials under limited circumstances may obtain MSDS information. The nondisclosure provision was the subject of considerable respondent discontent. It was overturned by a U.S. District Court in August 1988, many months after the survey was completed.[2]

In Massachusetts, the names of citizens who had filed petitions under the community RTK portion of the state law were a matter of public record. Regional agency representatives supplied lists of names. Of the 56 citizens whose names were listed, 42 had filed successful petitions--that is, petitions that had elicited information from the employer. The other 14 had filed unsuccessful petitions. In contrast to the New Jersey procedure, the survey was not sent to the significant number of people who have requested information from the Massachusetts Department of Health. Moreover, after the survey was completed, I learned that many of the petitions were filed by multiple petitioners, as the law allows for copetitioning. Only the first named petitioners were on the mailing list, however, because these were the only names provided by the DEQE regional offices.

A questionnaire similar to that for New Jersey was mailed to successful petitioners with one cover letter and to unsuccessful petitioners with another letter. Since the latter had never received any information, they were simply asked to report their experiences with the program. Seven questionnaires were returned as undeliverable. Twenty responses were received from the remaining forty-nine; of these, one answered no questions, saying that to do so would violate the nondisclosure requirement. A second respondent stated that he had never filed a right-to-know petition. The eighteen usable responses constitute a 37 percent response rate.

The Massachusetts questionnaire was considerably abbreviated in comparison with the New Jersey form; because citizens could not discuss the information obtained with anyone else, the questions concerning spreading information and actions taken were omitted. References to state departments were changed appropriately.

The questionnaires sent to both states provided an opportunity for respondents to supply a first name and a telephone number. Many did express willingness to speak with me in more detail. Telephone interviews lasted up to half an hour and supplied many of the details of the experiences reported in the larger study.

Although I had expected to receive replies from citizens interested in hazardous materials in the community, the New Jersey pool of respondents turned out to comprise mostly people who had requested information in order to fulfill the requirements of their jobs, including consultants, facility managers, and so on. The answers to many questions, including one asking what sort of event prompted the request for information, reflected this situation. Results are reported in

Table A-1. Table A-2 shows the kinds of information people had requested.

TABLE A-1 Events Prompting Requests for Information

	New Jersey		Mass.		N.J. DEP	
Part of my job	30	(42%)	1	(6%)	11	(39%)
An odor	8	(11%)	12	(67%)	2	(7%)
Health complaints	12	(17%)	2	(11%)	6	(21%)
Reports of a spill or leak	10	(14%)	2	(11%)	4	(14%)
Reports of a cancer cluster	3	(4%)	4	(22%)	2	(7%)
Reports of other illnesses	6	(8%)	12	(67%)	3	(11%)
Proposed facility to be built	4	(6%)	0		1	(4%)
Training received in the workplace	11	(15%)	3	(17%)	4	(14%)
General interest	15	(21%)	2	(11%)	3	(11%)
Air emissions	2	(3%)	4	(22%)	2	(7%)
Denial of right by employer	2	(3%)	0		1	(4%)
Nearness to an existing facility	3	(4%)	18	(100%)	2	(7%)
Activist group	1	(1%)	3	(17%)	0	
Other	3	(4%)	2	(11%)	1	(4%)
Known dangerous substance/ labels	2	(3%)	0		0	

TABLE A-2 Kinds of Information Requested (New Jersey)

Hazardous substance fact sheets	51	(72%)
Workplace survey	36	(51%)
Right to know brochure	24	(34%)
Environmental Survey Part 1	23	(32%)
Environmental Survey Part 2	21	(30%)
Emergency Services Information Survey	16	(23%)
All facilities in an area	9	(13%)
All facilities with a specific substance	4	(6%)
Other	5	(7%)

TABLE A-3 Actions Taken and Proposed as a Result of RTK Information (N\%)

| | Actions Taken | | Actions Proposed | |
	N.J.	Mass.	N.J.	Mass.
Shared it with coworkers	31\44	--	17\24	--
Job-related actions	28\39	0	6\9	0
Shared it with friends	12\17	--	9\13	--
Provided it to a doctor	10\14	1\6	11\15	1\6
Provided it to a public official	9\13	1\6	12\17	0
Provided it to a lawyer	7\10	4\22	6\9	4\22
Provided it to a union official	6\8	--	7\10	--
Community facility tour/inspection	1\1	0	0	0
Organized others to ask for info	--	8\44	--	3\17
Other	0	6\33	5\7	0
None	8\11	7\39	19\27	2\11
Ask for water to be tested	--	4\22	--	2\11
Ask for more info	0	3\17	0	0

Table A-3 displays the answers to questions about the kinds of action people had taken and proposed to take as a result of their RTK requests. In New Jersey, the largest groups were those who intended to take job-related actions, such as "provide information to employees" or "improve safety practices," and those who shared information with coworkers. Other actions included sharing it with friends or providing it to a public official. Although the survey had included a response "provided it to a newspaper," no one reported having done so. In light of the concern often expressed that right to know is really the right to sue, it is interesting that only 10 percent of the respondents report having provided information to a doctor or to a lawyer. The actions that people expect to take differ little from the ones already taken; sharing information with coworkers and public officials ranks high, followed by providing it to a doctor. One-fourth of the respondents expect to take no further action.

There were some striking differences and also some notable similarities between the respondents in the two states. The New Jersey respondents included a large number of people who were making requests as part of their jobs; all Massachusetts respondents were acting primarily as private citizens concerned about a particular facility, usually about health effects from emissions. Largely as a result of the very different procedures followed in the two states, requests for information in Massachusetts were much more likely to result in a definitive outcome, with the facility installing a pollution-control device. Only one New Jersey respondent reported this kind of outcome; another had managed to use the information to persuade the facility manager to give neighbors a facility tour. Massachusetts residents were more likely to obtain information about RTK as employees or directly from DEQE, while New Jersey residents had a wider range of sources.

Respondents in both states were similar, however, in their reactions to the nature of information available and the procedures for obtaining the information. Nearly two-thirds in each state found the information understandable. The other third, however, felt strongly that the information was less useful: The most common complaint was that it was too technical or hard to understand; the second most common complaint was that more detailed information was needed. Many respondents in both states found the procedures for acquiring information too complex or slow, complaining about the number of telephone calls or letters needed to complete the process.

One of the most striking features of both pools of respondents was their small number. In New Jersey, where the right-to-know law had been in effect for almost three years when the survey was conducted, the number of community RTK requests to both major agencies was less than 200 and to DEP, which is most closely identified with community rather than employee RTK, was only 63. These numbers include no requests made to local lead agencies. In Massachusetts, 56 petitions had been filed in the year and a half the law had been in effect. Inclusion of the copetitioners, omitted because DEQE had not supplied the names, would have raised the number of potential respondents significantly.

There are several possible explanations for the relatively small number of requests received in both states. One is that citizens are simply not interested in right to know. Inasmuch as our pool included only citizens who had filed requests, the survey could shed no light on this hypothesis. Our respondents have suggested that the procedures for making requests constitute a serious impediment to right to know. Many citizens may have begun to make requests but were discouraged by the procedures, especially in Massachusetts, where even some of the respondents to the survey indicated that they had not filed formal RTK petitions because of the onerous procedural requirements. Many Massachusetts citizens are discouraged from filing petitions by the nondisclosure requirement; they believe that once they have received information they are inhibited from discussing any aspect of the case, even data familiar to them before they filed the petition. Several telephone respondents asked whether it was all right to talk to the interviewer, even though all questions concerned only procedures and not content.

Our respondents also indicated that it is not always easy to obtain information about the RTK program itself. Although many had learned about the community RTK program during workplace training, many others had learned about the program by accident. This finding suggests the need for additional outreach and publicity about the program--outreach that DEP in New Jersey is already proposing to undertake. The lack of funds specifically for outreach has been an impediment in both states.

A follow-up survey of New Jersey residents who have filed RTK requests with New Jersey DEP since September 1987 is in progress at this writing.

The Texas Voter Survey

The Texas telephone survey was conducted by a research team of students at the LBJ School of Public Affairs of the University of Texas at Austin under the direction of Robert Rickards and Laura Lein with grants from the Texas Employment Commission, the Texas Adult Probation Commission, and the Select Committee on Tax Equity. In addition to the questions reported here, the survey, whose general topic was the quality of community life, included questions about taxes and crime.

A random sample of 620 individuals eligible to register to vote in Texas was surveyed by telephone in February 1988. The 620 people constituted 60 percent of the eligible people who were contacted. The data analysis and interpretation presented here are solely my responsibility.

The first question about hazardous materials was "Are there hazardous materials in your community?" This question had an extraordinary number of nonrespondents--85--the highest number of nonrespondents to any question on the survey and more than 13 percent of the total. This high number of nonrespondents indicates a real lack of information about this subject. Of those who responded, 39 percent thought there were hazardous materials in their communities, 14 percent did not know, and the remaining 47 percent said there were not.

Another series of questions attempted to measure concern about hazardous materials. Each question was phrased as follows: "How concerned would you be with the (production, transportation, disposal) of hazardous materials in your community?" Respondents were asked to reply on a scale ranging from 1 to 7, with 1 reflecting lack of concern and 7 reflecting very high concern. The replies show a high degree of concern for the presence of hazardous materials in the community for any reason; in no case were less than two-thirds of the respondents very concerned (answering either 6 or 7), and in no case were more than one-eighth of the respondents generally unconcerned (answering either 2 or 1). However, respondents indicated a greater level of concern about the disposal of hazardous wastes, slightly less concern about manufacture, and the least about transport. We also asked whether respondents had heard about the new federal law (Title III), which we briefly described; 80 percent had not.

Whether or not they know about the new law, citizens often hear about possible new facilities in their communities. We asked people to suppose that a chemical company has applied for a permit to manufacture a cancer-causing substance in the community. First we asked, "On a scale from 1 to 7, how worried would you be, with 1 being 'not worried at all' and 7 being 'very worried'"? More than three-fourths of the respondents responded 6 or 7, thereby indicating considerable concern.

Having ascertained their level of concern, we then tried to determine whether respondents would take any of the kinds of community-related actions on which Title III is predicated. We asked how likely respondents would be to take the following actions: (1) talk to friends, family, or neighbors about the situation; (2) contact local officials or a government agency; (3) join a group or committee; and (4) organize a group or committee. The number of people quite likely to take these actions (indicated by responses 6 and 7) decreased markedly from the first action to the last. Although 75 percent of the respondents would talk to family and friends, and 60 percent would contact local officials, 52 percent would join a group, and 39 percent thought they would be likely to organize a group. It is to be expected that people are less willing to undertake the more arduous task of organizing a group than the relatively easy one of talking to family and friends.

Although the drop-off is significant, it is still striking that as many as two-fifths of the respondents were concerned enough to think that they might organize a group in response to the proposed presence of a new facility. We know that what people say they will do and what they actually do are quite different. Nevertheless, the reported willingness to organize seems to support the reported level of concern.

The Field Survey

The field survey was conducted by a research team of students at the LBJ School of Public Affairs under the direction of Leigh Boske and myself and was funded by a contract with the Texas Department of Highways and Public Transportation.

The eleven counties in the field survey were chosen on the basis of geographic location, population size, and apparent risk from hazardous materials. Some communities were chosen because of their participation in an industry-sponsored Community Awareness and Emergency Response program. El Paso, Ector, Harris, Brazoria, Travis, Dallas, and Cameron all have populations exceeding 100,000, whereas the remaining counties--Harrison, Calhoun, Coleman, and Gray--have smaller populations. Interviews were arranged with as many of the following as could be reached: representatives of the county judge's office, the fire department, the police department, the emergency medical services, the local media, the sheriff's office, the Department of Public Safety, local industry officials, the emergency management offices, and members of the LEPC. A survey instrument guided the interviews but researchers were free to ask other questions as applicable.

Of the eleven counties we surveyed, nine had appointed their LEPCs by November 1987; seven had met at least once by the time the research teams visited. Travis County, which had not formed its LEPC in November, did so in January and has taken a much more active role since then. The sample mirrored the statewide data; as late as March 1988, nearly 20 percent of the counties had not formed their LEPCs. In our sample, 22 percent did not have LEPCs.

Interviewees in the field survey were asked to name the primary hazardous materials risks in their counties. Transportation elicited the highest concern, with county officials especially worried about highways and railroads. This concern results in large part from the unpredictable nature of highway hazardous materials transport. Not only are the county officials unable to control what substances pass through their counties, they often feel frustration at having to plan for some unforeseen accident involving an unknown chemical. Concern was exacerbated by the fact that major transportation routes often go through the middles of towns.

This result differs from the comments in the telephone survey, in which most LEPC chairpeople seemed to believe that they were at low risk if there were no processing or manufacturing facilities in their jurisdictions and virtually disregarded risks posed by transportation.

One chairman from a rural county did mention that his county's major risk arose from transportation, but he complained that Title III does not cover those risks very well. Many of the county officials expressed concern or dissatisfaction over what they perceived to be the patchwork of state statutes regarding hazardous materials. Some counties felt frustrated by what they believed to be a lack of interest on the part of the state in helping them to understand what is expected of LEPCs and local officials.

The eleven counties differ in their motivations and abilities to implement Title III. Those with CAER programs have been more advanced in developing emergency plans and mobilizing response capabilites. Nevertheless, all counties identified several common concerns. First, every county official mentioned the lack of funding for implementing Title III. County officials also mentioned the lack of resources for emergency response training and the need for resources to collect, compile, and store MSDS or chemical lists from local industries. Counties do not have enough money for either computer facilities or experienced personnel to run the computer. Yet, without computerization, the MSDSs or chemical lists will be unusable for any of their intended purposes: community right to know, emergency planning, or emergency response.

Another concern of county officials is the LEPCs' lack of power to enforce the collection of MSDSs or chemical lists. They were especially concerned that smaller facilities would either unwillingly or unknowingly fail to comply with the Title III regulations. The Dallas respondents mentioned that the LEPC was hampered because it is not a policy body.

Another concern expressed by respondents in the field survey was lack of community or public awareness of the dangers posed by hazardous materials. Title III can presumably help rectify this problem. Other counties expressed the opposite concern--that citizens would overrate the risks from hazardous materials. Coleman County respondents, for example, voiced the fear that the public would be unnecessarily confused by the additional information Title III would make available. In the telephone survey, concern about the public's ability to understand and use the data was the second most frequently mentioned problem. Several chairpeople noted that although the right-to-know provisions will work only with citizen involvement, their experiences suggest that people do not want to take the time to read or learn about these issues. A few chairpeople said that people would take an interest only when something happened to affect them immediately. One chairman argued that LEPCs do not have to publicize the right-to-know provisions; instead, "people should take responsibility for themselves."

The field survey was conducted in November 1987, before counties had had much chance to begin implementing Title III. Respondents were most aware of and interested in the emergency planning and response portions of the law, in part because the CAER program already focused on these issues. They were worried about acquiring the resources necessary to implement all portions of the law, especially those that depend on acquisition and management of the extensive records required by the law--emergency planning and community RTK.

The telephone survey in April found little change in the kinds of concerns expressed. Because respondents were not asked about implementation or about emergency response or planning, we have no comparison with the earlier survey on these issues. However, officials, especially in smaller counties, seemed still to be overwhelmed by the complexity of the law and the new institutions it has been creating.

Telephone Surveys of LEPC Chairpeople

The telephone survey of LEPC chairpeople was conducted by Leticia Flores in partial fulfillment of requirements for a course at the LBJ School of Public Affairs. The presentation of the survey results is a joint effort of Ms. Flores and myself.

Counties whose LEPC chairperson would be interviewed were selected by assigning each county a three-digit number between 001 and 243. Texas has 254 counties, but the 11 visited in the field survey were excluded to guard against bias. The number 015 was picked from a random number table, and every fifth county (obtained by dividing the 243 by desired sample of 45 = 5.4 = 5) was drawn. The chairpeople received letters explaining the purpose of the survey and informing them that an interviewer would call. Of the 45 chairpeople, 36 participated in the survey, a response rate of 80 percent. Three declined to participate because they did not know enough about Title III. Three counties either did not have a chairperson or anyone willing to be identified as chairperson. Repeated phone calls failed to reach three chairpeople.

The sample could engender misleading results. The most serious consequences of excluding the 11 counties visited in the earlier study were the loss of three major metropolitan areas, two border counties, and two counties dependent on the oil industry. As a result of this exclusion and the nonresponse of some putative interviewees, the sample did not include any counties in far East Texas or the Rio Grande

Valley, nor did it include any border counties, which are poorer than average and face the problem of unregulated international hazardous materials transportation. The results of the field survey suggest, however, that the absence of some counties has not seriously affected the results of the telephone survey under consideration here.

By March 1988, nearly 20 percent of counties statewide had still not formed LEPCs, although the statutory deadline was September 17, 1987. The Division of Emergency Management of the Texas Department of Public Safety, therefore, appointed chairpeople and committees for them. In this sample, one-third of the chairpeople were appointed, a larger proportion than in the state as a whole. Not responding to legislative requirements may indicate ignorance, lack of interest, or even an attitude of willful noncompliance.

All eleven chairpeople visited in the fall field survey were local officials, but only 61 percent of the respondents in this survey were local officials. The 39 percent who were private citizens included an attorney, a rancher, and employees of major chemical producers. Even among the local officials, positions ranged from director of a major city's emergency management office to county judge. The wide range of knowledge, interest, and resources among the chairpeople also affected the results. Only half of the committees had met by the time of the survey. The attitudes of their leaders were, therefore, not based on actual experience in implementing Title III.

One factor that affects perception of the need to know is the level of perceived risk in the county. Nearly 50 percent of all chairpeople placed their counties in the "low" risk-level group. Only two respondents ranked their counties' risk levels in the highest risk category. They replied in the same way to the four attitudinal questions and mostly favored citizen outreach and right-to-know. Considering only those who placed their counties in the three lower risk categories, in general, the higher the perceived risk level, the more likely a chairperson was to believe that LEPCs should publicize the right-to-know provisions and to think that it is important for citizens to know about hazardous materials in the community.

The chairpeople showed a wide range of knowledge or interest in Title III. Some were familiar with it in detail and were working to implement it and use it in their counties. Others knew of it in terms of the emergency response plan required by the state but did not know any of the other provisions. Several barely knew more than its name. The varying level of knowledge and commitment, coupled with the lack of funding, are probably going to keep Title III from being very effective for most of the state's counties. One chairman talked about the LEPC as "the government," expressing a common confusion about the exact role of the newly created organizations.

Conclusion

Although three of these surveys had some methodological flaws (the Texas voter survey is the exception), their results may be used to gain insight into the workings of Title III. After these surveys were conducted, additional surveys were made by other researchers in other states, as noted in this book. In general, their findings confirmed or provided additional evidence for the findings of the four surveys reported here.

Notes

1. Letter to me from MaryBeth Smuts, director, Right-to-Know Program, Massachusetts Department of Health, March 23, 1988.
2. *Lawlor* v. *Shannon*, CIV. A. No. 86-2516-MC, U.S. District Court Massachusetts (1988 WL 96609 D. Mass.).

Acronyms

CAER--Community Awareness and Emergency Response (program of the Chemical Manufacturers Assocation)
CAMEO™--Computer-Aided Management of Emergency Operations
CAS--Chemical Abstract Service
CD-ROM--Compact disk/read only memory (form of data storage)
CEPP--Chemical Emergency Preparedness Program
CERCLA--Comprehensive Environmental Response, Compensation, and Liability Act of 1980, often called "superfund"
CMA--Chemical Manufacturers Association
DEM--Division of Emergency Management (Texas)
DEP--Department of Environmental Protection (New Jersey)
DEQE--Department of Environmental Quality Engineering (Massachusetts)
DOH--Department of Health (New Jersey)
DOT--Department of Transportation (federal)
EPA--Environmental Protection Agency (federal)
EPDs--Emergency Planning Districts
FEMA--Federal Emergency Management Agency (federal)
FOIA--Freedom of Information Act
HCA--Hazard Communication Act (used here for the Texas statute)
HCS--Hazard Communication Standard (promulgated by OSHA)
LEPC--Local Emergency Planning Committee (created by Title III)
MSDSs--Material Safety Data Sheets
NIMBY--Not in my back yard
NIOSH--National Institute for Occupational Safety and Health
NLM--National Library of Medicine
NOAA--National Oceanographic and Atmospheric Administration (federal)
OMB--Office of Management and Budget (federal)
OSHA--Occupational Safety and Health Administration (federal)
ppm--Parts per million
RC--Risk communication
SARA--Superfund Amendments and Reauthorization Act (the Emergency Planning and Community Right to Know Act was embodied in Title III of SARA)

SERC--State Emergency Response Commission (established under Title III)

SIC codes--Standard Industrial Classification codes (20-39 are manufacturing industries)

TRI--Toxic Release Inventory (the database of section 313 emissions reports)

Index